ILLINOIS CENTRAL COLLEGE
PN6122.L53
STACKS
Contemporary American speeches;
A12900 305385

WITHDRAWN

WADSWORTH PUBLISHING COMPANY, INC.
BELMONT, CALIFORNIA

CONTEMPORARY AMERICAN SPEECHES

A SOURCEBOOK OF SPEECH FORMS AND PRINCIPLES

Wil A. Linkugel
University of Kansas

R. R. Allen
University of Wisconsin

Richard L. Johannesen
Indiana University

L.C. Cat. Card No. 65–21112
Printed in the United States of America

THIRD PRINTING: JUNE 1966

PREFACE

Contemporary American Speeches is dedicated to the belief that acquisition of speaking skills is best achieved through three complementary lines of study: *theory,* from which the student may gain a basic understanding of the speech act; *example,* through which the student may evaluate precept in the light of real and varied instances of public discourse; and *practice,* in which the student may apply rhetorical principles to the creation of speeches.

The study of speeches, in the tradition of humane studies, gives a student a view of man seeking to adapt to his social environment. By examining the issues on which others have spoken, the forms their expressions have taken, and the principles that have made their thoughts clear and impelling, the student of speech may know more of himself and of man in general. He may compare the topics he chooses for his speeches with those that are of vital concern to leaders in society. He may perceive his own skills and achievements in proper perspective. He may establish standards of excellence with which to judge the quality of our contemporary public dialogue.

This book is concerned with speech *forms* and *principles.* It has long been recognized that speeches serve diverse social purposes. Through speech, man may seek to inform and to persuade his fellow men. He may inform others about established knowledge and the products of his personal inquiry. He may try to persuade men concerning propositions of fact or propositions of personal and social values. He may wish to create or induce concern for man's significant problems and construct programs to improve and direct social action. To these ends, this book presents examples of speeches that embrace *six major speech forms:* Imparting Knowledge, Augmenting Knowledge, Affirming Propositions of Fact, Affirming Propositions of Value, Creating Concern for Problems, and Affirming Propositions of Policy. Integral to each of these speech forms are the rhetorical principles discussed in speech textbooks. By studying important speeches of contemporary American speakers, the student will find that these principles become meaningful tools for communicating effectively, through speech, in contemporary American society. With this objective in mind, we have noted examples of major speech principles in the speeches collected here and have catalogued them in an Index of Rhetorical Principles.

We wish to acknowledge our indebtedness to the many people who have given us permission to reprint the speeches in this book. Especially important in this respect has been the cooperation of Thomas F. Daly, Jr., of *Vital Speeches of the Day*. We wish further to acknowledge indebtedness to Professor Karl Dallinger of Illinois State University, Normal, Illinois, and Professor Bruce Kendall of Purdue University for reading and reviewing the manuscript prior to its publication and for offering invaluable criticism and advice.

W. A. L.
R. R. A.
R. L. J.

CONTENTS

NOTE TO THE TEACHER

Teaching by example is an ancient practice. Isocrates used the study of speeches as one of his principal teaching devices. Cicero, himself an assiduous student of speeches, advocated the study of Greek and Roman speech models to all aspiring orators. Quintilian said, "It is from . . . authors worthy of our study that we must draw our stock of words, the variety of our figures and our methods of composition." Goodrich noted that "He who would teach eloquence must do it chiefly by examples." Burke studied Demosthenes; Webster studied Burke; and Wilson studied Webster.

We have found that students, by testing precept against real and varied speech examples, come to view theory as a foundation for their own critical analysis and as a guide for their own creative efforts. By considering not only the rhetorical choices they must make but also the choices others have made, students become more critical and demanding of their own efforts and the efforts of their classmates and, ultimately, develop standards of excellence that they take with them beyond the classroom.

While the question "Why study speeches?" may be answered in detail (and Chapter 1 tries to do this for the student), the question of how to study speeches remains for the most part unanswered. The final answer can be provided only by the individual teacher. Nonetheless, the study of speeches as embodied in *Contemporary American Speeches* may contribute to any of the varied approaches that a basic speech course may take.

For the performance course that provides student speaking experience in the various speech forms, this collection is an obvious supplement. Chapters 3 through 8 provide speeches representative of each form. By studying these speeches, the student may discover the nature of the choices that a speaker makes in fulfilling each of the most important purposes of public discourse.

For the course in speech fundamentals or public speaking with a strong emphasis on speech principles, this book provides examples by which principles may be tested, judged, and reinforced. It should not be assumed that the speeches in this book are without imperfections; rather, they were chosen as representative examples that illuminate important rhetorical principles. We have also prepared an Index to Rhetorical Principles, which catalogues examples of the major precepts found in the speeches. We have made no attempt to index every example of a principle but have listed those that are the most illustrative. In some instances, we have cited whole speeches as being especially useful in studying certain principles. Additionally, we have prepared headnotes that call attention to those principles warranting special consideration in the discussion of a specific speech. These headnotes should guide the student's thinking about speech principles as he reads each address. We think that the teacher will find the index and the headnotes useful in teaching the principles of a basic speech course.

For the performance course that encourages student performance on the dominant issues of our time, this book provides examples of speeches that deal with significant thoughts, values, and issues. Since excellence of form in itself is no virtue, we have included only speeches rich in content. We have also tried to find speeches with subject matter that is relatively timeless.

This book also provides a rich fund of speeches that a student may critically explore and evaluate in *a course in criticism of contemporary American speaking.* Chapter 1 ("Why Study Speeches?") provides as meaningful a rationale for such a course, as it does for a performance course in speech fundamentals. The speeches we have collected represent the rhetoric and thought of major figures from diverse fields of contemporary American society.

The basic plan and organization of this book, based on our experience, is functional. Part One, *The Study of Speeches,* consists of two chapters. Chapter 1 ("Why Study Speeches?") asks the student and teacher to consider a rationale for studying speeches. In Chapter 2 ("Gaining a Perspective"), we have presented a view of the essential components of public address, defined the general nature of the speaker's choices in adapting to his environment, and focused on the nature of the major speech forms that public discourse produces.

Parts Two and Three focus on the basic speech purposes of *in-*

forming and *persuading.* We have tried to increase the meaningfulness of these broad concepts by classifying the functions of speeches within these categories. Part Two, *Speaking to Inform,* consists of two chapters: "Speeches That Impart Knowledge" and "Speeches That Augment Knowledge." Part Three, *Speaking to Persuade,* consists of four chapters: "Speeches That Affirm Propositions of Fact," "Speeches That Affirm Propositions of Value," "Speeches That Create Concern for Problems," and "Speeches That Affirm Propositions of Policy." The chapters follow a consistent format. Each begins with a brief introduction to the nature of the speech form and the constraints that influence the choices the speaker has in presenting that type of speech. A variety of speeches representative of the chapter's speech form is then included for analysis.

The authors hope that the student's study of the choices men have made in giving social utility to ideas may help him to understand the nature of the rhetorical act and his relation to it.

PART ONE

THE STUDY OF SPEECHES

Chapter One

WHY STUDY SPEECHES?

Only as the constant companions of Demosthenes, Cicero, Burke, Fox, Channing, and Webster can we hope to become orators.
Woodrow Wilson

In the study of speeches, as in all other learning, the thoughtful student will attempt to define the role of such inquiry in his personal and social development. This chapter is meant to stimulate your thinking about the importance of such study in your speech training and in your general intellectual development. We hope that the discussion will help you, a twentieth-century student, to perceive the implications of the insightful words of Woodrow Wilson concerning the study of speeches.

WE STUDY SPEECHES TO INCREASE OUR KNOWLEDGE OF MAN

That a student considers his college education important is demonstrated by his devotion of four years of his life to its demands. He makes such a dedication expecting that, some place along the way, there will evolve a body of knowledge, a habit of thought, a system of values upon which all of his future decisions will fundamentally rest. In so doing, he seeks not only the development of marketable intellectual skills, but an understanding of self and society as well. He seeks to become not a lawyer but a *man* who practices law, not a teacher but a *man* who teaches, not a businessman but a *man* who engages in business, not a scientist but a *man* who studies the physical world about him.

A student may take varied paths in his effort to understand

himself as man. Each liberal study, be it philosophy, literature, history, speech, or any other, holds such promise—and rightfully so. Nothing made by man is alien to the student in search of humane understanding. Emerson said: "Raphael paints wisdom, Handel sings it, Phidias carves it, Shakespeare writes it, Wren builds it, Columbus sails it, Luther preaches it, Washington arms it, Watt mechanizes it." In each of these studies the student may find evidence of man's creative struggle with his environment. From each of these studies the student may gain insight into his own life.

All liberal studies may convey a view of man making choices in an effort to adapt to his environment. But what better time to know him than in those moments when he speaks to other men?

In studying speeches, the student may see man making choices in the articulation of the master ideals of our civilization. He may see him electing that which degrades our common humanity. He may see him making enlightened judgments on the great social, moral, and political issues of our own and other times. He may see him concocting themes of hatred and bigotry. Whatever else may accrue from such endeavor, the study of speeches will contribute to our understanding of the potentialities and limitations of man's nature.

While a speech is only one of several forms of human reflection, it nevertheless has an element of uniqueness. A painting encompasses the elements of thought and form; a speech is composed of language. A poem embraces thought, language, and form; a speech is conveyed by sound. Literature, interpreted orally, makes use of thought, language, form, and sound; a speech is at once more urgent and real, more literal and spontaneous. Since a speech is a unique product of man's creativity, it demands understanding, as does a painting or a poem, a statue, or a scroll. The study of speeches thus accords a fuller insight into man's expressive behavior.

In a democratic society, man's social existence gives rise to forces that compel him to speak. He may speak to be seen and to be heard, to impress others and to impress himself, to question and to answer, to persuade and to dissuade, to teach and to learn. His subject may be grand or mundane, important or trivial, simple or complex, but he will speak. The student who would understand himself should examine the forces that have compelled other men to speak. The student who would know himself will find no better way than comparing the content and manner of his own speaking with that of other men. We study speeches that we may better understand ourselves.

WE STUDY SPEECHES TO DERIVE STANDARDS FOR THE CRITICAL APPRAISAL OF PUBLIC DISCOURSE

Today's speech student tends to find our rhetorical world confusing. While favoring the public expression of our social purpose and identity, he often finds such expressions grandiose and trite. While approving the public dialogue as an instrument of social decision making, he often finds such dialogues one-sided and irrational. While a protagonist of the free and full dissemination of the *truth* to the public, he often is offended by the articulation of these "truths" in watered and distorted forms under pressures of mass understanding and acceptance. Although the student of speech should be encouraged to question the matter and manner of the public dialogue, his criticism should not be superficial. Let it be based upon sound critical standards derived from an incisive analysis of varied instances of public discourse.

Let him so sharpen his tools of analysis and judgment that he may put to a test the worth and truth of a speaker's assertions. In the study of speeches, the student may acquire a broad familiarity with issues that have compelled men to speak. Our communion with the past, the freedom of our citizens, the quality of our private and public life, our hopes for the future—all these are manifest in the public dialogue. Through an awareness of the significant issues of our time, the student may judge the wisdom of the speaker's choices. He may evaluate the speaker's interpretation of the world about him. He may reject the unimportant issue and the petty thought as the strawmen of feeble intellects. By reading widely of the speeches of the present and the past, the student may also appraise the truth and validity of a speaker's assertions. He may test the sufficiency of the speaker's proof and deny the specious inference and the faulty deduction. No responsible and enlightened person will base such judgments on unexamined prejudices but on sound critical standards derived from careful study and reflection and from analysis of vital public speeches.

But he should not stop here. Public discourse does not exist in a social vacuum. It is not soliloquy; it seeks always to influence the hearer and to change his behavior. If ideas are to have social utility, they must be transformed from private conceptions into meaningful public statements. The speaker must so develop and project his thoughts that they give direction to those who listen. The means he selects are the basis for the critic's judgment. Is the speaker's organization appropriate? Is his delivery effective? Is his style impelling?

In the study of speeches, the student may see men making choices in their efforts to adapt ideas to their audiences. Through such study he may learn not only of the choices to be made, but of the choices that others have made. He may find men, in their finer moments, giving ennobling and inspiring expression to our political purposes. He may see them speaking responsibly to the great social problems of our time. He may see them enlisting popular support in worthy causes. He may see them conveying the essence of significant thoughts with compelling clarity, force, and beauty. Because of these observations, he may reject the expression that is feeble and unworthy. He may deny the appeal that is base and degrading. He may condemn the unethical strategy and the mean social purpose. He may develop standards for the judicious appraisal of public discourse—the merit of the speaker's ideas and his means of public expression.

WE STUDY SPEECHES TO ENLARGE AND DEEPEN OUR UNDERSTANDING OF RHETORICAL THEORY

The student of speech, faced with a body of precepts set forth in a contemporary basic speech textbook, will often fail to give just importance to the ideas expressed. The text, he may claim, is too much concerned with the larynx and pharynx and the physiological processes of speech; too firm in its adherence to inviolate rules; too committed to the perpetuation of useless names and distinctions; too verbose in the expression of common sense. Any body of principles divorced from the context that gave it being may seem drab and useless. But if these principles are viewed in their proper context, they tend to become meaningful and even intellectually stimulating.

Rhetorical theory was born of man's attempt to systematize his observations of the purposive and dynamic public interactions of other men. In the fifth century B.C., the first body of rhetorical precepts emerged from Corax's observations of the attempts of his fellow citizens of Syracuse to give social order to a society newly emerged from tyranny. In the centuries that followed, countless other men recorded their observations of identifiable speech principles. While those who followed owed a great debt to those who preceded them, each sought to redefine and reconceptualize the art of speaking in a manner consistent with his own perceptions of public address as it occurred in his own culture and in his own time.

Like most of his predecessors, the author of a modern speech textbook must acknowledge his debt to the great rhetorical tradition.

His task, however, is not the perpetuation of the intellectual faults of eminent men. Rather he seeks to test and temper the principles of the art of speech communication. He must blend with the old the particular insights of the new—insights gleaned from the scholarship of his own and related disciplines—insights gathered from his own judicious observation of public discourse. Building on the rhetorical philosophies of the past with the knowledge of the present, our modern theorist seeks to create not a memorial to the past, but a structure consistent with the needs and realities of his age. Such work is vital and meaningful, not drab or devoid of intellectual stimulation.

Is it strange that that which is bright with intellectual challenge in process often seems boring in product? Not really. The excitement of the intellectual search for precepts by one man is easily lost when relegated to a body of generalizations for the consumption of another. It is not that the theory is bad; it is just that theory alone, divorced from the world from which it was abstracted, is inadequate.

Would it not be best, then, for the student of speech to seek out his own precepts? Not really. The perceptive student, skilled in listening to popular instances of communication and afforded such great examples as Burke, Churchill, and Roosevelt, could derive his own theory of speech. But at what expense of time? At what expense to progress? Each student would have to begin anew his quest for order and meaning, as helplessly alone as if no one else had ever walked his way.

While the problem is not fully solved by presenting the student with the generalizations of another's mind, concisely arranged, neither is it fully solved by presenting the student with a body of speech masterpieces, past and present, with the caution to keep "an open mind and vigilant eye." The study of a speech textbook is, like the study of examples of public discourse, one important element in the training of the student of speech. Preference for one should not lead to a discarding of the other. A speech textbook is a body of generalizations drawn from the author's contemplation of the long tradition of rhetorical theory, the scholarship of his day, and his own perceptions of human communication. It exists not to inhibit, but to stimulate. The good student will put the precepts of a textbook to the pragmatic test of actual public life. He will realize, as did Quintilian, that "rhetoric would be a very easy and small matter, if it could be included in one short body of rules, but rules must generally be altered to suit the nature of each individual case, the time, the occasion, and the necessity itself . . ." By testing the generalizations of a textbook in the light of real and varied instances of public discourse, the student will learn to challenge, question, and compare; and, ultimately, he will develop for himself a theory of speech both comprehensive and personal.

WE STUDY SPEECHES TO DEVELOP AN APPRECIATION FOR EMINENCE IN PUBLIC ADDRESS

In 1852, Chauncey Goodrich, Professor of Rhetoric at Yale College, reviewed his teaching philosophy in the preface to his work *Select British Eloquence.* He wrote:

> My object was not only to awaken in the minds of the class that love of genuine eloquence which is the surest pledge of success, but to aid them in catching the spirit of the authors read, and, by analyzing passages selected for the purpose, to initiate the pupil in those higher principles which (whether they were conscious of it or not) have always guided the great masters of the art, till he should learn the *unwritten* rules of oratory, which operate by a kind of instinct upon the mind, and are far more important than any that are found in the books.

This passage has merit today for the student who would be more than a follower of blueprints. It recommends that those students who would develop an appreciation for eminence in public address, a love of eloquence, look beyond textbook principles to the unwritten rules of the art. It suggests the importance of developing taste, a sense of the rightness, or the strength, or the felicity of a thought or an expression through exposure to speeches. Such an appreciation of eminence serves to inspire the student to seek in his own work only the highest level of excellence.

The student who has come to acquire this appreciation for eminence will reject trivial subjects. He will understand that a concern for significant ideas has been at the heart of great oratory from ancient times. Demosthenes spoke for the freedom of a city. Churchill spoke for the survival of a nation. Roosevelt spoke for the freedom of man. Kennedy spoke for peace in a divided world. Rhetorical eminence presupposes worthy ideas to express, ideas that merit the attention and efforts of the speaker and the concern of the audience.

But rhetorical excellence depends on eminence of manner as well as eminence of matter. Given significance of ideas, great public address demands an expression that renders the idea in a striking and compelling way, giving it life and vitality. This view is something of a departure from the thinking of those theorists of the past who asserted that expression is simply that use of language which is required to give thought its natural expression. John Henry Newman, the nineteenth-century English writer, said, "Thought and speech are inseparable from each other. Matter and expression are parts of one: Style is a thinking out into language." Joubert, a late eighteenth- and early nineteenth-century French philosopher, maintained that "as soon as a thought has reached its full perfection, the word springs into being, offers itself, and clothes the thought." Such thinking suggests that a thought, like nature, has an inherent form; as the form of a flower is implicit in the seed from which it is born, so too is the form of a thought implicit in the germ of the idea that gives rise to its expression. But as the seed of a flower is influenced by the environment in which it is planted, so too is a thought influenced by the peculiarities of the rhetorical environment in which it is nourished.

Much attention has been given to style as one aspect of this rhetorical environment. Buffon, in an address to the French Academy in 1753, said: "The style is the man himself." This statement does not deny the importance of thought to expression. It suggests, rather, that both thought and expression reflect the personality of the speaker. Wackernagel, a nineteenth-century German scholar, defined style in this way:

> Style is no lifeless mask laid upon the substance of thought: it is the living play of the countenance, the play of living feature, produced by the expressive soul within. Or, again, it is simply an investiture of the substance, a drapery; yet the folds of the drapery are caused by the posture of the limbs that the drapery veils, and it is the soul, once more, that alone has given the limbs such movement and position.

While eminence in expression is determined by content, it is also determined by the speaker himself.

But there are other aspects of style in this rhetorical environment. Eminence in public address demands not only that a man with a unique personality express a worthy thought; it also demands that his thought be expressed in such a way that it will have the intended effect on a given audience, at a given time, in a given setting. To be effective, speech style must possess a human quality, since public address is public above all else. It presupposes the purposeful interaction of a man communicating with other men. It is not enough that a man has an idea worthy of expression; he must strikingly illuminate the thought in a manner that compels others to attend, understand, and accept. Roosevelt dispelled panic with the expression, "The only thing we have to fear is fear itself." Churchill imparted strength with the expression, "This was their finest hour." Kennedy inspired dedication with the expression, "Ask not what your country can do for you—ask what you can do for your country." Martin Luther King generated hope with the expression, "I have a dream." Rhetorical eminence is a worthy thought expressed in a compelling way by a speaker to an audience.

In the study of speeches, the student may acquire an appreciation for eminence in public address—an appreciation that transcends the body of precepts set forth in textbooks. He may find dynamic inspiration in the notable works of others that will stimulate him to seek only those subjects for speeches worthy of intelligent concern. Further, by reading speeches that reflect the purposive interaction of other speakers with their audiences, he may acquire an intimate sense of the rightness, appropriateness, and artistry of language that will help him to express himself with greater force. He can acquire personal excellence in no better way.

For Further Reading

ON SPEECH AS A HUMANE STUDY

Nichols, Marie Hochmuth, *Rhetoric and Criticism,* Louisiana State University Press, 1963. Chapter 1 analyzes rhetoric and public address as a humane study—as a study of man making enlightened choices in a rhetorical context.

Wilson, John F., and Carroll C. Arnold, *Public Speaking as a Liberal Art,* Allyn and Bacon, 1964. Chapter 1 probes speech as a liberal study showing man apprehending truths about himself and his environment and communicating them to others.

ON THE CRITICAL APPRAISAL OF SPEECHES

Hochmuth, Marie, "The Criticism of Rhetoric," in *A History and Criticism of American Public Address,* Vol. 3, David McKay Co., 1955, pp. 1–24. Discusses the nature of criticism in general and the process of speech criticism in particular.

Thonssen, Lester, and A. Craig Baird, *Speech Criticism,* The Ronald Press, 1948. Chapter 1 examines the nature of rhetorical criticism; chapters 8–17 detail preliminary aspects and standards of judgment for rhetorical criticism.

Wilson, John F., and Carroll C. Arnold, *Public Speaking as a Liberal Art*, Allyn and Bacon, 1964. Chapter 12 presents a methodology for the critical appraisal of speeches.

ON RHETORICAL THEORY

Aristotle, *Rhetoric*. The definitive ancient treatise on the art of rhetoric.

Clark, Donald Lemen, *Rhetoric in Greco-Roman Education*, The Columbia University Press, 1957. Chapter 2 explains what the ancients meant by rhetoric; chapter 4 presents the five ancient rhetorical canons of invention, organization, style, delivery, and memory; chapter 5 discusses how the ancients used speech models for study and emulation.

Wilson, John F., and Carroll C. Arnold, *Public Speaking as a Liberal Art*, Allyn and Bacon, 1964. Chapter 2 presents an overview of the historical development of rhetorical theory.

ON EMINENCE IN PUBLIC ADDRESS

Baird, A. Craig, *Rhetoric, A Philosophical Inquiry*, The Ronald Press, 1965. Chapter 8 discusses language and style in relation to rhetoric from a philosophical point of view.

Buffon, "Discourse on Style," in Lane Cooper, *Theories of Style*, The Macmillan Co., 1907, chap. 6. A brief essay focusing on the intimate connection between a man and his style of discourse.

Longinus, "On the Sublime," in Cooper, *Theories of Style*, chap. 4. A classic treastise on sublimity in discourse, with emphasis on its necessity for grandeur of thought.

Orwell, George, *Shooting an Elephant and Other Essays*, Harcourt, Brace & World, Inc., 1950, pp. 77–92. Discussion of "Politics and the English Language"; identifies common pitfalls in language usage in speech and writing.

Wackernagel, Wilhelm, "Selections from Poetics, Rhetoric, and the Theory of Style," in Cooper, *Theories of Style*, chap. 1. Discusses the relation of rhetoric to theories of style and prose.

Chapter Two

GAINING A PERSPECTIVE

Socrates: *I am contented with the admission that rhetoric is of two sorts: one, which is a mere flattery and disgraceful declamation; the other, which is noble and aims at the training and improvement of the souls of the citizens, and strives to say what is best, whether welcome or unwelcome, to the audience; but have you ever known such a rhetoric; or if you have, and can point out any rhetorician who is of this stamp, who is he?* Plato, *Gorgias*

This book is a collection of speeches that exemplify the major forms and principles of public address in contemporary American society. Rationale for the study of speeches has been presented in the preceding chapter; it thus remains for us to place in perspective the underlying philosophy and the procedural patterns for the use of this book.

THE ART OF RHETORIC

Rhetoric is a term with varied and vague meanings today. Major dictionaries, reflecting the popular confusion, list numerous definitions. Among those commonly cited are the following: the speech of stereotyped politicians—empty, misleading, insincere, and high-flown; an oratorical display or exaggeration; highly figurative language, commonly called "purple patches"; the art of prose writing; and, originally, the art of oratory. *Rhetoric, oratory,* and *eloquence* all come from roots meaning *to speak.* Quintilian, the Roman schoolmaster, translated the Greek word for *rhetoric* into Latin with the words *oratoria* and *eloquentia,* and he placed the art of rhetoric at the center of his educational system. Aristotle thought that rhetoric had the capacity to prevent the triumph of fraud and injustice, to instruct popular audiences, to help a person see both sides of an issue, and to help provide a dignified and distinctive means of self-defense. There were those who abused the art of rhetoric in classical times, just as today, but, for most, the word had a noble meaning.

As used in this text, *rhetoric* is the art of selecting and adapting ideas for the achievement of a desired response through verbal communication. Defined in this way, the rhetorical act involves the making of choices: choices relating to the matter of communication—what subjects may be chosen, what issues they embrace, and what values they embody; choices relating to the manner of communicating the mind's perceptions in order to produce a desired effect on one's listeners. It is important to the welfare of a democratic society that both of these orders of choices be ethical and enlightened. Not only must a speaker be discerning in his perception of truth, but he must succeed in articulating this truth to others as a guide for their personal and social behavior. Each speaker must decide for himself the ethical balance point between his own idea in its pure form and the idea modified to achieve maximum impact with a specific audience.

Let us examine, for a moment, two scenes that depict men making reasoned judgments concerning their worlds and responsible choices that relate the expression of their judgments to others.

The first scene took place at Faneuil Hall, Boston, on December 8, 1837. A meeting had been called to protest the action of a mob that had shot and killed the Reverend E. P. Lovejoy in Alton, Illinois, for his printing of an editorial censuring the mob burning of a live Negro. More than 5,000 people were assembled in the great hall when James T. Austin, attorney general of the Commonwealth, rose to defend the slayers of Lovejoy by comparing them with the mob that had accomplished the Boston Tea Party. His speech was loudly cheered. At that moment, Wendell Phillips, relatively unknown and only twenty-six years old, hurried to the platform and, despite heckling, delivered a reply that won the acclaim of the audience and the action of the assembly. "Mr. Chairman," he said:

> We have need for the freest discussion of these resolutions, and the events which gave rise to them. [Cries of "Question," "Hear him," "Go on," "No gagging," etc.] I hope I shall be permitted to express my surprise at the sentiments of the last speaker—surprise not only at such sentiments from such a man, but at the applause they have received within these walls. . . .
>
> The gentleman says Lovejoy was presumptuous and impru-

> dent,—he "died as the fool dieth." And a reverend clergyman of the city tells us that no citizen has a right to publish opinions disagreeable to the community. If any mob follows such publication, on *him* rests its guilt. He must wait, forsooth, till the people come up to it and agree with him. This libel on liberty goes on to say that the want of right to speak as we think is an evil inseparable from republican institutions. If this be so, what are they worth? Welcome the despotism of the Sultan, where one knows what he may publish and what he may not, rather than the tyranny of this many-headed monster, the mob, where we know not what we may do or say, till some fellow-citizen has tried it, and paid for the lesson with his life.

The second scene took place in the United States Senate on October 6, 1917. As people rarely reason their way into war, in times of war, emotion, rather than reason, guides the social hand. In the throes of wartime hysteria, the nation's soul and her organs of expression cry out for persecution of those suspected of disloyalty. As one of six senators who had voted against entrance into World War I, Robert M. LaFollette was the target of invective and slanderous abuse. When in early October 1917, an Associated Press wire included a recklessly libelous attack under the banner, "District Judge Would Like to Take Shot at Traitors in Congress," LaFollette could remain silent no longer. "Mr. President," he said, "I rise to a question of personal privilege."

> If I alone had been made the victim of these attacks, I should not take one moment of the Senate's time for their consideration . . . Neither the clamor of the mob nor the voice of power will ever turn me by the breadth of a hair from the course I mark out for myself, guided by such knowledge as I can obtain and controlled and directed by a solemn conviction of right and duty.
>
> But, sir, it is not alone Members of Congress that the war party in this country has sought to intimidate. . . .
>
> It appears to be the purpose of those conducting this campaign to throw the country into a state of terror, to coerce public opinion, to stifle criticism, and suppress discussion of the great issues involved in this war.
>
> I think all men recognize that in time of war the citizen must surrender some rights for the common good which he is entitled to enjoy in time of peace. But, sir, the right to control their own Government according to constitutional forms is not one of the rights that the citizens of this country are called upon to surrender . . .
>
> Rather in time of war the citizen must be more alert to the preservation of his right to control his government. He must be watchful of the encroachment of the military upon the civil

power. He must beware of those precedents in support of arbitrary action by administration officials which, excused on the pleas of necessity in war time, become the fixed rule when the necessity has passed and normal conditions have been restored.

In these two examples some rather striking parallels exist. In each case a man rose to protest the rule of the mob over individual liberty. In each case a man exhibited courage in standing fast for his convictions in the face of mob hostility. These speakers were not preoccupied with purple patches or empty, misleading, and insincere oratorical exaggerations. In each case a man exercised choices—moral judgments concerning his world, ethical and pragmatic judgments concerning the communication of his convictions to other men. Such is the rhetorical act.

In seeking to define the nature of this art, rhetorical theorists have identified those dimensions common to all instances of public discourse. First, there is a man with an idea and a speech purpose—the *speaker.* Governed by his physical, intellectual, and experiential characteristics, the speaker seeks to choose, structure, and present his message so as to elicit a desired response. Next, there is the *audience,* whose members see the rhetorical context through individual lenses. They may view the speaker as trustworthy, expert, and of good will, or they may set up emotional blocks to the speaker's message because his image and his reputation strike them unfavorably. They may view the speaker's thesis as interesting, wise, accurate, and of unquestionable merit, or they may erect barriers to the speaker's message because his ideas run contrary to the beliefs, attitudes, and values that their personal experiences have dictated to them. Finally, there is the *situation* in which the speech occurs: a place—a college classroom, the United States Senate, an ancient synagogue, or London's Hyde Park; a time—fourth-century Athens, twentieth-century Washington, December 7, 1941, November 22, 1963, or before lunch or after; a raison d'être—a prep-school commencement, a Rotary Club meeting, a Presidential inaugural, a murder trial, a United Nations Security Council meeting, a business association luncheon, or a scientific conference.

In addition to the dimensions of speaker, audience, and situation, speech theorists have identified four variables common to the speech itself. In attempting to elicit a desired response, the speaker makes choices concerning each of these four variables. Through the process that rhetoricians call *invention,* or the discovery and selection of the central idea and its supports, the speaker utilizes whatever evidence, reasoning, and appeals to audience motives and values will substantiate his message. The remaining three variables involve transmission of the idea. The speaker selects relevant patterns of *organization* to provide structure and design. Furthermore, the speaker employs impelling symbolization through *language* best suited to himself, his subject, the audience, and the setting. Finally, the speaker uses *delivery* to get his idea across to the audience. Whether he uses the impromptu, extemporaneous, manuscript, or memorized methods of delivery, he employs both voice and body to reinforce the meaning and feeling embodied in his message.

Standard speech textbooks contain general principles concerning these dimensions and variables as they pertain to all types of speeches. By including these principles, these sources seek to provide a foundation for purposive and responsible public address that the student may use as a guide for his speaking behavior. We will not discuss all of these principles. Rather, we will present examples of speeches illustrating them. Additionally, the introduction to each chapter will focus on the nature of the constraints that influence the choices a speaker must make in adapting principles to that speech form.

THE FORMS OF SPEECHES

From ancient times, men have sought to classify those social contexts that give rise to public discourse. They have done so in order to understand the nature of the rhetorical act better and to formulate principles by which it might be taught. In 336 B.C. Aristotle saw men in law courts trying to secure justice concerning past action. Accordingly, he identified one class of speeches as *forensic*. In a second instance, he witnessed men deliberating about problems and the best courses of action for their successful solution. He saw statesmen in the political assembly giving counsel and advice about the practicality and advisability of future policies. He saw men in legislative chambers seeking to exhort or dissuade those who could decide future action. These speeches he classified as *deliberative*. Finally, he observed men at ceremonial gatherings praising the virtuous and eulogizing the noble dead. At other times he beheld men launching vitriolic attacks against others at public gatherings. These speeches of praise and blame he labeled *epideictic*.

As Aristotle profited from appraising the speeches of his day, so too may the modern scholar of rhetoric profit from an examination of contemporary speeches. As we survey twentieth-century public address, we see men in public gatherings translating technical information into popular terms; we see men vividly describing and graphically narrating an experience or event. We classify this type of speaking as *imparting knowledge.* At other times we see men publicly probing for definitive meanings, searching for the causes of natural and social phenomena, and seeking out the implications of things and events. In these instances men are *augmenting knowledge.* In other situations we see lawyers seeking decisions concerning the legality of actions and politicians asking for the acceptance of what they validate as facts. These speakers are *affirming propositions of fact.* In still other situations, we see dramatic and literary critics applying criteria to art forms to establish a judgment concerning their quality; we see social critics asking for the acceptance of a personal or a social good that involves ethical and moral standards; or we see clergymen preaching funeral sermons in tribute to deceased parishioners. When men seek to intensify, formulate, or change human values, we label their efforts as ones *affirming propositions of value.* On some occasions we observe speakers seeking to make people vitally aware of those problems that hinder personal and social fulfillment. These men are *creating concern for problems.* Finally, we see men constructing and advocating programs for the solution of perplexing problems and for the ultimate betterment of mankind. This effort we call *affirming propositions of policy.*

Recognizing the importance of these major speech forms in society and the different kinds of speaking behavior that they embrace, most teachers provide students with speaking experiences approximating these forms or experiences that involve principles basic to them. Therefore, the six chapters that follow present both speech examples and theoretical expositions of the speech forms to guide the student in his own creative efforts.

The speeches in the following chapters may guide the student toward the realization of his own speaking potential through an awareness of the rhetorical efforts of others. In such study he will find that a sound process of invention is rooted in a liberal education, in honesty and validity of means and ends, and in incisiveness and exhaustiveness of inquiry and induction.

For Further Reading

ON THE ART OF RHETORIC

Baird, A. Craig, *Rhetoric, A Philosophical Inquiry,* The Ronald Press, 1965. This book presents a philosophical discussion of the art of rhetoric.

Brembeck, Winston L., and William S. Howell, *Persuasion: A Means of Social Control,* Prentice-Hall, 1952. Chapter 24 discusses the ethics of persuasion, especially the authors' social-utility approach.

Bryant, Donald C., "Rhetoric: Its Functions and Its Scope," *Quarterly Journal of Speech,* Vol. 39 (December 1953), pp. 401–424. Examines in depth rhetoric as informative and persuasive discourse.

Hochmuth, Marie, "The Criticism of Rhetoric," in *History and Criticism of American Public Address,* Vol. 3, David McKay Co., 1955, pp. 1–23. Examines the dimensions and variables of speaker, audience, place, purpose, time, and form.

Minnick, Wayne C., *The Art of Persuasion,* Houghton Mifflin Co., 1957. Chapter 12 probes various approaches to the ethics of persuasion.

Wallace, Karl R., "An Ethical Basis of Communication," *The Speech Teacher,* Vol. 4 (January 1955), pp. 1–9. Outlines four guidelines for ethical choices and conduct in speaking.

Weaver, Richard M., "Language Is Sermonic," in *Dimensions of Rhetorical Scholarship,* ed. Roger Nebergall, University of Oklahoma Department of Speech, 1963, pp. 49–64. Focuses on the nature, rationale, and argumentative approaches of sound rhetoric.

ON THE FORMS OF SPEECHES

Bryant, Donald C., and Karl R. Wallace, *Fundamentals of Public Speaking,* 2nd ed., Appleton-Century-Crofts, 1960, chap. 7. Presents a detailed discussion of the nature of informative speaking.

Ehninger, Douglas, and Wayne Brockriede, *Decision by Debate,* Dodd, Mead & Co., 1963, chap. 14. Discusses affirming propositions of definition, fact, value, and policy.

Walter, Otis M., and Robert L. Scott, *Thinking and Speaking,* The Macmillan Co., 1962, chap. 8–13. Discusses speeches that deal with problems, causes, solutions, values, and definitions.

ON THE INVENTION OF SPEECH IDEAS

Harrington, Elbert W., "A Modern Approach to Invention," *Quarterly Journal of Speech,* Vol. 47 (December 1962), pp. 373–378. Discusses the significant facets of a sound invention process.

St. Onge, Keith R., *Creative Speech,* Wadsworth Publishing Co., 1964. Chapter 17 presents some suggested guidelines for thought to aid the speaker in his preparation. Part Two of this book, pages 215–464, pinpoints, briefly discusses, and provides a short bibliography for each of 60 important contemporary speech issues.

Wilson, John F., and Carroll C. Arnold, *Public Speaking as a Liberal Art,* Allyn and Bacon, 1964. Chapter 5 examines the basic process of invention, including some general lines of thought to aid the speaker in his hunt for appropriate ideas and methods.

PART TWO

SPEAKING TO INFORM

Chapter Three

SPEECHES THAT IMPART KNOWLEDGE

There are social contexts that give rise to public discourse as a medium for imparting knowledge. In certain of these moments, the social purpose of speech is fully met by the public address that increases an audience's understanding of an event, fact, process, or concept. A professor of sociology, for example, discusses the major value systems of the American Negro with his students. A psychiatrist explains the nature of mental illness for a lay audience. In other of these moments, a speaker imparts knowledge as ancillary to the fulfillment of other speech purposes. A historian describes an event as a basis for appraising its historical significance. A civil-rights leader narrates a story of social injustice in order that he may elicit a fuller commitment to the cause of social tolerance. A senator explains a piece of legislation as a prelude to urging its adoption. Whether increasing an audience's understanding is the sole purpose of a speech or a secondary purpose, the goal of imparting knowledge imposes distinctive constraints on a speaker's behavior—constraints that strongly influence the choices he may make.

CONSTRAINTS IMPOSED BY SPEECH PURPOSE

When a speaker stands before a group in seeking to fulfill this speech purpose, he reports and clarifies the accumulated knowledge of past and present generations. Neither judge nor advocate, he is, for that moment, a source of knowledge concerning established facts and ideas. To fulfill his goal of securing popular understanding, he must communicate knowledge with *accuracy*, *completeness*, and *unity*. Wilson and Arnold have put it this way:

> The speaker who undertakes to explain how a tape recorder works will err seriously if he alleges that all tape recorders use

> vacuum tubes for sound amplification (many use transistors), he will err in a different way if he neglects to discuss the playback systems most recorders have, and he will err in another fashion if he does not make it clear that the entire mechanical system exists to preserve sound and re-present it for later examination. . . . His listeners may not reject him as a person for his error of fact, his omission, and his disregard for the total meaning of his material; but they will not understand tape recorders unless they understood them before. Why? The speaker did not put into his discourse those things that must be there if talk is to inform or teach: accuracy, completeness, unity.[1]

Given a specific body of knowledge to impart, a speaker must select those facts and ideas that an audience must have to gain understanding. His choices are as varied as the subjects about which he speaks. He may choose to classify and define, to compare and contrast, to use exact bits of evidence and broad generalizations drawn from the testimony of others. Whatever his choices, if he is to achieve this purpose, he must provide an accurate, complete, and unified representation of a body of knowledge.

CONSTRAINTS IMPOSED BY A PARTICULAR AUDIENCE

But it is not enough that a speaker knows the essential components of a truth. In seeking to impart knowledge to a particular audience at a particular time, he must transform his perceptions of established facts and concepts into symbols that evoke an understanding in those who listen. He must, at once, be faithful to the integrity of the truth that he seeks to impart and to the demands of the particular audience addressed.

That these demands need not be incompatible may be demonstrated by an example. Let us assume that you wish to clarify the processes of induction and deduction to an audience of workers who have come to your campus. Through numerous encounters with these terms you have concluded that *induction* is a method of systematic investigation that seeks to discover, analyze, and explain particular cases or facts in order to determine the existence of a general law embracing these facts, whereas *deduction* is a process by which a

[1] John F. Wilson and Carroll C. Arnold, *Public Speaking as a Liberal Art* (Boston: Allyn and Bacon, 1964), pp. 165–166.

particular conclusion about an instance is drawn from the application of a general law. In appraising your audience you recognize that while these terms are meaningful to you, they represent an unfamiliar level of conceptual abstraction to your audience. The rhetorical problem is clear. The solution is not.

In 1866, Thomas Henry Huxley was faced with this precise problem. The rhetorical choices that he made in explaining these processes to a group of English workingmen in his speech entitled "The Method of Scientific Investigation" are demonstrated in the following paragraphs.

> Suppose you go into a fruiterer's shop, wanting an apple—you take one up, and, on biting, you find it is sour; you look at it, and see that it is hard and green. You take another one and that too is hard, green, and sour. The shopman offers you a third; but, before biting it, you examine it, and find that it is hard and green, and you immediately say that you will not have it, as it must be sour, like those that you have already tried.
>
> Nothing can be more simple than that, you think; but if you will take the trouble to analyze and trace out into its logical elements what has been done by the mind, you will be greatly surprised. In the first place, you have performed the operation of induction. You found that, in two experiences, hardness and greenness in apples went together with sourness. It was so in the first case, and it was confirmed by the second. True, it is a very small basis, but still it is enough to make an induction from; you generalize the facts, and you expect to find sourness in apples where you get hardness and greenness. You found upon that a general law, that all hard and green apples are sour; and that, so far as it goes, is a perfect induction. Well, having got your natural law in this way, when you are offered another apple which you find is hard and green, you say, "All hard and green apples are sour; this apple is hard and green, therefore this apple is sour." That train of reasoning is what logicians call a syllogism, and has all its various parts and terms—its major premise, its minor premise, and its conclusion. And, by the help of further reasoning, which, if drawn out, would have to be exhibited in two or three other syllogisms, you arrive at your final determination. "I will not have that apple." So that, you see, you have, in the first place, established a law by induction, and reasoned out the special conclusion of the particular case.

In this instance, Huxley chose to impart only a very basic understanding of the processes of induction and deduction by showing them to be inherent in a commonplace happening familiar to the workers who comprised his audience. He chose not to treat the subtleties of form and fallacy. Did he compromise the integrity of the truth in order to win popular understanding? Most critics think not. While he simplified these processes, he did not misrepresent them. His illustration accurately portrays their essential nature. And it is complete in the sense of comprehensively demonstrating the specific purpose of the speech: to show that "there is not one here who has not in the course of the day had occasion to set in motion a complex train of reasoning, of the very same kind, though differing of course in degree, as that which a scientific man goes through in tracing the causes of natural phenomena." His speech possesses unity in providing a systematic development through which the listener may gain a clear grasp of the total meaning. In seeking to adapt this specific truth to his particular audience, Huxley was compelled to choose that knowledge which he might properly treat within the constraints imposed by time and audience.

What are these constraints? Basically they are of two essential types. The first order of constraints involves the *interest* that the speaker's subject holds for the audience. Since understanding is the goal of the speech designed to impart knowledge, the speaker must create in his audience a reason for concentrating on the information he wishes to transmit. Creating this interest is not always an easy task. Often the speaker must explain technical, detailed, and abstract concepts to an audience less interested than he in his subject. Under the circumstances, it becomes the speaker's task to enliven and vitalize his material. As a study of the choices that one speaker made, let us again return to the illustration employed by Huxley. In appraising his audience, Huxley realized that for the average English workingman of his time the scientific method represented an esoteric construct of little interest or significance to all but the chosen few—the disciples of science. By making his individual audience member "you," the chief participant in his illustration, by choosing a familiar common environment as the setting, and by selecting suspense words, "suppose" and "you will be greatly surprised," as major transitional devices, he gave to his material a sense of vitality, realism, suspense, and urgency that it did not naturally possess. He chose a hypothetical illustration for this purpose; others have selected metaphors, narratives, comparisons, contrasts, real and figurative analogies, and specific examples. Consequently, a speaker who is inventive need not worry about losing his audience even when he is talking on an unusual or difficult subject.

The second order of constraints that an audience imposes on a speaker seeking to impart knowledge concerns the *meaning* the speaker's subject holds for the audience. Even a highly motivated audience may lack the substantive, linguistic, and conceptual skills essential to understanding an idea presented in its most pure form. In recognition of these constraints, Huxley chose to move from a simple illustration to a complex generalization, to develop a common understanding of a process before attaching labels to it, and to use periodic summations of that which had been established. Others have used restatement and repetition, topical and chronological patterns of organization, strong transitions and introductory statements, synonyms and negation, comparison and contrast, examples and statistics, description and narration, photographs and films, blackboards and diagrams, gestures and movement, questions and answers, and varied patterns of rate and pitch.

CONCLUSION

Imparting knowledge is one of the primary and ancillary functions that speeches serve in society. When a speaker seeks to fulfill this purpose, he must be aware of the particular constraints that govern his speech behavior. He must be aware of the need for imparting his knowledge with *accuracy, completeness,* and *unity*. He must be aware of the demands that varied audiences impose on the choices he makes in giving *interest* and *meaning* to a body of knowledge. In other words, he must be faithful to the integrity of his perception of truth while adapting to the demands of his audience.

In the speeches that compose the remainder of this chapter, the student is encouraged to examine the choices others have made in giving impelling expression to facts and concepts so that others may understand. Study and evaluate the speeches from the standpoint of the constraints set forth in this chapter and from the standpoint of the speech principles cited in each headnote. In the first speech, "Healthier than Healthy," Karl A. Menninger strives to make meaningful for a lay audience some basic aspects of our knowledge about mental health. Carl Rogers, addressing a university faculty and staff about "What We Know about Psychotherapy," seeks to report and clarify research findings concerning psychotherapy. In the third speech, representatives of the Bell System report and explain the Telstar project, a major scientific breakthrough in electronic space communications. Lastly, in "Love, Law, and Civil Disobedience," Martin Luther King, Jr., explains the philosophy of a social movement—Negro nonviolence.

For Further Reading

Andersen, Martin, Wesley Lewis, and James Murray, *The Speaker and His Audience,* Harper & Row, 1964. Chapter 13 discusses the use of visual aids in communication. Chapter 17 presents an analysis of speaking to increase understanding.

Bryant, Donald C., and Karl R. Wallace, *Fundamentals of Public Speaking,* 3rd ed., Appleton-Century-Crofts, 1960. Chapters 7–10 explain methods of amplification, use of visual aids, organization, and introductions and conclusions in informative speaking.

Gilman, Wilbur, Bower Aly, and Hollis White, *The Fundamentals of Speaking,* 2nd ed., The Macmillan Co., 1964, pp. 62–82. A discussion of informative speaking, including twelve obstacles to imparting knowledge.

Hance, Kenneth G., David C. Ralph, and Milton J. Wiksell, *Principles of Speaking,* Wadsworth Publishing Co., 1962. Chapter 13 provides an insightful discussion of the informative process and the special types of informative speaking.

Larrabee, Harold A., *Reliable Knowledge,* Houghton Mifflin Co., 1945. The entire book explains in detail the use of logic—induction and deduction—in the establishment of reliable knowledge. Chapters 1 and 2 are of special value as they discuss man's external and internal sources of knowledge and make meaningful the concept of "reliable" knowledge.

Petrie, Charles R., Jr., "Informative Speaking: A Summary and Bibliography of Related Research," *Speech Monographs,* Vol. 30 (June 1963), pp. 79–91.

Reid, Loren, *First Principles of Public Speaking,* 2nd ed., Artcraft Press, 1962. Chapters 9–12 present profusely illustrated discussions on narration, exposition, visual aids, and introductions and conclusions in informative speaking.

Weinberg, Harry L., *Levels of Knowing and Existence,* Harper & Row, 1959. Chapters 1 and 2 present basic concepts about knowing and existence relevant to imparting knowledge.

HEALTHIER THAN HEALTHY

Karl Menninger

Dr. Karl Menninger, a renowned lecturer and psychiatrist, helped his father, Charles F. Menninger, start the Menninger Clinic for Psychiatric Research in Topeka, Kansas, in 1919; and in 1941, he and his brother William (Will) founded the Menninger Foundation for psychiatric treatment, education, and research in Topeka. Dr. Menninger is the author of several books on psychiatry and mental health, including Why Men Fail, *1918;* The Human Mind, *1930;* Man Against Himself, *1938;* Love Against Hate, *1942; and* Theory of Psychoanalytic Technique, *1958. He delivered this speech, "Healthier than Healthy," to an audience of laymen in the Chautauqua, New York, Amphitheater on April 5, 1958.*

This address is an exposition of four professional observations about mental illness. Dr. Menninger, before developing his major point, initially seeks to remove existing misconceptions about mental illness in the minds of his audience. The student is invited to examine the order in which Dr. Menninger presents these observations. What psychological advantage does he gain through the order of arrangement he uses? In a more general sense, why is order of arrangement even a factor for a speaker to consider if his primary target is understanding?

Since Dr. Menninger is addressing a lay audience, his message must be made especially interesting, clear, and meaningful. To this end, he employs interest devices, such as dialogue and example, extensively. Do these devices serve purposes other than the generation of listener interest? When discussing any technical subject with a lay audience, one of the foremost challenges to the speaker is to translate jargon into meaningful language. How successful is Dr. Menninger in this quest?

The digression on the evils of capital punishment, which occurs in the latter part of the speech, is understandable when one realizes that Dr. Menninger is past vice president of the American League to Abolish Capital Punishment. However, this departure interferes with the successful accomplishment of his speech purpose. First, it directs attention away from the central subject of the speech; second, it makes him an open advocate for a cause in the minds of his audience, rather than a professional man merely imparting knowledge about his field of specialization. And as an advocate, there is the danger that his total message may be judged in the light of audience values concerning capital punishment. This danger of arousing the prejudices of the listener is an important reason why a speaker is wise not to editorialize or digress from his subject when his primary objective is to impart knowledge.

1 I want to report four observations to you. I would call these "facts," except that I have an aversion for the expression, "Let's get the facts." One of the most untruthful things possible, you know, is a collection of facts, because they can be made to appear so many different ways. I was somewhat interested in sleight of hand when I was younger, and what always intrigued me was that the obvious facts could be so untruthful. It was a fact that here something was and a minute later it was there. It was a fact but it wasn't the truth, because what was over there wasn't what was here. There was something phoney about it.

2 Here are four observations I want you to consider. The first observation is that mental illness is something that may occur in the lives of any of us. It always develops rather unexpectedly. Nobody plans to get mentally ill, you know, and nobody expects to get mentally ill. We all expect we may get pneumonia or we may get a bad cold next winter. We expect physical illnesses of certain kinds, but no one expects a mental illness.

3 Nevertheless, mental illness does come; it strikes down friends and acquaintances, the prominent and the lowly, rich victims and poor ones. It is no respecter of persons. It may come to any one of us.

4 I do not want you to be alarmed by this statement. But I do want to break through the barrier of misapprehensions that divides the world into "those people"—meaning this time those impossible, outlandish, afflicted "crazy" people—and "us"—us sane, sensible people. That is the perfectly understandable, aristocratic view, but it is a mistaken one.

5 Mental illness used to be thought of only in the extreme forms or stages which render its victims incapacitated by reason of such symptoms as overwhelming depressions, paralyzing fear, delusional misapprehensions, or uncontrolled impulses toward unprofitable or undesirable behavior. Such individuals have to be taken in hand and cared for, even over their protests. True.

6 But surely many of us have experienced *some* degree of depression, some inhibition from irrational fear, some loss of self-control in social behavior. And, while it is true that one swallow does not make a summer, these *are* the symptoms of mental illness, and mental illness can be mild in degree, or severe, and it can be "in between."

7 This, of course, is not quite like the notion of some physical diseases. One can have many degrees of arthritis. But one either *has*

malaria or does not have it. The same is true with many other diseases. But in the case of mental illness, it seems that any of us can—indeed, all of us *do*—have some degree of it, at some times.

8 That is my first observation. Now for a second observation.

9 The general notion has long prevailed that, once mental illness has appeared, the victim is doomed. The illness progresses, the disability increases, the specter of dementia looms inevitably ahead. "Once insane, always insane," they said. Mental illness is incurable. Kindly and well-meaning doctors in state hospitals sometimes used to counsel relatives to go home and try to forget their poor father or sister or whoever it was; "He can never recover and you should remake your life as if he were dead."

10 This all seems incredible to us today, because we have quite the opposite view. Most attacks of mental illness subside; most of the patients recover. The trend of mental illness is *usually* back toward health, not toward permanent disability and incurability, and we believe that we know some ways to encourage that return to health, one of which is the sustained and sustaining love of friends and relatives. This is something *they* can do, while the doctors (and nurses and therapists) do what *they* can; all contribute to the patient's recovery from mental illness.

11 The third observation I am going to make is that some mental illnesses seem to recover for a while and then stop and other mental illnesses recover slowly and others may recover more rapidly but may recur. They come back again. People often ask me, "You say that eighty-five to ninety per cent of all the patients in the state hospitals that you know about are out within a year. How many of them come back?" They always say this with a knowing look in their eye. "Ah, we've got you there." They haven't got me at all. I admit that something like a fifth of them come back, perhaps even as many as a fourth. "Well," they say, "in other words, they weren't cured." "Well, I do not agree with that. I have had pneumonia three or four times and I don't consider that I wasn't cured of it." Well, I guess I am likely to have another attack. I expect to get over it if I do. Similarly, I think people with a mental illness can have another attack. It is something they will recover from, in all probability. But now you see this is a different attitude. This attitude of, "He is probably a little crazy underneath and just waiting for it to appear," is the old medieval, suspicious, devil-possession attitude toward mental illness which we psychiatrists and those interested in mental health wish so much that the public could learn to renounce. They will learn to renounce it when they have had more experience. That is why we wish everybody could have more exposure, more contact, and more communication with the mentally ill. It is a pity that every one of you can't visit some of our patients and make life a little more enjoyable for them. Go and read to them if you like; go and talk with them; go and chat with them about things; they would enjoy it. They would like to have you. You do have to be screened by the hospital authorities, but they will be glad to do it. Most state hospitals now have hundreds of volunteers.

12 The fourth observation I wanted to make is that some patients may have a mental illness and then get well, and then may even get "weller"! I mean they get better than they ever were. They get even better than they were before. This is an extraordinary and little-realized truth—and it constitutes the main point of my talk today. Take an instance familiar to all of you. Abraham Lincoln was undoubtedly a far more productive, a far bigger man, and a far broader and wiser man after his attack of mental illness than he was before. Prior to it he had seemed to fail at everything—in his profession, in politics, in love. After his terrible year of depression, he rose to the great heights of vision and accomplishment for which we all know him. And Lincoln is not the only one; there are many others, but he is a conspicuous one. Now I ask you, does this occur in physical illness?

13 It was noticed in England by a very observing doctor, Dr. Jenner, that some of the milkmaids caught a disease called "cowpox." They subsequently seemed to be a little healthier in some respects than did the other people. Particularly when smallpox came, which was one of the great plagues of the world, as you know, it was noticed that these milkmaids didn't get it. From that it was gradually discovered through a process of some numerous steps that if you get cowpox, you are in some way or other protected against getting smallpox. Now this idea of inoculation, giving you one disease to prevent your getting another, is a kind of a way of making you "weller" than you were before, in that you are protected against something that you previously haven't been protected against. Cowpox being less serious than smallpox, most of us are glad to have it. Of course most of us have had it now. Cowpox got to be one of the great popular diseases of the world and everybody tried to get it, just as we try to have our little girls and boys get the German measles to protect them against serious trouble later.

14 Now for another illustration. People who have arthritis noticed long ago that if they have a fever of some kind from another cause, their arthritis gets much better. So the treatment was tried of giving them a fever artificially in various ways. We tried giving them an abscess. Now an abscess is pretty painful, but not necessarily as painful as the arthritis, and so a severe abscess will sometimes seem to improve the arthritis. We have better ways of producing fever now with fever machines which don't cause infections. I am just giving you the principle.

15 Another discovery with which you are probably familiar was made accidentally when a drug being used experimentally seemed to cause convulsions. It was not meant to cause them, but after the convulsions had occurred it was noticed that some of the sick people were improved in ways that had no relation to the disease for which they were being treated. This is the way that electroshock and insulin shock were discovered, by accident during an attempt to cure some other condition—diabetes, for example. The point that I am trying to develop is the old principle that sometimes one illness can, in some way or other, drive out another illness.

16 I remember an old story which I am sure you have heard. My dentist told it to me when I was just a little boy. If a tooth was to be extracted he would guarantee that the pain would go away if I would do exactly what he told me. Of course I said, "Well what is it?" He said, "I will give you a hatpin, and when I tell you, stick the hatpin the full length right in your leg and you won't notice that your tooth hurts!" That principle sort of stuck with me and I wrestled with it quite a while! Then I ran across the fact that Hippocrates, who was a kind of father of scientific medicine, believed in what he called the healing powers of nature. However, he thought that nature was outside the body. He didn't think of the body as being nature so much at first. Later he did. He thought sunshine and fresh air were great healers, but he also noticed that a great many diseases were cured if *hemorrhoids* developed! Now why on earth he made that observation—and I doubt the accuracy of it—I don't know. The question is, supposing that that were true; how would we be able to repeat that experiment of nature in a therapeutic way? I don't know.

17 This idea that illnesses can be replaced or changed is one that I am asking you to concentrate on because I want to go back now to mental illnesses. We have thought for a long time that various drugs could cure illnesses in various ways by neutralizing the infection, or by stimulating certain responses in the body to combat them. Now I want to invite your thinking for a few minutes on what the word "recovery" means. In what way does the hatpin illness cause one to recover from a dental illness, so to speak?

18 Suppose you think of somebody who is ill—not yourself, somebody else; there one can be more objective. He is ill, but somebody says he has recovered. Now who says he has recovered? Let's say that *he* says he is recovered. What does he mean? I suppose he means that he doesn't have any pain any more; or perhaps he means that he doesn't have the disability he had had . . . he doesn't limp so much, or he can move his arm more freely; or perhaps he merely means that he doesn't feel so hopeless and the world looks bright again; or maybe he means that he is not so aware of a rapid degeneration and disintegration of his corporal frame and in that sense feels that death is somewhat postponed. Obviously, none of us recovers from death. In one way of looking at it, we are all marching slowly, slowly, slowly toward disintegration. From that we never recover. We know that we don't recover from that progressive march, and what we recover from subjectively is discomfort rather than disease in that sense, or from a particularly rapid disintegration, or from disability.

19 Now look at it from the standpoint of the observer. The observer cannot see the pain, and he cannot feel the pain. He can only be told about it. If the patient says "I have pain," you have to believe it; or if he says, "I don't have pain," you accept that. But the observer, who might be a physician, has other ways of examining. *You* may say you feel perfectly well and think you have recovered, but *I* don't think so. The doctor may say, "I think you have recovered," and the patient says, "I don't think I have, as I still feel awful." Or it may be the other way. The physician may say, "I have evidence from tests and from X-ray that you haven't recovered. You'll have to stay in bed a few more days." But the patient says, "But doctor, I feel fine. I want to get up." Now you have two judges. You could have another judge, couldn't you? What do the neighbors say? They may say, "Well, *he* may think he has recovered and the doctor may think so, but *I* don't think so. And I'll tell you why." And they tell you. Well, the neighbors have a point of view about this and it is one that we shouldn't neglect. Maybe the neighbors are the best judge of all; they may say, "He has never done a constructive thing for this community. He doesn't act like there was anybody but him on this earth. I don't call that recovery."

20 Suppose the neighbors say, "Oh, he looks fine; he has recovered." Let's suppose that the doctor says, "I have X-rayed you, I've made some blood tests, I have made some urine tests, I have observed you, I have taken your temperature, etc., and I think you have recovered." Suppose the patient himself says, "I am glad I have. The doctor says I have recovered, the neighbors say I have recovered, my wife says I have recovered; I guess I have recovered." Now suppose we give psychological tests to such an individual. A psychologist might conceivably say, "He is able to fool people pretty well, even himself, but he just thinks he has recovered. He hasn't recovered." In what way hasn't he recovered? He still continues to think loosely. He continues to misjudge people slightly. He still tends to project the blame to others. The question of whether and to what degree a person has recovered is all relative and is capable of being judged differently by different people.

21 This abstract case I am giving you, you may find a little dull. Let me give you a more dramatic one and you will see immediately what it means. Suppose I ask you if a certain person in your community, who has done a violent crime, has recovered. First you will say, "Recovered from what?" I'll ask you, "Did you think he was sick?" "Well," you say right away, "I don't think a healthy-minded person would do what he did." Well, then you assume that he must have been sick. "Do you think he has recovered?" "No, I don't. I think he is dangerous." Very well, let's all agree with you for the moment. Let's say, here is a person whose illness took a form worse than cancer, worse than pneumonia, worse than hemorrhoids, worse than diabetes, worse than any of these things. It took the form that made him hurt one of his fellow men. He has become dangerous. Certainly, then, somebody has to deny him liberty for a while. Let's leave vengeance and punishment and smug righteousness out of it. Let's just treat him objectively and say, "This is a dangerous person and he mustn't be in the position to hurt other people as he has a tendency to do. So let's watch him. We will watch him all year, and we will watch him next year, and the next, and the next." So we do, and this man develops a good many talents and becomes useful and decorous. Has he recovered? Let's ask the doctor to examine him. The doctor examines him and says, "I find no sickness. I find no evidence of sickness." Let's ask the people who have been in his vicinity—his neighbors. They say, "Well, he doesn't offend us. He is not a difficult person for us to adjust ourselves to. We find nothing that can be called a sickness. If he had one, so far as we are concerned, he is recovered." Then let's ask the person himself. He will say, "I think I am perfectly safe to be trusted. I don't think I would hurt anybody. I think I am recovered." Then let's ask the psychologist.

22 Now suppose they all agree. There will still be other people in the general public who will say, "We don't think he has recovered. We don't think he has ceased to be dangerous. We don't want him near us." You ask them on what basis they say that and they reply, "We just don't think he has. We don't want to believe that this could be possible." Now this isn't just a theoretical matter; it is one of the most puzzling problems for the federal government and the state government at the present time.

23 We don't want to be responsible for releasing people who are going to be dangerous, but we are just as alarmed today about retaining people in custody at your expense—and a very considerable expense—who are not only not dangerous but who are capable of doing splendid things, doing useful things and being community assets. The man committed his crime, but in my opinion that does not justify the state in committing a crime. That is why I am irrevocably, to the last ditch, opposed to capital punishment. I think the state has no right to commit a crime any more than an individual does, and taking peoples' lives is a crime and immoral in my opinion. Besides being immoral, it is unscientific, and it frequently defeats justice. It constantly leads people to be so afraid to take any responsibility of saying that a man is dangerous that they find him not guilty.

24 Nevertheless it is hard to say, when an individual has been detained in public custody for a while, that he is well enough to go. Everybody in the country has been angered, at times, by reading that such-and-such a terrible crime had been committed by a man who was recently discharged from such-and-such a prison. You know why. Many times the prison officials would like very much to keep the man; they know he is dangerous, but the judge didn't sentence him to stay until he was cured, or until he was recovered. The judge sentenced him to five years according to the statutes of the state law, or whatever it is. Therefore he served five years and then he is out. Penological people are very much distressed by this because the men that ought to be released they can't release and men they ought not to release they have to release, and this is because of the present rigid structure of the penal system.

25 I want to talk about the fact that people improve and we don't know how to handle people who have improved. If you have pneumonia, or if you have bronchitis or a bad cold, you don't feel as well as before you had it. You wait until it has run its course and then you say, "I am well again. I am just as well as ever. I am my old self." Of course you are not your old self. You are a different self because time has moved on. You have learned something. Maybe the cold did you some good. You theoretically could be better. Now in the case of mental illness it is very definitely and obviously true that frequently you are better.

26 Mental illness is frequently an experience from which the individual learns and profits and develops and grows. The fact that this can happen seems to me to illustrate a principle which some clergymen might seize upon to make the basis of quite a little inspirational thinking. Even Nietzsche, who was far from being a clergyman, said something like this: "This secret spake life herself unto me. 'Behold, I am that which must ever surpass itself.' " Now this tendency to constantly surpass one's previous state of existence is, of course, from the biological standpoint, comparable to growth. So we say of a person, "Is this man living up to his maximum potentialities?"

27 Have you read *Christie's Big Toe?* It is an incredible story. In a little tenement crowded with eleven or twelve children, one child who was born a spastic was regarded as being mentally deficient. He was noticed, however, scratching with his toe, which was the one part of his anatomy over which he had any continuous control. Gradually he began to draw with his toe and then to write, and under the guidance of his very busy mother ultimately to go beyond that and get some excellent training at one of the fine places in New York. Ultimately he wrote his autobiography, which is a unique document of the boy who could communicate only with his right big toe at first.

28 The ill individual narrows his vision till he ceases to see the multiplicity of opportunities. Is the recovered individual now a constructive social factor? Is he giving to the world as well as receiving from it? Giving money is a very good criterion, in a way, of a person's mental health. Generous people are rarely mentally ill people. On the other hand, let's not get critical of some of our stingy friends. Remember that stinginess is an illness. Stinginess is a symptom of some kind of a fear, so that they don't dare give of themselves even if they have money. They might run out. My dear friends, of course you are going to run out. You can't take it with you! I don't know how many hundreds of my patients are now asleep in the graveyard, leaving behind them far more money than they could handle. Far more money than their children can amicably divide, causing endless trouble and worry and oftentimes injury.

29 I remember I said to a man, "What on earth are you going to do with all that money?" He said, "Just worry about it, I suppose!" I said, "Well, do you get that much pleasure out of worrying about it?" "No, but I get such terror when I think of giving some of it to somebody." I said, "Well, you have quite a symptom there. But you are not alone in it. That is a fairly common symptom at your age. You are older, now, aren't you?" "Yes, I'm fifty-seven now, but I still feel just like I did when I didn't have anything."

30 Sometimes some people have a mental illness and grow beyond that. They begin suddenly to see they want to have fun in the broad sense of the word. They want to grow. They want to enjoy the gratitude of people. "I want to enjoy trees, I want to enjoy music, I want to enjoy the world." This represents a kind of growth that we frequently see in our patients who have been mentally ill and some who don't know that they have been mentally ill, and even some who haven't been ill at all. I think, in short, that this is my notion of the gradual and progressive growth that we all make in the direction of mental health. This is what I think mental hygiene is. Now, as I have been speaking perhaps you have been thinking, "Well that is what is done at Chautauqua." That is the whole spirit of Chautauqua and that is what I meant you to think. That is what I think mental health is.

WHAT WE KNOW ABOUT PSYCHOTHERAPY—OBJECTIVELY AND SUBJECTIVELY

Carl Rogers

Dr. Carl Rogers, Professor of Psychology and Psychiatry at the University of Wisconsin, is a prominent author and lecturer in the field of psychotherapy. The following text represents the essence of a speech Dr. Rogers delivered in the spring of 1960 to a faculty and staff forum at the California Institute of Technology.

One of the reasons for including Dr. Rogers' address in this book is that it offers an interesting comparison and contrast to Dr. Menninger's lecture, "Healthier than Healthy." Dr. Menninger spoke to a lay audience; Dr. Rogers, to the faculty and staff of an institution of higher learning. A pertinent question is whether Dr. Rogers' lecture would have to be altered significantly if it were to be given to an audience similar to the one addressed by Dr. Menninger. What, if any, changes would you suggest that might make this speech more interesting and meaningful for you as a member of a lay audience?

In the first section of this speech Dr. Rogers says that all his generalizations are based upon empirical evidence, but he never refers to any specific studies. The student reading this speech may profitably raise the question whether the audience addressed by Dr. Rogers viewed his information as complete and accurate. Under what circumstances might it be prudent for a speaker to cite specific sources for the information contained in an informative speech?

The second part of this speech is devoted to making the exposition of knowledge in the first part meaningful by placing it in a subjective context. How successful is Dr. Rogers' effort? What rhetorical devices are especially useful in making ideas meaningful?

This speech is reprinted by permission from Carl Rogers, On Becoming a Person: A Therapist's View of Psychotherapy *(Boston: Houghton Mifflin, 1961), pp. 59–69. Copyright © 1961 by Carl R. Rogers.*

1 In the field of psychotherapy considerable progress has been made in the last decade in measuring the outcomes of therapy in the personality and behavior of the client. In the last two or three years additional progress has been made in identifying the basic conditions in the therapeutic relationship which bring about therapy, which facilitate personal development in the direction of psychological maturity. Another way of saying this is that we have made progress in determining those ingredients in a relationship which promote personal growth.

2 Psychotherapy does not supply the motivation for such development or growth. This seems to be inherent in the organism, just as we find a similar tendency in the human animal to develop and mature physically, provided minimally satisfactory conditions are provided. But therapy does play an extremely important part in releasing and facilitating the tendency of the organism toward psychological development or maturity, when this tendency has been blocked.

3 I would like, in the first part of this talk, to summarize what we know of the conditions which facilitate psychological growth, and something of what we know of the process and characteristics of that psychological growth. Let me explain what I mean when I say that I am going to summarize what we "know." I mean that I will limit my statements to those for which we have objective empirical evidence. For example, I will talk about the conditions of psychological growth. For each statement one or more studies could be cited in which it was found that changes occurred in the individual when these conditions were present which did not occur in situations where these conditions

were absent, or were present to a much lesser degree. As one investigator states, we have made progress in identifying the primary change-producing agents which facilitate the alteration of personality and of behavior in the direction of personal development. It should of course be added that this knowledge, like all scientific knowledge, is tentative and surely incomplete, and is certain to be modified, contradicted in part, and supplemented by the painstaking work of the future. Nevertheless there is no reason to be apologetic for the small but hard-won knowledge which we currently possess.

4 I would like to give this knowledge which we have gained in the very briefest fashion, and in everyday language.

5 It has been found that personal change is facilitated when the psychotherapist is what he *is,* when in the relationship with his client he is genuine and without "front" or façade, openly being the feelings and attitudes which at that moment are flowing *in* him. We have coined the term "congruence" to try to describe this condition. By this we mean that the feelings the therapist is experiencing are available to him, available to his awareness, and he is able to live these feelings, be them, and able to communicate them if appropriate. No one fully achieves this condition, yet the more the therapist is able to listen acceptantly to what is going on within himself, and the more he is able to be the complexity of his feelings, without fear, the higher the degree of his congruence.

6 To give a commonplace example, each of us senses this quality in people in a variety of ways. One of the things which offends us about radio and TV commercials is that it is often perfectly evident from the tone of voice that the announcer is "putting on," playing a role, saying something he doesn't feel. This is an example of incongruence. On the other hand each of us knows individuals whom we somehow trust because we sense that they are being what they are, that we are dealing with the person himself, not with a polite or professional front. It is this quality of congruence which we sense which research has found to be associated with successful therapy. The more genuine and congruent the therapist in the relationship, the more probability there is that change in personality in the client will occur.

7 Now the second condition. When the therapist is experiencing a warm, positive and acceptant attitude toward what *is* in the client, this facilitates change. It involves the therapist's genuine willingness for the client to be whatever feeling is going on in him at that moment,—fear, confusion, pain, pride, anger, hatred, love, courage, or awe. It means that the therapist cares for the client, in a nonpossessive way. It means that he prizes the client in a total rather than a conditional way. By this I mean that he does not simply accept the client when he is behaving in certain ways, and disapprove of him when he behaves in other ways. It means an outgoing positive feeling without reservations, without evaluations. The term we have come to use for this is unconditional positive regard. Again research studies show that the more this attitude is experienced by the therapist, the more likelihood there is that therapy will be successful.

8 The third condition we may call empathic understanding. When the therapist is sensing the feelings and personal meanings which the client is experiencing in each moment, when he can perceive these from "inside," as they seem to the client, and when he can successfully communicate something of that understanding to his client, then this third condition is fulfilled.

9 I suspect each of us has discovered that this kind of understanding is extremely rare. We neither receive it nor offer it with any great frequency. Instead we offer another type of understanding which is very different. "I understand what is wrong with you"; "I understand what makes you act that way"; or "I too have experienced your trouble and I reacted very differently"; these are the types of understanding which we usually offer and receive, an evaluative understanding from the outside. But when someone understands how it feels and seems to be *me,* without wanting to analyze me or judge me, then I can blossom and grow in that climate. And research bears out this common observation. When the therapist can grasp the moment-to-moment experiencing which occurs in the inner world of the client as the client sees it and feels it, without losing the separateness of his own identity in this empathic process, then change is likely to occur.

10 Studies with a variety of clients show that when these three conditions occur in the therapist, and when they are to some degree perceived by the client, therapeutic movement ensues, the client finds himself painfully but definitely learning and growing, and both he and his therapist regard the outcome as successful. It seems from our studies that it is attitudes such as these rather than the therapist's technical knowledge and skill, which are primarily responsible for therapeutic change.

11 You may well ask, "But why does a person who is seeking help change for the better when he is involved, over a period of time, in a relationship with a therapist which contains these elements? How does this come about?" Let me try very briefly to answer this question.

12 The reactions of the client who experiences for a time the kind of therapeutic relationship which I have described are a reciprocal of the therapist's attitudes. In the first place, as he finds someone else listening acceptantly to his feelings, he little by little becomes able to listen to himself. He begins to receive the communications from within himself—to realize that he *is* angry, to recognize when he is frightened, even to realize when he is feeling courageous. As he becomes more open to what is going on within him he becomes able to listen to feelings which he has always denied and repressed. He can listen to feelings which have seemed to him so terrible, or so disorganizing, or so abnormal, or so shameful, that he has never been able to recognize their existence in himself.

13 While he is learning to listen to himself he also becomes more acceptant of himself. As he expresses more and more of the hidden and awful aspects of himself, he finds the therapist showing a consistent and unconditional positive regard for him and his feelings. Slowly he moves toward taking the same attitude toward himself, accepting himself as he is, and therefore ready to move forward in the process of becoming.

14 And finally as he listens more accurately to the feelings within, and becomes less evaluative and more acceptant toward himself, he also moves toward greater congruence. He finds it possible to move out from behind the façades he has used, to drop his defensive behaviors, and more openly to be what he truly is. As these changes occur, as he becomes more self-aware, more self-acceptant, less defensive and more open, he finds that he is at last free to change and grow in the directions natural to the human organism.

15 Now let me put something of this process in factual statements, each statement borne out by empirical research. We know that the client shows movement on each of a number of continua. Starting from wherever he may be on each continuum I will mention, he moves toward the upper end.

16 In regard to feelings and personal meanings, he moves away from a state in which feelings are unrecognized, unowned, unexpressed. He moves toward a flow in which ever-changing feelings are experienced in the moment, knowingly and acceptingly, and may be accurately expressed.

17 The process involves a change in the manner of his experiencing. Initially he is remote from his experiencing. An example would be the intellectualizing person who talks about himself and his feelings in abstractions, leaving you wondering what is *actually* going on within him. From such remoteness he moves toward an immediacy of experiencing in which he lives openly *in* his experiencing, and knows that he can turn to it to discover its current meanings.

18 The process involves a loosening of the cognitive maps of experience. From construing experience in rigid ways, which are perceived as external facts, the client moves toward developing changing, loosely held construings of meaning in experience, constructs which are modifiable by each new experience.

19 In general, the evidence shows that the process moves away from fixity, remoteness from feelings and experience, rigidity of self-concept, remoteness from people, impersonality of functioning. It moves toward fluidity, changingness, immediacy of feelings and experience, acceptance of feelings and experience, tentativeness of constructs, discovery of a changing self in one's changing experience, realness and closeness of relationships, a unity and integration of functioning.

20 We are continually learning more about this process by which change comes about, and I am not sure that this very brief summary conveys much of the richness of our findings.

21 But let me turn to the outcomes of therapy, to the relatively lasting changes which occur. As in the other things I have said I will limit myself to statements borne out by research evidence. The client changes and reorganizes his concept of himself. He moves away from perceiving himself as unacceptable to himself, as unworthy of respect, as having to live by the standards of others. He moves toward a conception of himself as a person of worth, as a self-directing person, able to form his standards and values upon the basis of his own experience. He develops much more positive attitudes toward himself. One study showed that at the beginning of therapy current attitudes toward self were four to one negative, but in the final fifth of therapy self-attitudes were twice as often positive as negative. He becomes less defensive, and hence more open to his experience of himself and of others. He becomes more realistic and differentiated in his perceptions. He improves in his psychological adjustment, whether this is measured by the Rorschach test, the Thematic Apperception Test, the counselor's rating, or other indices. His aims and ideals for himself change so that they are more achievable. The initial discrepancy between the self that he is and the self that he wants to be is greatly diminished. Tension of all types is reduced—physiological tension, psychological discomfort, anxiety. He perceives other individuals with more realism and more acceptance. He describes his own behavior as being more mature and, what is more important, he is seen by others who know him well as behaving in a more mature fashion.

22 Not only are these changes shown by various studies to occur during the period of therapy, but careful follow-up studies conducted six to eighteen months following the conclusion of therapy indicate that these changes persist.

23 Perhaps the facts I have given will make it clear why I feel that we are approaching the point where we can write a genuine equation in this subtle area of interpersonal relationships. Using all of the research findings we have, here is a tentative formulation of the crude equation which I believe contains the facts.

24 The more that the client perceives the therapist as real or genuine, as emphatic, as having an unconditional regard for him, the more the client will move away from a static, fixed, unfeeling, impersonal type of functioning, and the more he will move toward a way of functioning marked by a fluid, changing, acceptant experiencing of differentiated personal feelings. The consequence of this movement is an alteration in personality and behavior in the direction of psychic health and maturity and more realistic relationships to self, others, and the environment.

25 Up to this point I have spoken of the process of counseling and therapy objectively, stressing what we know, writing it as a crude equation in which we can at least tentatively put down the specific terms. But let me now try to approach it from the inside, and without ignoring this factual knowledge, present this equation as it occurs subjectively in both therapist and client. I want to do this because therapy in its occurrence is a highly personal, subjective experience. This experience has qualities quite different from the objective characteristics it possesses when viewed externally.

26 To the therapist, it is a new venture in relating. He feels, "Here is this other person, my client. I'm a little afraid of him, afraid of the depths in him as I am a little afraid of the depths in myself. Yet as he speaks, I begin to feel a respect for him, to feel my kinship to him. I sense how frightening his world is for him, how tightly he tries to hold it in place. I would like to sense his feelings, and I would like him to know that I understand his feelings. I would like him to know that I stand with him in his tight, constricted little world, and that I can look upon it relatively unafraid. Perhaps I can make it a safer world for him. I would like my feelings in this relationship with him to be as clear and transparent as possible, so that they are a discernible reality for him, to which he can return again and again. I would like to go with him on the fearful journey into himself, into the buried fear, and hate, and love which he has never been able to let flow in him. I recognize that this is a very human and unpredictable journey for me, as well as for him, and that I may, without even knowing my fear, shrink away within myself, from some of the feelings he discovers. To this extent I know I will be limited in my ability to help him. I realize that at times his own fears may make him perceive me as uncaring, as rejecting, as an intruder, as one who does not understand. I want fully to accept these feelings in him, and yet I hope also that my own real feelings will show through so clearly that in time he cannot fail to perceive them. Most of all I want him to encounter in me a real person. I do not need to be uneasy as to whether my own feelings are 'therapeutic.' What I am and what I feel are good enough to be a basis for therapy, if I can transparently *be* what I am and what I feel in relationship to him. Then perhaps he can be what he is, openly and without fear."

27 And the client, for his part, goes through far more complex sequences which can only be suggested. Perhaps schematically his feelings change in some of these ways. "I'm afraid of him. I want help, but I don't know whether to trust him. He might see things which I don't know in myself—frightening and bad elements. He seems not to be judging me, but I'm sure he is. I can't tell him what really concerns me, but I can tell him about some past experiences which are related to my concern. He seems to understand those, so I can reveal a bit more of myself.

28 "But now that I've shared with him some of this bad side of me, he despises me. I'm sure of it, but it's strange I can find little evidence of it. Do you suppose that what I've told him isn't so bad? Is it possible that I need not be ashamed of it as a part of me? I no longer feel that he despises me. It makes me feel that I want to go further, exploring *me,* perhaps expressing more of myself. I find him a sort of companion as I do this—he seems really to understand.

29 "But now I'm getting frightened again, and this time deeply frightened. I didn't realize that exploring the unknown recesses of myself would make me feel feelings I've never experienced before. It's very strange because in one way these aren't new feelings. I sense that they've always been there. But they seem so bad and disturbing I've never dared to let them flow in me. And now as I live these feelings in the hours with him, I feel terribly shaky, as though my world is falling apart. It used to be sure and firm. Now it is loose, permeable and vulnerable. It isn't pleasant to feel things I've always been frightened of before. It's his fault. Yet curiously I'm eager to see him and I feel more safe when I'm with him.

30 "I don't know who I am any more, but sometimes when I *feel* things I seem solid and real for a moment. I'm troubled by the contradictions I find in myself—I act one way and feel another—I think one thing and feel another. It is very disconcerting. It's also sometimes adventurous and exhilarating to be trying to discover who I am. Sometimes I catch myself feeling that perhaps the person I am is worth being, whatever that means.

31 "I'm beginning to find it very satisfying, though often painful, to share just what it is I'm feeling at this moment. You know, it is really helpful to try to listen to myself, to hear what is going on in me. I'm not so frightened any more of what *is* going on in me. It seems pretty trust-worthy. I use some of my hours with him to dig deep into myself to know what I *am* feeling. It's scary work, but I want to *know*. And I do trust him most of the time, and that helps. I feel pretty vulnerable and raw, but I know he doesn't want to hurt me, and I even believe he cares. It occurs to me as I try to let myself down and down, deep into myself, that maybe if I could sense what is going on in me, and could realize its meaning, I would know who I am, and I would also know what to do. At least I feel this knowing sometimes with him.

32 "I can even tell him just how I'm feeling toward him at any given moment and instead of this killing the relationship, as I used to fear, it seems to deepen it. Do you suppose I could be my feelings with other people also? Perhaps that wouldn't be too dangerous either.

33 "You know, I feel as if I'm floating along on the current of life, very adventurously, being me. I get defeated sometimes, I get hurt sometimes, but I'm learning that those experiences are not fatal. I don't *know* exactly *who* I am, but I can feel my reactions at any given moment, and they seem to work out pretty well as a basis for my behavior from moment to moment. Maybe this is what it *means* to be *me*. But of course I can only do this because I feel safe in the relationship with my therapist. Or could I be myself this way outside of this relationship? I wonder. I wonder. Perhaps I could."

34 What I have just presented doesn't happen rapidly. It may take years. It may not, for reasons we do not understand very well, happen at all. But at least this may suggest an inside view of the factual picture I have tried to present of the process of psychotherapy as it occurs in both the therapist and his client.

TELSTAR

Starting in 1955 with eight speakers, the Volunteer Speakers Program of the Bell Telephone System now includes more than 5,000 employees who have devoted a portion of their free time to speaking before audiences. By 1963, the annual audience of Bell Telephone Volunteer Speakers numbered in excess of 11 million people.

The "Telstar" speech, one of many given by representatives of the Bell System, was written by members of the public relations staff of the American Telephone and Telegraph Company and was released for use by Volunteer Speakers in July 1962. Approximately 550 speakers were trained to deliver this speech to audiences in communities served by the Bell System. The audiences to whom this speech was addressed included business and professional organizations, school and church groups, and social clubs.

The speeches presented by the Bell System represent an interesting study in speech purposes. Most audiences consider these speeches informative and entertaining. Representatives of the Bell System view them, in an ultimate sense, as part of a public relations program that seeks to inspire popular appreciation of the services Bell renders. To what extent is "Telstar" successful in achieving both of these purposes?

In imparting knowledge of the nature of satellite communication and the developments that made such communication possible, "Telstar" must be judged by standards of accuracy, completeness, *and* unity. *Having been approved by the scientists responsible for the research and technology leading to this achievement, the speech was judged by its authors as having met these constraints. Would you agree? The constraints of* interest *and* meaning *must also be evaluated. Through visual aids, careful explanation, and illustrations, Bell System speakers sought to reduce scientific technology to visual and auditory symbols with* meaning *for the lay audiences addressed. Which of these devices do you consider most effective?*

This text is an edited version of a speech presented by Volunteer Speakers of the Bell Telephone Companies and is printed by permission of the Bell System.

1 On July 10, 1962, at 4:35 A.M., a Delta rocket blazed off pad 17 at Cape Canaveral carrying the Bell System's Telstar Satellite. It was a "shot heard around the world!"

2 The launch of the experimental satellite by the National Aeronautics and Space Administration opens up an entirely new approach to global communications. Stated in somewhat technical terms, Telstar is now in orbit testing the actual use and reliability of "active" satellites for the transmission of broadband microwave radio signals. But the implication of that mouthful of words could touch the lives of all of us in many wonderful ways. The concept of space communications is nothing short of fantastic even in this fast-moving world where yesterday's science fiction is today's fact. Telstar gives us a chance to test the use of space for international business and personal telephone calls. It heralds the advent of "live" overseas telecasts from the cultural and entertainment centers of Europe. It might be interesting, for example, to watch the changing of the guard at Buckingham Palace. Or, the Olympic games in Tokyo. Even perhaps a fashion show direct from Paris.

3 Telstar comes in a small package like so many other amazing devices in our miniaturized wonder world of electronics. This little sphere of aluminum and magnesium is 34½ inches in diameter—only slightly larger than a beach ball. But it's worth more than its weight in gold. Four hundred Bell Telephone Laboratories scientists, engineers and technicians worked on the development of Telstar and associated microwave experiments. More than 15,000 components had to be put together, inspected and tested before it could be boosted into the blue. This cutaway view [Fig. 1] gives you an idea of how compactly the equipment is packed into the satellite. The electronic equipment is sealed in a 20-inch aluminum canister which is suspended inside the housing with nylon cord lacings. This helped absorb blast-off shock and space vibrations.

4 Let's take a close look for a moment at Telstar now orbiting the earth at an altitude varying from about 590 to 3,500 miles [Fig. 2]. At the top is a spiral antenna which sends out tracking signals and information about the satellite's performance. It also receives the command to turn Telstar "on" or "off" from the command tracker on the ground. In the dark squares are some of the 3,600 solar cells that are mounted on the exterior of the satellite. They are protected by coverings of clear, man-made sapphire. These solar cells charge 19 small batteries that provide Telstar's power. One of the things we are most interested in knowing is the effect of space radiation on the solar cells.

These four specially prepared silicon diodes are giving us that information. Around the middle of the satellite, in the small squares, are the receiving and transmitting antennas. In all, Telstar relays to earth 115 different measurements and data on operating conditions every minute. Now, why are satellites going to be so necessary in modern communication?

5 During 1962, the existing 700 overseas circuits, terminating in all parts of the world, handled over 5,000,000 calls. Reliable estimates say that by 1980, overseas requirements will approach 100 million calls and that kind of volume will take 10,000 circuits. This tremendous increase is due to the expansion of our international trade which means more foreign voice communications and much more information in the form of data will have to be transmitted. In fact, within a few years, we expect that this business of data machines in our country talking to similar machines in foreign lands may make up at least half of the total overseas traffic.

6 An interesting possibility was brought up recently by a group of prominent medical men. They want to establish a world-wide communications diagnostic center. This would allow for almost instant diagnosis of even the rarest diseases anywhere in the world. It could also mean that your medical history, including such things as television pictures of electrocardiograms, could be transmitted instantly to Rome, Cairo or wherever you happened to require treatment by specialists. Benefits such as these certainly point up the need for forging ahead rapidly with satellite communications. Not only that, but our government's defense needs are constantly expanding, even into the remote corners of the world.

7 Another important consideration is that satellite communications can make it possible for you to see on television, "live," the great news events of the world, when they happen, regardless of where they happen. Present underseas telephone cables do not have the ability to carry television programs. The last point I would make here is the extreme importance of having alternate facilities, so that if one system is put out of operation for any reason, there is another one available that can still do the job. We do this now on land, supplementing underground cables with microwave radio routes, and by building alternate systems *around* large cities so communications could continue uninterrupted even if large cities were destroyed in the event of war. You are no doubt aware of the fact, that calls travel by these microwave radio routes, as well as by long distance cable. Let me mention something here about how microwave sends telephone calls—because

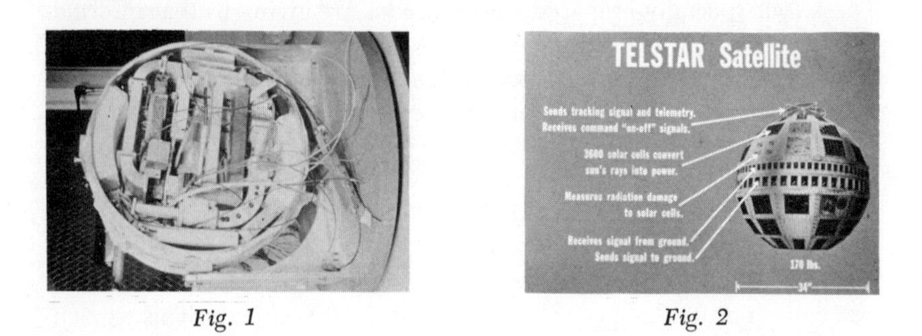

Fig. 1 *Fig. 2*

this is actually the transmission technique used by the Telstar satellite.

8 The Bell System built the first transcontinental microwave system early in the 1950's—a system of more than 100 towers, spaced at approximately 30-mile intervals across the United States. Since that time, we have been able to satisfy our customers' needs for additional telephone circuits as well as for cross-country or network television. Microwave has one disadvantage, however, which shows up when we come to the ocean. That is, the waves won't bend! Instead of following the curvature of the earth, they continue right out into space [Fig. 3]. Obviously then, we would either have to float microwave towers at 30-mile intervals across the ocean or face the equally impractical task of building one tower in the middle of the ocean high enough so that it would capture the signal for reamplification.

9 If we built such a "tower," it would have to be about 475 miles high [Fig. 4]. The answer then is to build our "towers in the sky" to supplement our present and future cables and to allow for diversification. And this is exactly what communication satellites are.

10 There are at least two altitudes in which satellites might be placed. One is a medium range (3,000 to 7,000 miles) system of

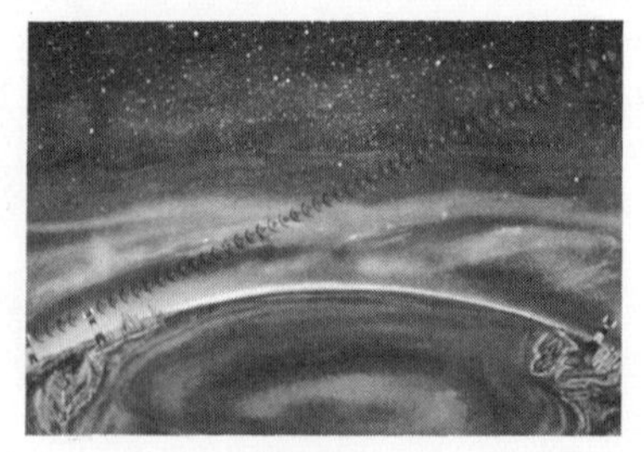

Fig. 3

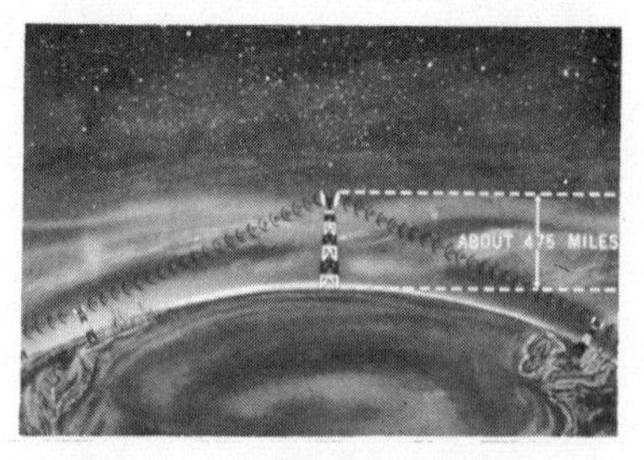

Fig. 4

Fig. 5

Fig. 6

encircling the earth with a number of satellites in random orbit [Fig. 5]. We would then relay our signal as necessary with at least one being always in view from any place on earth. The other possibility is to place three satellites, which would obviously have to be more powerful, in a fixed orbit about 22,000 miles up [Fig. 6]. At this altitude they would rotate at the same speed as the earth, always seeming to hang in the same position in the sky. A big problem here is getting a powerful enough launch vehicle to put the satellite in the precise orbit required at such a height. At this time, no one knows just how many communications satellites will be needed. Both systems have advantages and disadvantages and the final finished product may well be a combination of the two.

11 I'd like to mention here the Transistor and Bell Solar Battery, which are two of the key elements in Telstar. Without these two inventions and some others developed by the scientists at the Bell Telephone Laboratories, these things we are doing in space would almost certainly not have been possible. The transistor, on the left [Fig. 7], was invented at the Labs in 1948 and since that time has come to be known as the "Mighty Midget." Practically overnight, the transistor made miniaturization possible. Its other chief properties are its light

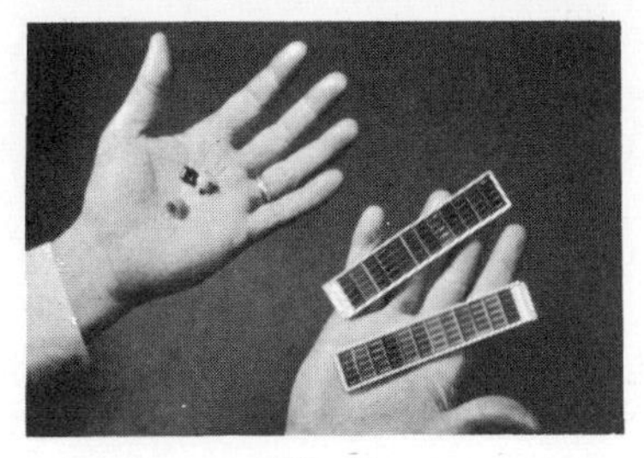

Fig. 7

Fig. 8

weight, its low-power requirements and its reliability. The solar cells, held in the right hand, came along a few short years later, also a result of Bell Labs scientists' efforts, and are the first practical devices for converting the sun's energy into useful amounts of electricity.

12 There are several other scientific break-throughs important to space communications, and the combined story makes as exciting a talk as the satellite itself. An interesting thing is that most of these developments came about with no specific thought of satellite communications. There is, for example, the MASER. MASER stands for "microwave amplification by stimulated emission of radiation." It is an amplifier which reduces by one hundred times the noise inherent in the very best receiving amplifiers of only a few years ago. The central element in the MASER is a man-made ruby crystal, cooled by liquid helium to 456 degrees below zero Fahrenheit. This is only two degrees above absolute zero.

13 Working right along with the MASER is the traveling wave tube shown here [Fig. 8], which can boost a satellite's signal strength 10,000 times. This was produced back in 1943. If you have any doubt that these things are necessary, let me point out that the power received from the satellite is only one billionth of a watt. It gets pretty weak after traveling several thousand miles through space.

14 Another stepping stone in the path that led to Telstar was in August of 1960 when the Project Echo *balloon* satellite was successfully launched. It was used for telephone experiments by Bell System scientists in New Jersey. Echo was simply a highly reflective mirror in the sky. It had no equipment aboard, as Telstar does, but its shiny surface permitted us to bounce voice signals back to earth, just as light reflected from a mirror. Echo looks simple now, but it was quite a step toward practical space communications. It was an immediate success. And it caught the public's fancy. Millions of people watched nightly for it to pass over at the times predicted in the newspapers or on news broadcasts and they still do! Echo is still up there, perhaps a little worse for wear but scientists are still conducting communications tests with it. To make communicating by satellite practical, however, we had to do more than just bounce the signal off a passive satellite like the Echo balloon. *This* we have achieved . . . with Telstar . . . which is capable of receiving, amplifying and retransmitting huge amounts of information over an extremely broad band of frequencies. We have been talking up to now primarily about the satellite itself. Of course we need more than a satellite to have satellite communications. There are other considerations.

15 The main one is the very complex ground stations needed to track and connect the space-relayed information to the nation's existing communications network where it can do its work. Ground stations have been built in the U.S. and in Great Britain and France. Italy and West Germany have theirs under construction. The Bell System's principal ground station is located on a 1,100-acre tract of land near Andover, Maine. Some of the considerations that led us to select this location were these: first, it is protected by a ring of hills and is away from concentrations of radio sources that might interfere. Also it is near good highways and is readily accessible to the Bell System telephone network. Lastly, it is almost the nearest site to Europe available and this is important since we're testing overseas communication by satellite.

16 We in the Bell System are glad to have played a part in the development of present domestic and international communications. We are also pleased with the contribution of the transistor, solar battery, traveling wave tube and the MASER in Communications Technology. But we are happiest of all because the dramatic accomplishments of Telstar have moved the world closer to the realization of world-wide satellite communications. On the evening of July 10, 1962, Telstar marked up these firsts in communications history:

17 One, it handled the first telephone calls by active satellite.

18 Two, it received and transmitted the first television picture of the American flag waving against the background of the Andover radome. This television transmission, was also received in France and England, thereby accomplishing the first overseas telecast. If you were at your own television sets that night, you saw some of this yourself.

19 Three, press association news stories were sent by way of the satellite, using the dataspeed device, a Bell System development which sends and receives 1,000 words a minute.

20 And four, representatives from the press used Telstar to transmit the news photo of the day—a telephoto of the satellite itself.

21 No question about it, July 10th was a spectacular day in the history of communications. And leaders all over the Free World spoke of the scientific achievement and the possibilities it brought for greater international understanding.

LOVE, LAW, AND CIVIL DISOBEDIENCE

Martin Luther King, Jr.

Dr. Martin Luther King, Jr., a Nobel Prize winner and a leader in the national nonviolent movement for Negro civil rights, delivered this address at the annual meeting of the Fellowship of the Concerned, November 16, 1961. The Fellowship of the Concerned is an organization of Presbyterian ministers and laymen that provides encouragement and financial assistance to churchmen whose stand on racial and social issues has put them under critical pressure.

Dr. King attempts to clarify the philosophy behind the nonviolent student movement for Negro civil rights to a friendly audience. To achieve this end, he enumerates the foremost characteristics of the movement and explains its rationale. Similar to the approach used by Dr. Menninger in "Healthier than Healthy," Dr. King uses an unfolding organizational approach in which he states each characteristic as he begins to discuss it. This procedure can easily lead to stilted and overworked transitions. Is this true of Dr. King's address? It is also important that transitions show a clear progression of ideas. Do Dr. King's ideas progress as effectively as Dr. Menninger's?

This speech demonstrates the important role definition may play in informative speaking. Dr. King analyzes the different meanings of the word love *in order to make explicit in what sense the word may be applied to the participants of the movement. When to define and how to define is a question that always presents itself to the informative speaker. Was it essential for Dr. King to define the word* love *carefully? What mode of definition does he employ? Are there other terms he could profitably have defined?*

Dr. King has been called a man with a very distinctive style. In which respects is style important in informative speaking? Does Dr. King's style in this speech seem more appropriate to persuasive than informative discourse?

This address points up the difficulty of placing speeches in precise, mutually exclusive categories, such as informative *or* persuasive. *While Dr. King explains the philosophy of the nonviolent student movement to a sympathetic audience, he may still, in some instances, formulate and intensify values through his manner of explanation. Exposition may have a persuasive impact. Are there any points in the speech at which Dr. King departs from the function of imparting knowledge and becomes an open advocate?*

This speech is reprinted by permission from Rhetoric of Racial Revolt, *ed. Roy L. Hill (Denver, Colo.: Golden Bell Press, 1964), pp. 345–356.*

1 Members of the Fellowship of the Concerned, of the Southern Regional Council, I need not pause to say how very delighted I am to be here today, and to have the opportunity of being a little part of this very significant gathering. I certainly want to express my personal appreciation to Mrs. Tilly and the members of the Committee, for giving me this opportunity. I would also like to express just a personal word of thanks and appreciation for your vital witness in this period of transition which we are facing in our Southland, and in the nation, and I am sure that as a result of this genuine concern, and your significant work in communities all across the South, we have a better South today and I am sure will have a better South tomorrow with your continued endeavor and I do want to express my personal gratitude and appreciation to you of the Fellowship of the Concerned for your significant work and for your forthright witness.

2 Now, I have been asked to talk about the philosophy behind the student movement. There can be no gain-saying of the fact that we confront a crisis in race relations in the United States. This crisis has been precipitated on the one hand by the determined resistance of reactionary forces in the South to the Supreme Court's decision in 1954 outlawing segregation in the public schools. And we know that at times this resistance has risen to ominous proportions. At times we find the legislative halls of the South ringing loud with such words as interposition and nullification. And all of these forces have developed into massive resistance. But we must also say that the crisis has been precipitated on the other hand by the determination of hundreds and thousands and millions of Negro people to achieve freedom and human dignity. If the Negro stayed in his place and accepted discrimination and segregation, there would be no crisis. But the Negro has a new sense of dignity, a new self respect, and new determination. He has reevaluated his own intrinsic worth. Now this new sense of dignity on the part of the Negro grows out of the same longing for freedom and human dignity on the part of the oppressed people all over the world;

for we see it in Africa, we see it in Asia, and we see it all over the world. Now we must say that this struggle for freedom will not come to an automatic halt, for history reveals to us that once oppressed people rise up against that oppression, there is no stopping point short of full freedom. On the other hand, history reveals to us that those who oppose the movement for freedom are those who are in privileged positions who very seldom give up their privileges without strong resistance. And they very seldom do it voluntarily. So the sense of struggle will continue. The question is how will the struggle be waged.

3 Now there are three ways that oppressed people have generally dealt with their oppression. One way is the method of acquiescence, the method of surrender; that is, the individuals will somehow adjust themselves to oppression, they adjust themselves to discrimination or to segregation or colonialism or what have you. The other method that has been used in history is that of rising up against the oppressor with corroding hatred and physical violence. Now of course we know about this method in western civilization, because in a sense it has been the hallmark of its grandeur, and the inseparable twin of western materialism. But there is a weakness in this method because it ends up creating many more social problems than it solves. And I am convinced that if the Negro succumbs to the temptation of using violence in his struggle for freedom and justice, unborn generations will be the recipients of a long and desolate night of bitterness. And our chief legacy to the future will be an endless reign of meaningless chaos.

4 But there is another way, namely the way of non-violent resistance. This method was popularized in our generation by a little man from India, whose name was Mohandas K. Gandhi. He used this method in a magnificent way to free his people from the economic exploitation and the political domination inflicted upon them by a foreign power.

5 This has been the method used by the student movement in the South and all over the United States. And naturally whenever I talk about the student movement I cannot be totally objective. I have to be somewhat subjective because of my great admiration for what the students have done. For in a real sense they have taken our deep groans and passionate yearnings for freedom, and filtered them in their own tender souls, and fashioned them into a creative protest which is an epic known all over our nation. As a result of their disciplined, non-violent, yet courageous struggle, they have been able to do wonders in the South, and in our nation. But this movement does have an underlying philosophy, it has certain ideas that are attached to it, it has certain philosophical precepts. These are the things that I would like to discuss for the few moments left.

6 I would say that the first point or the first principle in the movement is the idea that means must be as pure as the end. This movement is based on the philosophy that ends and means must cohere. Now this has been one of the long struggles in history, the whole idea of means and ends. Great philosophers have grappled with it, and sometimes they have emerged with the idea, from Machiavelli on down, that the end justifies the means. There is a great system of thought in our world today, known as Communism. And I think that with all of the weakness and tragedies of Communism, we find its greatest tragedy right here, that it goes under the philosophy that the end justifies the means that are used in the process. So we can read or we can hear the Lenins say that lying, deceit, or violence, that many of these things justify the ends of the classless society.

7 This is where the student movement and the non-violent movement that is taking place in our nation would break with Communism and any other system that would argue that the end justifies the means. For in the long run, we must see that the end represents the means in process and the ideal in the making. In other words, we cannot believe, or we cannot go with the idea that the end justifies the means because the end is pre-existent in the means. So the idea of non-violent resistance, the philosophy of non-violent resistance, is the philosophy which says that the means must be as pure as the end, that in the long run of history, immoral destructive means cannot bring about moral and constructive ends.

8 There is another thing about this philosophy, this method of non-violence which is followed by the student movement. It says that those who adhere to or follow this philosophy must follow a consistent principle of non-injury. They must consistently refuse to inflict injury upon another. Sometimes you will read the literature of the student movement and see that, as they are getting ready for the sit-in or stand-in, they will read something like this, "if you are hit do not hit back, if you are cursed do not curse back." This is the whole idea, that the individual who is engaged in a non-violent struggle must never inflict injury upon another. Now this has an external aspect and it has an internal one. From the external point of view it means that the individuals involved must avoid external physical violence. So they don't have guns, they don't retaliate with physical violence. If they are hit in the process, they avoid external physical violence at every point. But it also means that they avoid internal violence of spirit. This is why the love ethic stands so high in the student movement. We have a great deal of talk about love and non-violence in this whole thrust.

9 Now when the students talk about love, certainly they are not talking about emotional bosh, they are not talking about merely a sentimental outpouring; they're talking something much deeper, and I always have to stop and try to define the meaning of love in this context. The Greek language comes to our aid in trying to deal with this. There are three words in the Greek language for love, one is the word Eros. This is a beautiful type of love, it is an aesthetic love. Plato talks about it a great deal in his *Dialogue*, the yearning of the soul for the realm of the divine. It has come to us to be a sort of romantic love, and so in a sense we have read about it and experienced it. We've read about it in all the beauties of literature. I guess in a sense Edgar Allan Poe was talking about Eros when he talked about his beautiful Annabelle Lee, with the love surrounded by the halo of eternity. In a sense Shakespeare was talking about Eros when he said "Love is not love which alters when it alteration finds, or bends with the remover to remove; O' no! it is an ever fixéd mark that looks on tempests and is never shaken, it is the star to every wandering bark." (You know I remember that because I used to quote it to this little lady when we were courting; that's Eros.) The Greek language talks about Philia which was another level of love. It is an intimate affection between personal friends, it is a reciprocal love. On this level you love because you are loved. It is friendship.

10 Then the Greek language comes out with another word which is called the Agape. Agape is more than romantic love, agape is more than friendship. Agape is understanding, creative, redemptive, good will to all men. It is an overflowing love which seeks nothing in return. Theologians would say that it is the love of God operating in the human heart. So that when one rises to love on this level, he loves men not because he likes them, not because their ways appeal to him, but he loves every man because God loves him. And he rises to the point of loving the person who does an evil deed while hating the deed that the person does. I think this is what Jesus meant when he said "love your enemies." I'm very happy that he didn't say like your enemies, because it is pretty difficult to like some people. Like is sentimental, and it is pretty difficult to like someone bombing your home; it is pretty difficult to like somebody threatening your children; it is difficult to like congressmen who spend all of their time trying to defeat civil rights. But Jesus says love them, and love is greater than like. Love is understanding, redemptive, creative, good will for all men. And it is this idea, it is this whole ethic of love which is the idea standing at the basis of the student movement.

11 There is something else: that one seeks to defeat the unjust system, rather than individuals who are caught in that system. And that one goes on believing that somehow this is the important thing, to get rid of the evil system and not the individual who happens to be misguided, who happens to be misled, who was taught wrong. The thing to do is to get rid of the system and thereby create a moral balance within society.

12 Another thing that stands at the center of this movement is another idea: that suffering can be a most creative and powerful social force. Suffering has certain moral attributes involved, but it can be a powerful and creative social force. Now, it is very interesting at this point to notice that both violence and non-violence agree that suffering can be a very powerful social force. But there is this difference: violence says that suffering can be a powerful social force by inflicting the suffering on somebody else; so this is what we do in war, this is what we do in the whole violent thrust of the violent movement. It believes that you achieve some end by inflicting suffering on another. The non-violent say that suffering becomes a powerful social force when you willingly accept that violence on yourself, so that self-suffering stands at the center of the non-violent movement and the individuals involved are able to suffer in a creative manner, feeling that unearned suffering is redemptive, and that suffering may serve to transform the social situation.

13 Another thing in this movement is the idea that there is within human nature an amazing potential for goodness. There is within human nature something that can respond to goodness. I know somebody's liable to say that this is an unrealistic movement if it goes on believing that all people are good. Well, I didn't say that. I think the students are realistic enough to believe that there is a strange dichotomy of disturbing dualism within human nature. Many of the great philosophers and thinkers through the ages have seen this. It caused Ovid the Latin poet to say, "I see and approve the better things of life, but the evil things I do." It caused even St. Augustine to say "Lord, make me pure, but not yet." So that that is in human nature. Plato, centuries ago said that the human personality is like a charioteer with two headstrong horses, each wanting to go in different directions, so that within our own individual lives we see this conflict and certainly when we come to the collective life of man, we see a strange badness. But in spite of this there is something in human nature that can respond to goodness. So that man is neither innately good nor is he innately bad; he has potentialities for both. So in this sense, Carlyle was right when he said, that "there are depths in man which go down to the lowest hell, and heights which reach the highest heaven, for are not both heaven and hell made out of him, ever-lasting miracle and mystery that he is?" Man has the capacity to be good, man has the capacity to be evil.

14 And so the non-violent resister never lets this idea go, that there is something within human nature that can respond to goodness. So that a Jesus of Nazareth or a Mohandas Gandhi, can appeal to human beings and appeal to that element of goodness within them, and a Hitler can appeal to the element of evil within them. But we must never forget that there is something within human nature that can respond to goodness, that man is not totally depraved, to put it in theological terms, the image of God is never totally gone. And so the individuals who believe in this movement and who believe in non-violence and our struggle in the South, somehow believe that even the worst segregationist can become an integrationist. Now sometimes it is hard to believe that this is what this movement says, and it believes it firmly, that there is something within human nature that can be changed, and this stands at the top of the whole philosophy of the student movement and the philosophy of non-violence.

15 It says something else. It says that it is as much a moral obligation to refuse to cooperate with evil as it is to cooperate with good. Non-cooperation with evil is as much a moral obligation as the cooperation with good. So that the student movement is willing to stand up courageously on the idea of civil disobedience. Now I think this is the part of the student movement that is probably misunderstood more than anything else. And it is a difficult aspect, because on the one hand the students would say, and I would say, and all the people who believe in civil rights would say, obey the Supreme Court's decision of 1954 and at the same time, we would disobey certain laws that exist on the statutes of the South today.

16 This brings in the whole question of how can you be logically consistent when you advocate obeying some laws and disobeying other laws. Well, I think one would have to see the whole meaning of this movement at this point by seeing that the students recognize that there are two types of laws. There are just laws and there are unjust laws. And they would be the first to say obey the just laws, they would be the first to say that men and women have a moral obligation to obey just and right laws. And they would go on to say that we must see that there are unjust laws. Now the question comes into being, what is the difference, and who determines the difference, what is the difference between a just and an unjust law?

17 Well, a just law is a law that squares with a moral law. It is a law that squares with that which is right, so that any law that uplifts human personality is a just law. Whereas that law which is out of harmony with the moral is a law which does not square with the moral law of the universe. It does not square with the law of God, so for that reason it is unjust and any law that degrades the human personality is an unjust law.

18 Well, somebody says that that does not mean anything to me; first, I don't believe in these abstract things called moral laws and I'm not too religious, so I don't believe in the law of God; you have to get a little more concrete, and more practical. What do you mean when you say that a law is unjust, and a law is just? Well, I would go on to say in more concrete terms that an unjust law is a code that the majority inflicts on the minority that is not binding on itself. So that this becomes difference made legal. Another thing that we can say is that an unjust law is a code which the majority inflicts upon the minority, which that minority had no part in enacting or creating, because that minority had no right to vote in many instances, so that the legislative bodies that made these laws were not democratically elected. Who could ever say that the legislative body of Mississippi was democratically elected, or the legislative body of Alabama was democratically elected, or the legislative body even of Georgia has been democratically elected, when there are people in Terrell County and in other counties because of the color of their skin who cannot vote? They confront reprisals and threats and all of that; so that an unjust law is a law that individuals did not have a part in creating or enacting because they were denied the right to vote.

19 Now the same token of just law would be just the opposite. A just law becomes saneness made legal. It is a code that the majority, who happen to believe in that code, compel the minority, who don't believe in it, to follow, because they are willing to follow it themselves, so it is saneness made legal. Therefore the individuals who stand up on the basis of civil disobedience realize that they are following something that says that there are just laws and there are unjust laws. Now, they are not anarchists. They believe that there are laws which must be followed; they do not seek to defy the law, they do not seek to evade the law. For many individuals who would call themselves segregationists and who would hold on to segregation at any cost seek to defy the law, they seek to evade the law, and their process can lead on into anarchy. They seek in the final analysis to follow a way of uncivil disobedience, not civil disobedience. And I submit that the individual who disobeys the law, whose conscience tells him it is unjust and who is willing to accept the penalty by staying in jail until that law is altered, is expressing at the moment the very highest respect for law.

20 This is what the students have followed in their movement. Of course there is nothing new about this, they feel that they are in good company and rightly so. We go back and read the *Apology* and the *Crito,* and you see Socrates practicing civil disobedience. And to a degree academic freedom is a reality today because Socrates practiced civil disobedience. The early Christians practiced civil disobedience in a superb manner, to a point where they were willing to be thrown to the lions. They were willing to face all kinds of suffering in order to stand up for what they knew was right even though they knew it was against the laws of the Roman Empire.

21 We could come up to our own day and we see it in many instances. We must never forget that everything that Hitler did in Germany was "legal." It was illegal to aid and comfort a Jew, in the days of Hitler's Germany. But I believe that if I had the same attitude then as I have now I would publicly aid and comfort my Jewish brothers in Germany if Hitler were alive today calling this an illegal process. If I lived in South Africa today in the midst of the white supremacy law in South Africa, I would join Chief Luthuli and others in saying break these unjust laws. And even let us come up to America. Our nation in a sense came into being through a massive act of civil disobedience, for the Boston Tea Party was nothing but a massive act of civil disobedience. Those who stood up against the slave laws, the abolitionists, by and large practiced civil disobedience. So I think these students are in good company, and they feel that by practicing civil disobedience they are in line with men and women through the ages who have stood up for something that is morally right.

22 Now there are one or two other things that I want to say about this student movement, moving out of the philosophy of non-violence, something about what it is a revolt against. On the one hand it is a revolt against the negative peace that has encompassed the South for many years. I remember when I was in Montgomery, Ala., one of the white citizens came to me one day and said—and I think he was very sincere about this—that in Montgomery for all of these years we have been such a peaceful community, we have had so much harmony in race relations and then you people have started this movement and boycott, and it has done so much to disturb race relations, and we just don't love the Negro like we used to love them, because you have destroyed the harmony and the peace that we once had in race relations. And I said to him, in the best way I could say and I tried to say it in non-violent terms, we have never had peace in Montgomery, Ala., we have never had peace in the South. We have had a negative peace, which is merely the absence of tension; we've had a negative peace in which the Negro patiently accepted his situation and his plight, but we've never had true peace, we've never had positive peace, and what we're seeking now is to develop this positive peace. For we must come to see that peace is not merely the absence of some negative force, it is the presence of a positive force. True peace is not merely the absence of tension, but it is the presence of justice and brotherhood. I think this is what Jesus meant when he said, I come not to bring peace but a sword. Now Jesus didn't mean he came to start war, to bring a physical sword, and he didn't mean, I come not to bring positive peace. But I think what Jesus was saying in substance was this, that I come not to bring an old negative peace, which makes for stagnant passivity and deadening complacency, I come to bring something different, and whenever I come, a conflict is precipitated, between the old and the new, whenever I come a struggle takes place between justice and injustice, between the forces of light and the forces of darkness. I come not to bring a negative peace, but a positive peace, which is brotherhood, which is justice, which is the Kingdom of God.

23 And I think this is what we are seeking to do today, and this movement is a revolt against a negative peace and a struggle to bring into being a positive peace, which makes for true brotherhood, true integration, true person-to-person relationships. This movement is also revolt against what is often called tokenism. Here again many people do not understand this, they feel that in this struggle the Negro will be satisfied with tokens of integration, just a few students and a few schools here and there and a few doors open here and there. But this isn't the meaning of the movement and I think that honesty impels me to admit it everywhere I have an opportunity, that the Negro's aim is to bring about complete integration in American life. And he has come to see that token integration is little more than token democracy, which ends up with many new evasive schemes and it ends up with new discrimination, covered up with such niceties of complexity. It is very interesting to discover that the movement has thrived in many communities that had token integration. So this reveals that the movement is based on a principle that integration must become real and complete, not just token integration.

24 It is also a revolt against what I often call the myth of time. We hear this quite often, that only time can solve this problem. That if we will only be patient, and only pray—which we must do, we must be patient and we must pray—but there are those who say just do these things and wait for time, and time will solve this problem. Well the people who argue this do not themselves realize that time is neutral, that it can be used constructively or destructively. At points the people of ill will, the segregationists, have used time much more effectively than the people of good will. So individuals in the struggle must come to realize that it is necessary to aid time, that without this kind of aid, time itself will become an ally of the insurgent and primitive forces of social stagnation. Therefore, this movement is a revolt against the myth of time.

25 There is a final thing that I would like to say to you, this movement is a movement based on faith in the future. It is a movement based on a philosophy, the possibility of the future bringing into being something real and meaningful. It is a movement based on hope. I think this is very important. The students have developed a theme song for their movement, maybe you've heard it. It goes something like this "we shall overcome, deep in my heart, I do believe, we shall overcome," and then they go on to say another verse, "we are not afraid, we are not afraid today, deep in my heart I do believe, we shall overcome." So it is out of this deep faith in the future that they are able to move out and adjourn the councils of despair, and to bring new light in the dark chambers of pessimism. I can remember the times that we've been together, I remember that night in Montgomery, Ala., when we had stayed up all night, discussing the Freedom Rides, and that morning came to see that it was necessary to go on with the Freedom Rides, that we would not in all good conscience call an end to the Freedom Rides at that point. And I remember the first group got ready to leave, to take a bus for Jackson, Miss., we all joined hands and started singing together. "We shall overcome, we shall overcome." And something within me said, now how is it that these students can sing this, they are going down to Mississippi, they are going to face hostile and jeering mobs, and yet they could sing, "We shall overcome." They may even face physical death, and yet they could sing, "We shall overcome." Most of them realized that they would be thrown into jail, and yet they could sing, "We shall overcome, we are not afraid." Then something caused me to see at that moment the real meaning of the movement.

That students had faith in the future. That the movement was based on hope, that this movement had something within it that says somehow even though the arc of the moral universe is long, it bends toward justice. And I think this should be a challenge to all others who are struggling to transform the dangling discords of our Southland into a beautiful symphony of brotherhood. There is something in this student movement which says to us, that we shall overcome. Before the victory is won some may have to get scarred up, but we shall overcome. Before the victory of brotherhood is achieved, some will maybe face physical death, but we shall overcome. Before the victory is won, some will lose jobs, some will be called Communists, and reds, merely because they believe in brotherhood, some will be dismissed as dangerous rabble-rousers and agitators merely because they're standing up for what is right, but we shall overcome. That is the basis of this movement, and as I like to say, there is something in this universe that justifies Carlyle in saying no lie can live forever. We shall overcome because there is something in this universe which justifies William Cullen Bryant in saying truth crushed to earth shall rise again. We shall overcome because there is something in this universe that justifies James Russell Lowell in saying, truth forever on the scaffold, wrong forever on the throne. Yet that scaffold sways the future, and behind the dim unknown standeth God within the shadows, keeping watch above His own. With this faith in the future, with this determined struggle, we will be able to emerge from the bleak and desolate midnight of man's inhumanity to man, into the bright and glittering daybreak of freedom and justice. Thank you.

Chapter Four

SPEECHES THAT AUGMENT KNOWLEDGE

Sometimes a speaker's purpose is to probe the nature, genesis, and significance of a situation, event, movement, or idea. In such instances, the speaker goes beyond imparting a body of accepted fact. He draws upon information from varied sources in structuring a pattern of thought, a modus operandi, or a conception of reality not clearly expressed before. He presents his unique interpretation of the world about him. He asks the audience to understand and consider his conceptions, not that they necessarily accept his conclusions.

In some speeches, augmenting knowledge is a speaker's sole purpose. A sociologist explores the meaning of the term *mass culture*. A medical-research scientist probes the possible causes of arteriosclerosis. A political analyst appraises the impact of church affiliation on voting behavior. On other occasions, a speaker augments knowledge while fulfilling another of the social purposes of speech. For example, a politician defines political leadership prior to demonstrating that his party possesses qualities of leadership. A social worker examines the possible causes of juvenile delinquency before urging greater public concern. A Negro leader explores the political implications of racial violence as a basis for advocating a fuller commitment to the policy of nonviolent resistance. Whether augmenting knowledge is the sole objective of a speech or only one of its goals, the speaker must meet certain constraints.

CONSTRAINTS IMPOSED BY SPEECH PURPOSE

When a speaker addresses an audience for the purpose of augmenting knowledge, he seeks to convey some unique conception of the nature of things. He is a reporter and interpreter of a "truth" that he has ascertained through the process of inquiry. He is an investigator whose process of investigation is supposed complete and whose conclusions have been reached through that process. While the results of his inquiry may later be embodied in a proposition that he may persuade others to accept, he is not, for this moment, an advocate. Rather, he seeks to enlighten his hearers by asking them to consider with him those facts and those thought patterns on which he has based his own conclusions. His rhetorical choices are governed by the particular constraints of this speech function. These constraints demand that he convey an accurate view of the fields of observation comprising the basis for his analysis and a sufficiently complete view of the processes of analysis by which he derived his particular perceptions of truth. The speaker who distorts either the *substance* or the *process* of inquiry will fail to achieve this function.

The mass-communications analyst who seeks to augment our knowledge of the effects of televised debates on voter perception of Presidential candidates will fail in one respect if he neglects to report that his investigation was based on a population of 60 Republicans and 60 Democrats residing in and around Beaver Dam, Wisconsin. He will fail in another if he neglects to consider the specific tools of measurement he used for interpreting his data. Though his audience may not condemn his lack of accuracy and completeness in reporting, they will not understand the essential contribution of his research to our knowledge of the effects of campaign persuasion, the reason being that he has neglected to give the basis for his analysis and the processes through which he reached his conclusions.

The nature of the speaker's choices within these social constraints may be understood by examining the kinds of questions speakers frequently try to answer in augmenting knowledge.

Sometimes a speaker seeks to reveal and convey the true nature of a certain concept, process, event, or thing. The question he poses is "*What Is It?*" What is totalitarianism, democracy, or Chinese communism? What is extremism, conservatism, or expressionism? What is a slum, an enthymeme, or a civil right? What is a commencement speech, a literary critic, a hungry rat? While a speaker may answer these questions by simply discussing the results of others' explorations, he may, on occasion, wish to present his audience with his own research. If so, he must reveal the bases for his analysis—300 commencement speeches, selected examples of American literary criticism, or 100 white rats. He must also describe the process of analysis that he used: perhaps definition by comparison or contrast, definition by etymology or historical example, or definition by reported observation or survey.

At other times a speaker attempts to discover and pinpoint the major factor or factors that produced a situation, event, action, or idea. The question he poses is *"Why Is It?"* Why is deficit spending a prominent ingredient in our national economy? Why is the human being subject to coronary disease? Why is expressionism a force in the American theater? The choices a speaker may make in answering these questions are again governed by social constraints. Since his purpose is to enlighten his audience by contributing new insights into the forces responsible for known circumstances, he must reveal both his field of observation and the processes through which he reached his conclusions. Sometimes, a speaker may legitimately make an inference of causation about monkey behavior on the basis of careful personal observation of a dozen orangutans in a primate laboratory. On other occasions, the speaker's fields of observation must be wide and his processes of analysis complex in order that a reasonable degree of causal probability may be inferred.

At still another time, a speaker may begin with an event, idea, technique, or possible cause and ask, *"What Are Its Implications?"* For example, what are the economic implications of disarmament? What are the implications of our foreign policy in South East Asia? What are the effects of automation on the American economy? What are the effects of heterotransplants in the treatment of kidney disease? Here, as in the questions already considered, the choices a speaker may make in augmenting knowledge are governed by social constraints that necessitate a discussion of both the bases and processes of analysis. If, for example, the physicians in an audience at a medical convention are expected to understand the implications of a new surgical technique, the speaker must let them know both the number of instances in which the technique was employed (and the limitations imposed on his generalizations by his selection of patients) and the particular measures gauging its success, such as mortality rate, prolongation of life, and complete recovery.

Thus, whenever a speaker seeks to enlarge our total body of knowledge, he must report those observations and those processes of analysis by which he reached his unique perception of truth. His choices may be as varied as the subjects of his investigation. In exploring the nature, genesis and significance of natural laws and scientific phenomena, he may base his conclusions on a limited number of observed instances or specimens subjected to a certain precise treatment or analysis. In questions involving human conduct his inferences may require varied observations, the significance of which he has derived by statistical methods or the logical processes associated with definitional, causal, or interpretive analysis. In questions involving moral imperatives and philosophical truths, his conclusions may rest exclusively on the accepted processes of reasoning. Whatever his choices, if he is to achieve this social purpose, he must provide a sufficiently accurate and complete view of his field of observation and his processes of analysis, so that his audience may understand the particular contribution to knowledge his inquiry has unfolded.

CONSTRAINTS IMPOSED BY A PARTICULAR AUDIENCE

Just as when he speaks to impart knowledge, the speaker who would augment knowledge must consider the *interest* his subject holds for the audience. It is usually under ideal circumstances that a research scientist reports his findings to a convention of his fellows. In a less ideal moment, a college chaplain probes the meaning of sanctification while addressing students assembled for compulsory chapel during examination week. Though these examples represent extremes, they do suggest the vastly different orders of constraints that particular audiences may impose on a speaker. In the former instance the speaker is relatively free to proceed with his analysis without worrying about losing his audience. In the latter, the speaker must elect from a variety of choices those rhetorical devices that will capture his audience: humor or a sense of urgency, uniqueness or familiarity.

The speech to augment knowledge, like the speech to impart knowledge, is also an exercise in transforming the speaker's perceptions of truth into symbols that will have *meaning* for a particular audience. In this speech form, more than in any other, the speaker too frequently loses focus. His concern for the integrity of the truth he has discovered may cause him to overlook the audience he is addressing. We have all attended lectures at which the speaker made no observable attempt to adapt his ideas and materials to the level of his audience. "Here is my perception of truth," he seemed to say. "Take it—if you can—or leave it—if you must."

In fulfilling this speech purpose, a speaker must preserve the integrity of his inquiry while adapting his message to the substantive, linguistic, and conceptual abilities of his audience. Here, as in the speech that imparts knowledge, these demands are not incompatible. In the first place, the speaker should discuss only that portion of his total investigation which is compatible with his audience's level of comprehension. In choosing a focus for a particular speech he may reject certain concepts because they are too difficult, others because they are too elementary. In the second place, he should use those rhetorical devices that give his audience a faithful version of his inquiry. On some occasions he may wish to use technical language and direct exploration; on other occasions he may choose familiar language and amplify his subject through analogues, examples, or hypothetical illustrations.

CONCLUSION

One significant speech form is engendered by the primary and ancillary purpose that speech serves in augmenting knowledge. Whenever a speaker seeks to fulfill this social purpose, the rhetorical choices he may make are governed by certain constraints on his behavior. In order to achieve this purpose he must reveal to his audience, implicitly or explicitly, both the *fields of observation* and the *processes of analysis* that led to his conclusions. Whenever a speaker seeks to enlarge our total body of knowledge, he must also be aware of the demands that an audience places on his choices for giving *interest* and *meaning* to his unique perceptions of reality.

In the following speeches the student is asked to use the criteria developed in this chapter, and those special principles identified in each headnote, for studying and evaluating the choices other speakers have made when discussing their investigations. In the first speech, Lauralee Peters probes the question, "What Is Totalitarianism?" She uses certain analytical processes to arrive at a meaningful definition of a political term. Charles Beard, in "Written History as an Act of Faith," defines the nature of written history, thereby giving meaning to an academic discipline. In the last speech, Harry F. Harlow, a Wisconsin psychologist, reports and analyzes the causes and implications embodied in psychological research on monkeys in illuminating "The Nature of Love."

For Further Reading

Auer, J. Jeffery, *An Introduction to Research in Speech,* Harper & Row, 1959. Chapter 2 explores the nature of research and types of research studies.

Berlo, David, *The Process of Communication,* Holt, Rinehart and Winston, 1960. Chapter 11 gives insight into the nature and processes of definition.

Graves, Harold F., and Bernard S. Oldsey, *From Fact to Judgment,* The Macmillan Co., 2nd ed., 1963. Chapter 3 focuses on questions of meaning. Presents methods of defining and tells how to test definitions. Examples from essays are included.

Robinson, Richard, "Lexical Definition *and* Stipulative Definition," in Dudley Bailey, *Essays on Rhetoric,* Oxford University Press, 1965. This essay is reprinted from Richard Robinson's book, *Definition,* and consists of an intensive analysis of lexical and stipulative definitions.

Ruby, Lionel, *The Art of Making Sense,* J. B. Lippincott Co., 1954. Chapter 4 discusses definition from a semantic standpoint.

Stevenson, Charles L., *Ethics and Language,* Yale University Press, 1944. Chapter 9 discusses detached, intellectual definitions. Chapter 13 discusses persuasive definitions.

Walter, Otis, and Robert L. Scott, *Thinking and Speaking,* The Macmillan Co., 1962, pp. 163–171. Clear exposition of three important methods of definition.

WHAT IS TOTALITARIANISM?

Lauralee Peters

This analysis of totalitarianism *was prepared by a senior at the University of Kansas for a speech course in the summer of 1964. The assignment was to define an important term that does not have a commonly understood meaning. In arriving at her definition, the speaker uses three analytical processes: (1) she negates factors that do not represent true totalitarianism; (2) she explains the unique characteristics that make it different from other forms of government; and (3) she discusses the factors that give it special impetus.*

Negation is of special importance whenever a danger exists that listeners have prior misconceptions about the term to be defined. It also tends to make the speaker's definition more meaningful by contrast. Is the speaker's negation of misconceptions in this speech clear, meaningful, and complete? How essential to the success of this speech is the negation of misconceptions?

Testimony is a vital aspect of this speech. In a sense the speech represents an original synthesis of conceptions of other minds. It is apparent that the speaker's intent is to secure understanding of the materials and processes of her synthesis, as well as to secure understanding of the term totalitarianism. *Is Mrs. Peters' definition precise, clear, meaningful, and well supported?*

This speech is reprinted by permission of Mrs. Peters.

1 In the early 1930's a new word was coined in the language of the political scientist. Used at first to describe the changes occurring in Hitler's Germany and Stalin's Russia, the term *totalitarianism* soon enjoyed widespread usage. As with any complex term, however, its usage by laymen and newsmen looking for a convenient label has led to a dilution in its meaning. In the American press, for example, the term *totalitarianism* is applied to virtually anything which doesn't reek of democracy. Dictators, communists, strong military leaders and the like are all labelled totalitarian. In view of the present easy use, if not misuse, of this term, it is my purpose to attempt to arrive at some understanding of what the term *totalitarianism* actually means.

2 To begin with, totalitarianism does not mean simply any government which is not democratic in nature. To employ such a definition for the term would render it completely meaningless, for to be sure there are many forms of non-democratic rule in our present day world. Nor does the term *totalitarianism* denote any dictatorship. The dictatorships, for example, of most of South America and South East Asia, overthrown with great regularity as they are, reflect, not a totalitarian state, but a situation of intensified political struggle among the members of the power elite of the nation. What then does it mean?

3 To understand totalitarianism it is necessary for us to understand the unique aspects of a totalitarian state which make it different from other forms of government. J. A. Piekalkiewicz, professor of political science at the University of Kansas, has devoted considerable research and writing to the problem of defining totalitarianism. It is, he says, a system in which the group or party in control claims to have a complete and comprehensive plan or idea to answer all problems of a political, social, and economic nature in a given society. They claim to have, that is, a monopoly on truth and their monopoly includes the exclusion of all alternative solutions and all differing points of view. The solutions they have are total and comprehensive and the control they exercise over the people and the institutions of society is total and complete.

4 This definition, I think, helps us understand the unusual nature of the totalitarian state. Totalitarianism, for its existence, demands not only concentration of power in the hands of the government, but that this power be unlimited. Governmental power must be unlimited in two respects. First, it means complete government control of school curricula, newspapers, magazines, public and private utterances of individuals, in short all aspects of social and intellectual life. This control is maintained through extensive police forces with the power to eliminate any deviation or suspected deviation from the "official line." Second, there must be present a single-minded ideology which is all-encompassing in nature and to which devotion can be demanded of the people. The devotion is demanded not only to the ultimate ends of the society, but also to any means which the regime might employ. This is illustrated aptly by Arthur Koestler in his novel, *Darkness at Noon,* in which the central character is liquidated, not because he disagreed with the *end* of the Russian state under Stalin, but with certain minor aspects of the *means* being employed. Modern-day examples of the existence of such conditions include Hitler's Germany, Mussolini's Italy, and the Communist regime, particularly under Stalin. Another example of the totalitarian state which points to these characteristics is that of Paraguay under the rule of the Jesuits. Here was a state in which unlimited power was given to a government which possessed an all-encompassing ideology, in the form of the church, which demanded allegiance of the people.

5 N. A. Berdyaev, an early Marxist philosopher, wrote that at the basis of totalitarianism lies a reaction against fragmentation of human life and automatization of its various aspects. Thus the totalitarian state attempts to achieve a unity through the absolutization of the state, thereby hoping to achieve a unity of thought and purpose.

6 At this point we must ask the question, "Is totalitarianism compatible with modern technology and universal literacy?" Samuel Hendel in his book, *The Soviet Crucible,* says that it is an illusion to hold that totalitarianism is incompatible with these factors. Hendel notes that "It is precisely modern technology with its all-embracing means of communication, its high-speed transmission of commands and reports and armed force to any point in a country, its mass-communication and mass-conditioning techniques and the like, which for the first time makes it possible for total (undivided) power to aspire

to be totalist (all-embracing) power." It is, in fact, at this point that some political scientists distinguish between a totalitarian state and the absolute monarchy. According to one theorist, "It isn't that Louis the Fourteenth didn't try, he just didn't have the means available." Indeed this dependence on technology seems to be what Alexander Herzen, a nineteenth-century Russian liberal, foreboded when he wrote: "Some day Genghis Khan will return with the telegraph."

7 It is a fallacy to rely on universal literacy as a bulwark against totalitarianism. We need only to turn to modern Germany to see an example of one of the most highly literate and technologically trained peoples in the history of man adopting totalitarianism. Modern totalitarianism, in fact, requires that the people be able to read so that they can all be made to read the same thing at the same time. It is not the ability to read, but the ability to choose between alternative types of reading which is a potential—and only a potential—liberating element.

8 "Totalitarianism," then, describes, not every strong-arm regime, but rather a particular political system. This system depends on promulgating a single ideology through the undivided and all-encompassing power of the state. Attempts at establishing totalitarian states have met with varying success throughout history, but modern technology and methods of mass communication have given such attempts special impetus.

9 Perhaps the best description to date of the perfected totalitarian system is provided by George Orwell's novel *1984.* Orwell describes for us a state which has assumed almost infinite power over the lives of its people. Two-way telescreens placed in all public and private places enable the state to observe and listen to the citizens at all times; the Ministry of Truth rewrites history to agree with the party line and, using the telescreens, invades the lives of the people constantly with official propaganda; and finally a state language, Newspeak, is adopted, whose vocabulary expresses only those concepts the state deems desirable. Here we see the ultimate end of the totalitarian state. The utilization of *all* possible means of control to establish the ultimate supremacy of the state in *all* aspects of the people's lives.

WRITTEN HISTORY AS AN ACT OF FAITH

Charles A. Beard

Charles A. Beard, eminent American historian and author of well-known historical works, delivered this presidential address before the annual meeting of the American Historical Association at Urbana, Illinois, December 28, 1933. He made a searching analysis of the nature of written history.

Beard develops his speech differently from the speech on totalitarianism by Lauralee Peters. She proceeds inductively, advancing no explicit definition of totalitarianism until the end of her speech; Beard begins with a one-sentence definition of history and explains and defends it for the rest of his address. Both are useful approaches. Do you see any special advantages for either approach in terms of subject and audience?

Beard devotes most of his speech to negating other interpretations of written history; if he can successfully negate rival views, his own definition will stand. This analysis of other interpretations is of primary importance in this speech. Observe carefully the process of analysis Beard uses to achieve this end. Can you derive any general principles from it?

Beard uses a concise summary at the outset of his conclusion. Because of the length of his speech and the intellectual difficulty of his subject, this summary seems to add clarity to his message. Would most speeches profit from a summary?

Beard gave this speech to an audience of professional historians. The speech would have to be adapted considerably if it were to be given to a lay audience. What adaptations would you suggest? Perhaps organizational signposts? Simpler language? Use of illustrations? Explanations of special terminology, such as scientific method?

Definitions may be placed on a continuum. At one end, are the relatively detached, intellectual definitions of a person interested only in giving meaning to language. At the other extreme are the persuasive definitions of speakers interested in creating points of view that will influence the values of a group of listeners. The clergyman analyzing the meaning of Christian life *is trying, in all likelihood, to create a persuasive definition. Mrs. Peters' definition of totalitarianism is more detached than Beard's definition of history. Would you classify the intent of his definition as primarily informative or persuasive? Might his definition be placed approximately at the midpoint of the definitional continuum?*

This speech is reprinted by permission from The American Historical Review, *Vol. 39, 2 (January, 1934), pp. 219–229.*

1 History has been called a science, an art, an illustration of theology, a phase of philosophy, a branch of literature. It is none of these things, nor all of them combined. On the contrary, science, art, theology, and literature are themselves merely phases of history as past actuality and their particular forms at given periods and places are to be explained, if explained at all, by history as knowledge and thought. The philosopher, possessing little or no acquaintance with history, sometimes pretends to expound the inner secret of history,[1] but the historian turns upon him and expounds the secret of the philosopher, as far as it may be expounded at all, by placing him in relation to the movement of ideas and interests in which he stands or floats, by giving to his scheme of thought its appropriate relativity. So it is with systems of science, art, theology, and literature. All the light on these subjects that can be discovered by the human mind comes from history as past actuality.

2 What, then, is this manifestation of omniscience called history? It is, as Croce says, contemporary thought about the past. History as past actuality includes, to be sure, all that has been done, said, felt, and thought by human beings on this planet since humanity began its long career. History as record embraces the monuments, documents, and symbols which provide such knowledge as we have or can find respecting past actuality. But it is history as thought, not as actuality, record, or specific knowledge, that is really meant when the term history is used in its widest and most general significance. It is thought about past actuality, instructed and delimited by history as record and knowledge—record and knowledge authenticated by criticism and ordered with the help of the scientific method. This is the final, positive, inescapable definition. It contains all the exactness that is possible and all the bewildering problems inherent in the nature of thought and the relation of the thinker to the thing thought about.

[1] For a beautiful example, see the passages on America in the introduction to Hegel's *Philosophy of History*.

3 Although this definition of history may appear, at first glance, distressing to those who have been writing lightly about "the science of history" and "the scientific method" in historical research and construction, it is in fact in accordance with the most profound contemporary thought about history, represented by Croce, Riezler, Karl Mannheim, Mueller-Armack, and Heussi, for example. It is in keeping also with the obvious and commonplace. Has it not been said for a century or more that each historian who writes history is a product of his age, and that his work reflects the spirit of the times, of a nation, race, group, class, or section? No contemporary student of history really believes that Bossuet, Gibbon, Mommsen, or Bancroft could be duplicated to-day. Every student of history knows that his colleagues have been influenced in their selection and ordering of materials by their biases, prejudices, beliefs, affections, general upbringing, and experience, particularly social and economic; and if he has a sense of propriety, to say nothing of humor, he applies the canon to himself, leaving no exceptions to the rule. The pallor of waning time, if not of death, rests upon the latest volume of history, fresh from the roaring press.

4 Why do we believe this to be true? The answer is that every written history—of a village, town, county, state, nation, race, group, class, idea, or the wide world—is a selection and arrangement of facts, of recorded fragments of past actuality. And the selection and arrangement of facts—a combined and complex intellectual operation—is an act of choice, conviction, and interpretation respecting values, is an act of thought. Facts, multitudinous and beyond calculation, are known, but they do not select themselves or force themselves automatically into any fixed scheme of arrangement in the mind of the historian. They are selected and ordered by him as he thinks. True enough, where the records pertaining to a small segment of history are few and presumably all known, the historian may produce a fragment having an aspect of completeness, as, for example, some pieces by Fustel de Coulanges; but the completeness is one of documentation, not of history. True enough also, many historians are pleased to say of their writings that their facts are selected and ordered only with reference to inner necessities, but none who takes this position will allow the same exactitude and certainty to the works of others, except when the predilections of the latter conform to his own pattern.

5 Contemporary thought about history, therefore, repudiates the conception dominant among the schoolmen during the latter part of the nineteenth century and the opening years of the twentieth century—the conception that it is possible to describe the past as it

actually was, somewhat as the engineer describes a single machine. The formula itself was a passing phase of thought about the past. Its author, Ranke, a German conservative, writing after the storm and stress of the French Revolution, was weary of history written for, or permeated by, the purposes of revolutionary propaganda. He wanted peace. The ruling classes in Germany, with which he was affiliated, having secured a breathing spell in the settlement of 1815, wanted peace to consolidate their position. Written history that was cold, factual, and apparently undisturbed by the passions of the time served best the cause of those who did not want to be disturbed. Later the formula was fitted into the great conception of natural science—cold neutrality over against the materials and forces of the physical world. Truths of nature, ran the theory, are to be discovered by maintaining the most severe objectivity; therefore the truth of history may be revealed by the same spirit and method. The reasoning seemed perfect to those for whom it was satisfactory. But the movement of ideas and interests continued, and bondage to conservative and scientific thought was broken by criticism and events. As Croce and Heussi have demonstrated, so-called neutral or scientific history reached a crisis in its thought before the twentieth century had advanced far on the way.

6 This crisis in historical thought sprang from internal criticism—from conflicts of thought within historiography itself—and from the movement of history as actuality; for historians are always engaged, more or less, in thinking about their own work and are disturbed, like their fellow citizens, by crises and revolutions occurring in the world about them. As an outcome of this crisis in historiography, the assumption that the actuality of history is identical with or closely akin to that of the physical world, and the assumption that any historian can be a disembodied spirit as coldly neutral to human affairs as the engineer to an automobile have both been challenged and rejected. Thus, owing to internal criticism and the movement of external events, the Ranke formula of history has been discarded and laid away in the museum of antiquities. It has ceased to satisfy the human spirit in its historical needs. Once more, historians recognize formally the obvious, long known informally, namely, that any written history inevitably reflects the thought of the author in his time and cultural setting.

7 That this crisis in thought presents a distressing dilemma to many historians is beyond question. It is almost a confession of inexpiable sin to admit in academic circles that one is not a man of science working in a scientific manner with things open to deterministic and inexorable treatment, to admit that one is more or less a guesser in this vale of tears. But the only escape from the dust and storm of the present conflict, and from the hazards of taking thought, now before the historian, is silence or refuge in some minute particularity of history as actuality. He may edit documents, although there are perils in the choice of documents to be edited, and in any case the choice of documents will bear some reference to an interpretation of values and importance—subjective considerations. To avoid this difficulty, the historian may confine his attention to some very remote and microscopic area of time and place, such as the price of cotton in Alabama between 1850 and 1860, or the length of wigs in the reign of Charles II, on the pleasing but false assumption that he is really describing an isolated particularity as it actually was, an isolated area having no wide-reaching ramifications of relations. But even then the historian would be a strange creature if he never asked himself why he regarded these matters as worthy of his labor and love, or why society provides a living for him during his excursions and explorations.

8 The other alternative before the student of history as immense actuality is to face boldly, in the spirit of Cato's soliloquy, the wreck of matter and the crush of worlds—the dissolution of that solid assurance which rested on the formula bequeathed by Ranke and embroidered by a thousand hands during the intervening years. And when he confronts without avoidance contemporary thought about the nature of written history, what commands does he hear?

9 The supreme command is that he must cast off his servitude to the assumptions of natural science and return to his own subject matter—to history as actuality. The hour for this final declaration of independence has arrived: the contingency is here and thought resolves it. Natural science is only one small subdivision of history as actuality with which history as thought is concerned. Its dominance in the thought of the Western World for a brief period can be explained, if at all, by history; perhaps in part by reference to the great conflict that raged between the theologians and scientists after the dawn of the sixteenth century—an intellectual conflict associated with the economic conflict between landed aristocracies, lay and clerical, on the one side, and the rising bourgeois on the other.

10 The intellectual formulas borrowed from natural science, which have cramped and distorted the operations of history as thought, have taken two forms: physical and biological. The first of these rests upon what may be called, for convenience, the assumption of causation: everything that happens in the world of human affairs is determined by antecedent occurrences, and events of history are the illustrations or data of laws to be discovered, laws such as are found in hydraulics. It is true that no historian has ever been able to array the fullness of history as actuality in any such deterministic order; Karl Marx has gone further than any other. But under the hypothesis that it is possible, historians have been arranging events in neat little chains of causation which explain, to their satisfaction, why succeeding events happen; and they have attributed any shortcomings in result to the inadequacy of their known data, not to the falsity of the assumption on which they have been operating. Undiscouraged by their inability to bring all history within a single law, such as the law of gravitation, they have gone on working in the belief that the Newtonian trick will be turned some time, if the scientific method is applied long and rigorously enough and facts are heaped up high enough, as the succeeding grists of doctors of philosophy are ground out by the universities, turned loose on "research projects," and amply supplied by funds.

11 Growing rightly suspicious of this procedure in physico-historiography, a number of historians, still bent on servitude to natural science, turned from physics to biology. The difficulties and failures involved in all efforts to arrange the occurrences of history in a neat system of historical mechanics were evident to them. But on the other side, the achievements of the Darwinians were impressive. If the totality of history could not be brought into a deterministic system without doing violence to historical knowledge, perhaps the biological analogy of the organism could be applied. And this was done, apparently without any realization of the fact that thinking by analogy is a form of primitive animism. So under the biological analogy, history was conceived as a succession of cultural organisms rising, growing, competing, and declining. To this fantastic morphological assumption Spengler chained his powerful mind. Thus freed from self-imposed slavery to physics, the historian passed to self-imposed subservience to biology. Painfully aware of the perplexities encountered as long as he stuck to his own business, the historian sought escape by employing the method and thought of others whose operations he did not understand and could not control, on the simple, almost childlike, faith that the biologist, if not the physicist, really knew what he was about and could furnish the clue to the mystery.

12 But the shadow of the organismic conception of history had scarcely fallen on the turbulent actuality of history when it was scrutinized by historians who were thinking in terms of their own subject as distinguished from the terms of a mere subdivision of history. By an inescapable demonstration Kurt Riezler has made it clear that the organismic theory of history is really the old determinism of physics covered with murky words. The rise, growth, competition, and decline of cultural organisms is meaningless unless fitted into some overarching hypothesis—either the hypothesis of the divine drama or the hypothesis of causation in the deterministic sense. Is each cultural organism in history, each national or racial culture, an isolated particularity governed by its own mystical or physical laws? Knowledge of history as actuality forbids any such conclusion. If, in sheer desperation, the historian clings to the biological analogy, which school is he to follow—the mechanistic or the vitalistic? In either case he is caught in the deterministic sequence, if he thinks long enough and hard enough.

13 Hence the fate of the scientific school of historiography turns finally upon the applicability of the deterministic sequence to the totality of history as actuality. Natural science in a strict sense, as distinguished from mere knowledge of facts, can discover system and law only where occurrences are in reality arranged objectively in deterministic sequences. It can describe these sequences and draw from them laws, so-called. From a given number of the occurrences in any such sequence, science can predict what will happen when the remainder appear.

14 With respect to certain areas of human occurrences, something akin to deterministic sequences is found by the historian, but the perdurance of any sequence depends upon the perdurance in time of surrounding circumstances which cannot be brought within any scheme of deterministic relevancies. Certainly all the occurrences of history as actuality cannot be so ordered; most of them are unknown and owing to the paucity of records must forever remain unknown.

15 If a science of history were achieved, it would, like the science of celestial mechanics, make possible the calculable prediction of the future in history. It would bring the totality of historical occurrences within a single field and reveal the unfolding future to its last end, including all the apparent choices made and to be made. It would be omniscience. The creator of it would possess the attributes ascribed by the theologians to God. The future once revealed, humanity would have nothing to do except to await its doom.

16 To state the case is to dispose of it. The occurrences of history—the unfolding of ideas and interests in time-motion—are not identical in nature with the data of physics, and hence in their totality they are beyond the reach of that necessary instrument of natural science—mathematics—which cannot assign meaningful values to the imponderables, immeasurables, and contingencies of history as actuality.

17 Having broken the tyranny of physics and biology, contemporary thought in historiography turns its engines of verification upon the formula of historical relativity—the formula that makes all written history merely relative to time and circumstance, a passing shadow, an illusion. Contemporary criticism shows that the apostle of relativity is destined to be destroyed by the child of his own brain. If all historical conceptions are merely relative to passing events, to transitory phases of ideas and interests, then the conception of relativity is itself relative. When absolutes in history are rejected the absolutism of relativity is also rejected. So we must inquire: To what spirit of the times, to the ideas and interests of what class, group, nation, race, or region does the conception of relativity correspond? As the actuality of history moves forward into the future, the conception of relativity will also pass, as previous conceptions and interpretations of events have passed. Hence, according to the very doctrine of relativity, the skeptic of relativity will disappear in due course, beneath the ever-tossing waves of changing relativities. If he does not suffer this fate soon, the apostle of relativity will surely be executed by his own logic. Every conception of history, he says, is relative to time and circumstances. But by his own reasoning he is then compelled to ask: To what are these particular times and circumstances relative? And he must go on with receding sets of times and circumstances until he confronts an absolute: the totality of history as actuality which embraces all times and circumstances and all relativities.

18 Contemporary historical thought is, accordingly, returning upon itself and its subject matter. The historian is casting off his servitude to physics and biology, as he formerly cast off the shackles of theology and its metaphysics. He likewise sees the doctrine of relativity crumble in the cold light of historical knowledge. When he accepts none of the assumptions made by theology, physics, and biology, as applied to history, when he passes out from under the fleeting shadow of relativity, he confronts the absolute in his field—the absolute totality of all historical occurrences past, present, and becoming to the end of all things. Then he finds it necessary to bring the occurrences of history as actuality under one or another of three broad conceptions.

19 The first is that history as total actuality is chaos, perhaps with little islands of congruous relativities floating on the surface, and that the human mind cannot bring them objectively into any all-embracing order or subjectively into any consistent system. The second is that history as actuality is a part of some order of nature and revolves in cycles eternally—spring, summer, autumn, and winter, democracy, aristocracy, and monarchy, or their variants, as imagined by Spengler. The third is that history as actuality is moving in some direction away from the low level of primitive beginnings, on an upward gradient toward a more ideal order—as imagined by Condorcet, Adam Smith, Karl Marx, or Herbert Spencer.

20 Abundant evidence can be marshaled, has been marshaled in support of each of these conceptions of history as actuality, but all the available evidence will not fit any one of them. The hypothesis of chaos admits of no ordering at all; hence those who operate under it cannot write history, although they may comment *on* history. The second admits of an ordering of events only by arbitrarily leaving out of account all the contradictions in the evidence. The third admits of an ordering of events, also by leaving contradictions out of consideration. The historian who writes history, therefore, consciously or unconsciously performs an act of faith, as to order and movement, for certainty as to order and movement is denied to him by knowledge of the actuality with which he is concerned. He is thus in the position of a statesman dealing with public affairs; in writing he acts and in acting he makes choices, large or small, timid or bold, with respect to some conception of the nature of things. And the degree of his influence and immortality will depend upon the length and correctness of his forecast—upon the verdict of history yet to come. His faith is at bottom a conviction that something true can be known about the movement of history and his conviction is a subjective decision, not a purely objective discovery.

21 But members of the passing generation will ask: Has our work done in the scientific spirit been useless? Must we abandon the scientific method? The answer is an emphatic negative. During the past fifty years historical scholarship, carried on with judicial calm, has wrought achievements of value beyond calculation. Particular phases of history once dark and confused have been illuminated by research, authentication, scrutiny, and the ordering of immediate relevancies. Nor is the empirical or scientific method to be abandoned. It is the only method that can be employed in obtaining accurate knowledge of historical facts, personalities, situations, and movements. It alone can disclose conditions that made possible what happened. It has a value in itself—a value high in the hierarchy of values indispensable to the life of a democracy. The inquiring spirit of science, using the scientific method, is the chief safeguard against the tyranny of authority, bureaucracy, and brute power. It can reveal by investigation necessities and possibilities in any social scene and also offerings with respect to desirabilities to be achieved within the limits of the possible.

22 The scientific method is, therefore, a precious and indispensable instrument of the human mind; without it society would sink down into primitive animism and barbarism. It is when this method, a child of the human brain, is exalted into a master and a tyrant that historical thought must enter a caveat. So the historian is bound by his craft to recognize the nature and limitations of the scientific method and to dispel the illusion that it can produce a science of history embracing the fullness of history, or of any large phase, as past actuality.

23 This means no abandonment of the tireless inquiry into objective realities, especially economic realities and relations; not enough emphasis has been laid upon the conditioning and determining influences of biological and economic necessities or upon researches designed to disclose them in their deepest and widest ramifications. This means no abandonment of the inquiry into the forms and development of ideas as conditioning and determining influences; not enough emphasis has been laid on this phase of history by American scholars.

24 But the upshot to which this argument is directed is more fundamental than any aspect of historical method.

25 It is that any selection and arrangement of facts pertaining to any large area of history, either local or world, race or class, is controlled inexorably by the frame of reference in the mind of the selector and arranger. This frame of reference includes things deemed necessary, things deemed possible, and things deemed desirable. It may be large, informed by deep knowledge, and illuminated by wide experience; or it may be small, uninformed, and unilluminated. It may be a grand conception of history or a mere aggregation of confusions. But it is there in the mind, inexorably. To borrow from Croce, when grand philosophy is ostentatiously put out at the front door of the mind, then narrow, class, provincial, and regional prejudices come in at the back door and dominate, perhaps only half-consciously, the thinking of the historian.

26 The supreme issue before the historian now is the determination of his attitude to the disclosures of contemporary thought. He may deliberately evade them for reasons pertaining to personal, economic, and intellectual comfort, thus joining the innumerable throng of those who might have been but were not. Or he may proceed to examine his own frame of reference, clarify it, enlarge it by acquiring knowledge of greater areas of thought and events, and give it consistency of structure by a deliberate conjecture respecting the nature or direction of the vast movements of ideas and interests called world history.

27 This operation will cause discomfort to individual historians but all, according to the vows of their office, are under obligation to perform it, as Henry Adams warned the members of this Association in his letter of 1894. And as Adams then said, it will have to be carried out under the scrutiny of four great tribunals for the suppression of unwelcome knowledge and opinion: the church, the state, property, and labor. Does the world move and, if so, in what direction? If he believes that the world does not move, the historian must offer the pessimism of chaos to the inquiring spirit of mankind. If it does move, does it move backward toward some old arrangement, let us say, of 1928, 1896, 1815, 1789, or 1295? Or does it move forward to some other arrangement which can be only dimly divined—a capitalist dictatorship, a proletarian dictatorship, or a collectivist democracy? The last of these is my own guess, founded on a study of long trends and on a faith in the indomitable spirit of mankind. In any case, if the historian cannot know or explain history as actuality, he helps to make history, petty or grand.

28 To sum up contemporary thought in historiography, any written history involves the selection of a topic and an arbitrary delimitation of its borders—cutting off connections with the universal. Within the borders arbitrarily established, there is a selection and organization of facts by the processes of thought. This selection and organization—a single act—will be controlled by the historian's frame of reference composed of things deemed necessary and of things deemed desirable. The frame may be a narrow class, sectional, national, or group conception of history, clear and frank or confused and half conscious, or it may be a large, generous conception, clarified by association with the great spirits of all ages. Whatever its nature the frame is inexorably there, in the mind. And in the frame only three broad conceptions of all history as actuality are possible. History is chaos and every attempt to interpret it otherwise is an illusion. History moves around in a kind of cycle. History moves in a line, straight or spiral, and in some direction. The historian may seek to escape these issues by silence or by a confession of avoidance or he may face them boldly, aware of the intellectual and moral perils inherent in any decision—in his act of faith.

THE NATURE OF LOVE

Harry F. Harlow

This lecture by Harry F. Harlow, Professor of Psychology at the University of Wisconsin, was delivered as the presidential address at the sixty-sixth annual convention of the American Psychological Association in Washington, D.C., August 31, 1958. Professor Harlow's address, which is based upon psychological-research studies on monkeys, is concerned with all three questions set forth in this chapter's introductory essay: What is it? Why is it? What are its implications? *Harlow examines the last two questions in order to establish the real nature of love. Before he reports and analyzes his own research information, Harlow reviews related knowledge. What special purpose does this review serve in a speech that discusses primary research?*

Clarity is essential in the discussion of research data. Harlow's use of slides showing pictures and graphs obviously assist in fulfilling this objective. Yet a speaker wishing to augment knowledge must do more; he must make clear and meaningful the field of observation and the process of analysis. How well does Harlow perform these two functions?

Research reports tend to be dull. This dullness usually results from an overuse of specialized terms and an unimaginative presentation. Harlow's presentation, however, has considerable interest value. From what does this interest stem?

This address is reprinted by permission from The American Psychologist, *Vol. 13, (December 1958), pp. 673–685.*

1 Love is a wondrous state, deep, tender, and rewarding. Because of its intimate and personal nature it is regarded by some as an improper topic for experimental research. But, whatever our personal feelings may be, our assigned mission as psychologists is to analyze all facets of human and animal behavior into their component variables. So far as love or affection is concerned, psychologists have failed in this mission. The little we know about love does not transcend simple observation, and the little we write about it has been written better by poets and novelists. But of greater concern is the fact that psychologists tend to give progressively less attention to a motive which pervades our

entire lives. Psychologists, at least psychologists who write textbooks, not only show no interest in the origin and development of love or affection, but they seem to be unaware of its very existence.

2 The apparent repression of love by modern psychologists stands in sharp contrast with the attitude taken by many famous and normal people. The word "love" has the highest reference frequency of any word cited in Bartlett's book of *Familiar Quotations*. It would appear that this emotion has long had a vast interest and fascination for human beings, regardless of the attitude taken by psychologists; but the quotations cited, even by famous and normal people, have a mundane redundancy. These authors and authorities have stolen love from the child and infant and made it the exclusive property of the adolescent and adult.

3 Thoughtful men, and probably all women, have speculated on the nature of love. From the developmental point of view, the general plan is quite clear: The initial love responses of the human being are those made by the infant to the mother or some mother surrogate. From this intimate attachment of the child to the mother, multiple learned and generalized affectional responses are formed.

4 Unfortunately, beyond these simple facts we know little about the fundamental variables underlying the formation of affectional responses and little about the mechanisms through which the love of the infant for the mother develops into the multifaceted response patterns characterizing love or affection in the adult. Because of the dearth of experimentation, theories about the fundamental nature of affection have evolved at the level of observation, intuition, and discerning guesswork, whether these have been proposed by psychologists, sociologists, anthropologists, physicians, or psychoanalysts.

5 The position commonly held by psychologists and sociologists is quite clear: The basic motives are, for the most part, the primary drives—particularly hunger, thirst, elimination, pain, and sex—and all other motives, including love or affection, are derived or secondary drives. The mother is associated with the reduction of the primary drives—particularly hunger, thirst, and pain—and through learning, affection or love is derived.

6 It is entirely reasonable to believe that the mother through association with food may become a secondary-reinforcing agent, but this is an inadequate mechanism to account for the persistence of the infant-maternal ties. There is a spate of researches on the formation of secondary reinforcers to hunger and thirst reduction. There can be no question that almost any external stimulus can become a secondary

reinforcer if properly associated with tissue-need reduction, but the fact remains that this redundant literature demonstrates unequivocally that such derived drives suffer relatively rapid experimental extinction. Contrariwise, human affection does not extinguish when the mother ceases to have intimate association with the drives in question. Instead, the affectional ties to the mother show a lifelong, unrelenting persistence and, even more surprising, widely expanding generality.

7 Oddly enough, one of the few psychologists who took a position counter to modern psychological dogma was John B. Watson, who believed that love was an innate emotion elicited by cutaneous stimulation of the erogenous zones. But experimental psychologists, with their peculiar propensity to discover facts that are not true, brushed this theory aside by demonstrating that the human neonate had no differentiable emotions, and they established a fundamental psychological law that prophets are without honor in their own profession.

8 The psychoanalysts have concerned themselves with the problem of the nature of the development of love in the neonate and infant, using ill and aging human beings as subjects. They have discovered the overwhelming importance of the breast and related this to the oral erotic tendencies developed at an age preceding their subjects' memories. Their theories range from a belief that the infant has an innate need to achieve and suckle at the breast to beliefs not unlike commonly accepted psychological theories. There are exceptions, as seen in the recent writings of John Bowlby, who attributes importance not only to food and thirst satisfaction, but also to "primary object-clinging," a need for intimate physical contact, which is initially associated with the mother.

9 As far as I know, there exists no direct experimental analysis of the relative importance of the stimulus variables determining the affectional or love responses in the neonatal and infant primate. Unfortunately, the human neonate is a limited experimental subject for such researches because of his inadequate motor capabilities. By the time the human infant's motor responses can be precisely measured, the antecedent determining conditions cannot be defined, having been lost in a jumble and jungle of confounded variables.

10 Many of these difficulties can be resolved by the use of the neonatal and infant macaque monkey as the subject for the analysis of basic affectional variables. It is possible to make precise measurements in this primate beginning at two to ten days of age, depending upon the maturational status of the individual animal at birth. The macaque infant differs from the human infant in that the monkey is more mature at birth and grows more rapidly; but the basic responses relating to affection, including nursing, contact, clinging, and even visual and auditory exploration, exhibit no fundamental differences in the two species. Even the development of perception, fear, frustration, and learning capability follows very similar sequences in rhesus monkeys and human children.

11 Three years' experimentation before we started our studies on affection gave us experience with the neonatal monkey. We had separated more than 60 of these animals from their mothers 6 to 12 hours after birth and suckled them on tiny bottles. The infant mortality was only a small fraction of what would have obtained had we let the monkey mothers raise their infants. Our bottle-fed babies were healthier and heavier than monkey-mother-reared infants. We know that we are better monkey mothers than are real monkey mothers thanks to synthetic diets, vitamins, iron extracts, penicillin, chloromycetin, 5% glucose, and constant, tender, loving care.

12 During the course of these studies we noticed that the laboratory-raised babies showed strong attachment to the cloth pads (folded gauze diapers) which were used to cover the hardware-cloth floors of their cages. The infants clung to these pads and engaged in violent temper tantrums when the pads were removed and replaced for sanitary reasons. Such contact-need or responsiveness had been reported previously by Gertrude van Wagenen for the monkey and by Thomas McCulloch and George Haslerud for the chimpanzee and is reminiscent of the devotion often exhibited by human infants to their pillows, blankets, and soft, cuddly stuffed toys. Responsiveness by the one-day-old infant monkey to the cloth pad is shown in Figure 1, and an unusual and strong attachment of a six-month-old infant to the cloth pad is illustrated in Figure 2. The baby, human or monkey, if it is to survive, must clutch at more than a straw.

13 We had also discovered during some allied observational studies that a baby monkey raised on a bare wire-mesh cage floor survives with difficulty, if at all, during the first five days of life. If a wire-mesh cone is introduced, the baby does better; and, if the cone is covered with terry cloth, husky, healthy, happy babies evolve. It takes more than a baby and a box to make a normal monkey. We were impressed by the possibility that, above and beyond the bubbling fountain of breast or bottle, contact comfort might be a very important variable in the development of the infant's affection for the mother.

14 At this point we decided to study the development of

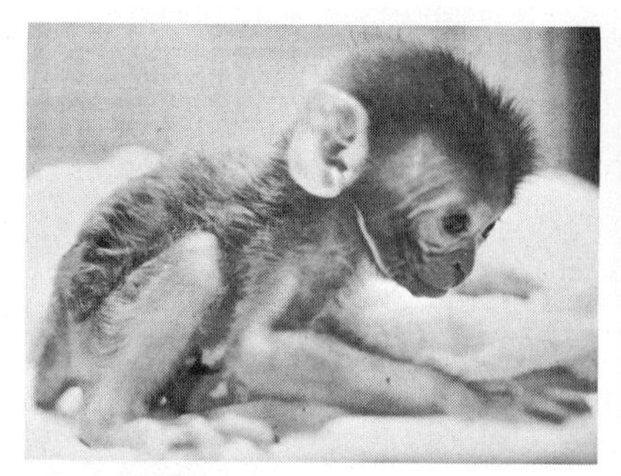

Fig. 1. Response to cloth pad by one-day-old monkey.

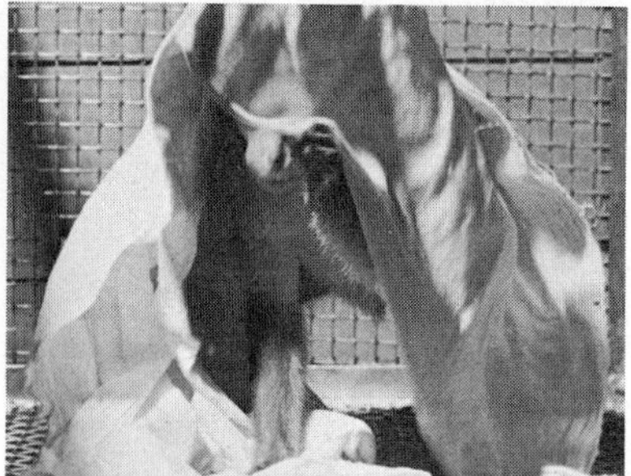

Fig. 2. Response to gauze pad by six-month-old monkey used in earlier study.

affectional responses of neonatal and infant monkeys to an artificial, inanimate mother, and so we built a surrogate mother which we hoped and believed would be a good surrogate mother. In devising this surrogate mother we were dependent neither upon the capriciousness of evolutionary processes nor upon mutations produced by chance radioactive fallout. Instead, we designed the mother surrogate in terms of modern human-engineering principles (Figure 3). We produced a perfectly proportioned, streamlined body stripped of unnecessary bulges and appendices. Redundancy in the surrogate mother's system was avoided by reducing the number of breasts from two to one and placing this unibreast in an upper-thoracic, sagittal position, thus maximizing the natural and known perceptual-motor capabilities of the infant operator. The surrogate was made from a block of wood, covered with sponge rubber, and sheathed in tan cotton terry cloth. A light bulb behind her radiated heat. The result was a mother, soft, warm, and tender, a mother with infinite patience, a mother available twenty-four hours a day, a mother that never scolded her infant and never struck or bit her baby in anger. Furthermore, we designed a mother-machine with maximal maintenance efficiency since failure of any system or function could be resolved by the simple substitution of black boxes and new component parts. It is our opinion that we engineered a very superior monkey mother, although this position is not held universally by the monkey fathers.

15 Before beginning our initial experiment we also designed and constructed a second mother surrogate, a surrogate in which we deliberately built less than the maximal capability for contact comfort. This surrogate mother is illustrated in Figure 4. She is made of wire-

Fig. 3. Cloth mother surrogate.

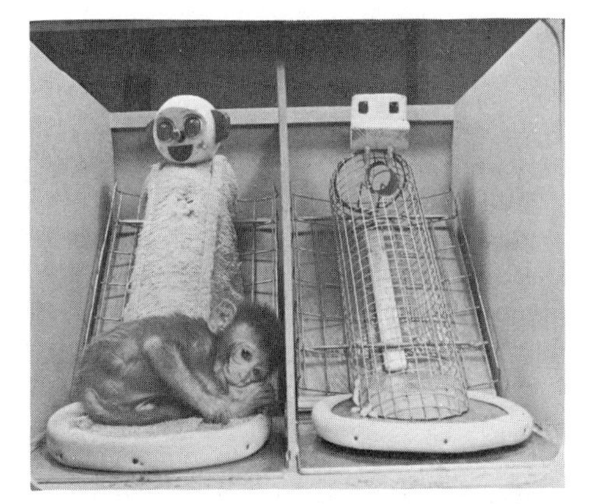

Fig. 4. Wire and cloth mother surrogates.

mesh, a substance entirely adequate to provide postural support and nursing capability, and she is warmed by radiant heat. Her body differs in no essential way from that of the cloth mother surrogate other than in the quality of the contact comfort which she can supply.

16 In our initial experiment, the dual mother-surrogate condition, a cloth mother and a wire mother were placed in different cubicles attached to the infant's living cage as shown in Figure 4. For four newborn monkeys the cloth mother lactated and the wire mother did not; and, for the other four, this condition was reversed. In either condition the infant received all its milk through the mother surrogate as soon as it was able to maintain itself in this way, a capability achieved within two or three days except in the case of very immature infants. Supplementary feedings were given until the milk intake from the mother surrogate was adequate. Thus, the experiment was designed as a test of the relative importance of the variables of contact comfort and nursing comfort. During the first 14 days of life the monkey's cage floor was covered with a heating pad wrapped in a folded gauze diaper, and thereafter the cage floor was bare. The infants were always free to leave the heating pad or cage floor to contact either mother, and the time spent on the surrogate mothers was automatically recorded. Figure 5 shows the total time spent on the cloth and wire mothers under the two conditions of feeding. These data make it obvious that contact comfort is a variable of overwhelming importance in the development of affectional responses, whereas lactation is a variable of negligible importance. With age and opportunity to learn,

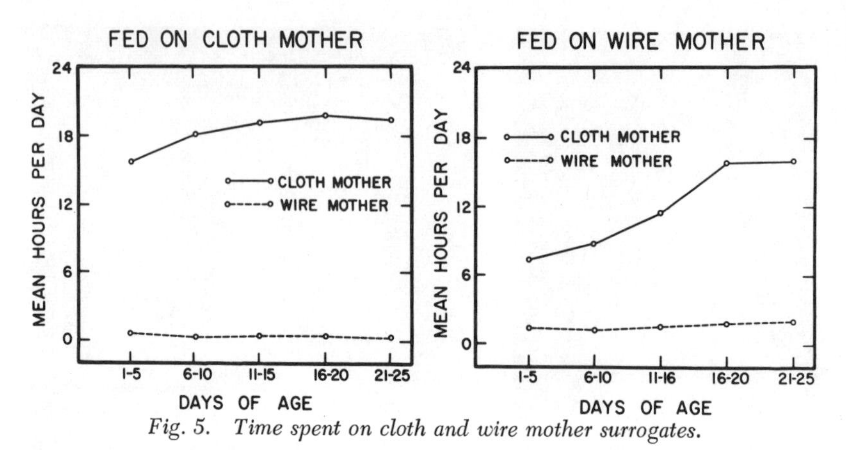

Fig. 5. Time spent on cloth and wire mother surrogates.

subjects with the lactating wire mother showed decreasing responsiveness to her and increasing responsiveness to the nonlactating cloth mother, a finding completely contrary to any interpretation of derived drive in which the mother-form becomes conditioned to hunger-thirst reduction. The persistence of these differential responses throughout 165 consecutive days of testing is evident in Figure 6.

17 One control group of neonatal monkeys was raised on a single wire mother, and a second control group was raised on a single cloth mother. There were no differences between these two groups in amount of milk ingested or in weight gain. The only difference between the groups lay in the composition of the feces, the softer stools of the wire-mother infants suggesting psychosomatic involvement. The wire mother is biologically adequate but psychologically inept.

18 We were not surprised to discover that contact comfort was an important basic affectional or love variable, but we did not expect it to overshadow so completely the variable of nursing; indeed, the disparity is so great as to suggest that the primary function of nursing

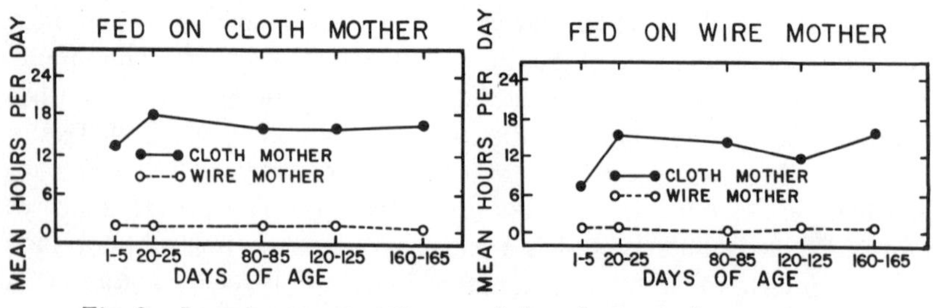

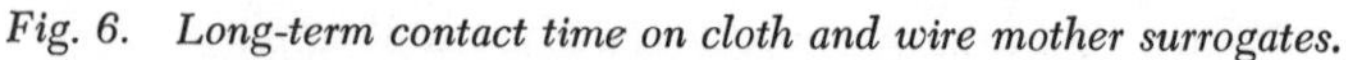
Fig. 6. Long-term contact time on cloth and wire mother surrogates.

as an affectional variable is that of insuring frequent and intimate body contact of the infant with the mother. Certainly, man cannot live by milk alone. Love is an emotion that does not need to be bottle- or spoon-fed, and we may be sure that there is nothing to be gained by giving lip service to love.

19 A charming lady once heard me describe these experiments; and, when I subsequently talked to her, her face brightened with sudden insight: "Now I know what's wrong with me," she said, "I'm just a wire mother." Perhaps she was lucky. She might have been a wire wife.

20 We believe that contact comfort has long served the animal kingdom as a motivating agent for affectional responses. Since at the present time we have no experimental data to substantiate this position, we supply information which must be accepted, if at all, on the basis of face validity [Figs. 7a–d].

21 One function of the real mother, human or subhuman, and presumably of a mother surrogate, is to provide a haven of safety for the infant in times of fear and danger. The frightened or ailing child clings to its mother, not its father; and this selective responsiveness in times of distress, disturbance, or danger may be used as a measure of the strength of affectional bonds. We have tested this kind of differential responsiveness by presenting to the infants in their cages, in the presence of the two mothers, various fear-producing stimuli such as the moving toy bear illustrated in Figure 8. A typical response to a fear stimulus is shown in Figure 9, and the data on differential responsiveness are presented in Figure 10. It is apparent that the cloth mother is highly preferred over the wire one, and this differential selectivity is enhanced by age and experience. In this situation, the variable of nursing appears to be of absolutely no importance: the infant consistently seeks the soft mother surrogate regardless of nursing condition.

22 Similarly, the mother or mother surrogate provides its young with a source of security, and this role or function is seen with special clarity when mother and child are in a strange situation. At the present time we have completed tests for this relationship on four of our eight baby monkeys assigned to the dual mother-surrogate condition by introducing them for three minutes into the strange environment of a room measuring six feet by six feet by six feet (also called the "open-field test") and containing multiple stimuli known to elicit curiosity-manipulatory responses in baby monkeys. The subjects were placed in this situation twice a week for eight weeks with no mother surrogate present during alternate sessions and the cloth mother pres-

Fig. 7a from *Zoo Guide*, Zoological Society of London

The Rhinoceros

The rhino's skin is thick and tough,
And yet this skin is soft enough
That baby rhinos always sense,
A love enormous and intense.

Fig. 7b by Sponholz

The Crocodile

Here is the skin they love to touch.
It isn't soft and there isn't much,
But its contact comfort will beguile
Love from the infant crocodile.

Fig. 7c from *All About Snakes*. By Bessie M. Hecht. © Copyright 1956 by Bessie M. Hecht. Reprinted by permission of Random House, Inc.

The Snake

To baby vipers, scaly skin
Engenders love 'twixt kith and kin.
Each animal by God is blessed
With kind of skin it loves the best.

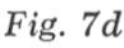

Fig. 7d

You see, all God's chillun's got skin.

Fig. 8. Typical fear stimulus.

Fig. 9. Typical response to cloth mother surrogate in fear test.

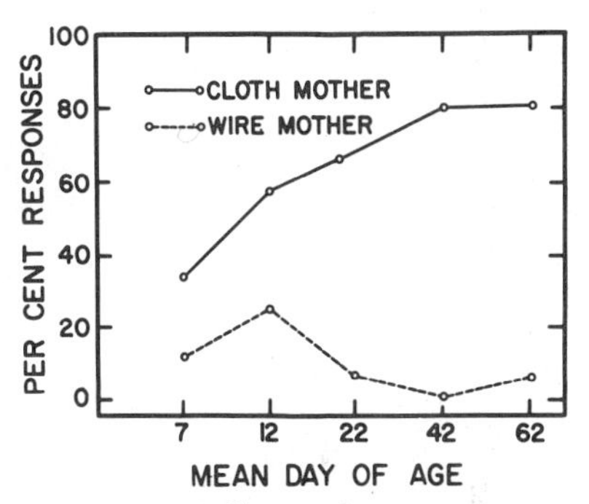

Fig. 10. Differential responsiveness in fear tests.

ent during the others. A cloth diaper was always available as one of the stimuli throughout all sessions. After one or two adaptation sessions, the infants always rushed to the mother surrogate when she was present and clutched her, rubbed their bodies against her, and frequently manipulated her body and face. After a few additional sessions, the infants began to use the mother surrogate as a source of security, a base of operations. As is shown in Figures 11 and 12, they would explore and manipulate a stimulus and then return to the mother before adventuring again into the strange new world. The behavior of these infants was quite different when the mother was absent from the room. Frequently they would freeze in a crouched position, as is illustrated in Figures 13 and 14. Emotionality indices such as vocalization, crouching, rocking, and sucking increased sharply, as shown in Figure 15. Total emotionality score was cut in half when the mother was present. In the absence of the mother some of the experimental monkeys would rush to the center of the room where the mother was customarily placed and then run rapidly from object to object, screaming and crying all the while. Continuous, frantic clutching of their bodies was very common, even when not in the crouching position. These monkeys frequently contacted and clutched the cloth diaper, but this action never pacified them. The same behavior occurred in the presence of the wire mother. No difference between the cloth-mother-fed and wire-mother-fed infants was demonstrated under either condition. Four control infants never raised with a mother surrogate showed the same emotionality scores when the mother was absent as the experimental infants showed in the absence of the mother, but the controls' scores were slightly larger in the presence of the mother surrogate than in her absence.

23 Some years ago Robert Butler demonstrated that mature monkeys enclosed in a dimly lighted box would open and reopen a door hour after hour for no other reward than that of looking outside the box. We now have data indicating that neonatal monkeys show this same compulsive visual curiosity on their first test day in an adaptation of the Butler apparatus which we call the "love machine," an apparatus designed to measure love. Usually these tests are begun when the monkey is 10 days of age, but this same persistent visual exploration has been obtained in a three-day-old monkey during the first half-hour of testing. Butler also demonstrated that rhesus monkeys show selectivity in rate and frequency of door-opening to stimuli of differential attractiveness in the visual field outside the box. We have utilized this principle of response selectivity by the monkey to measure strength of affectional responsiveness in our infants in the baby version of the Butler box. The test sequence involves four repetitions of a test battery in which four stimuli—cloth mother, wire mother, infant monkey, and empty box—are presented for a 30-minute period on successive days. The first four subjects in the dual mother-surrogate group were given a single test sequence at 40 to 50 days of age, depending upon the availability of the apparatus, and only their data are presented. The second set of four subjects is being given repetitive tests to obtain information relating to the development of visual exploration. The apparatus is illustrated in Figure 16. The data obtained from the first four infants raised with the two mother surrogates are presented in the middle graph of Figure 17 and show approximately equal responding to the cloth mother and another infant monkey, and no greater responsiveness to the wire mother than to an empty box. Again, the results are

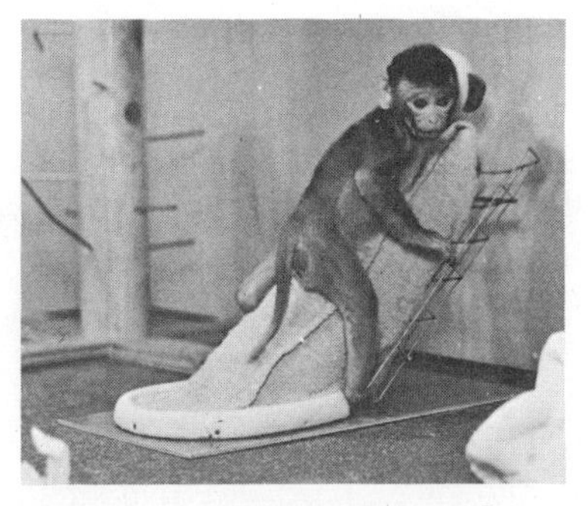

Fig. 11. Response to cloth mother in the open-field test.

Fig. 12. Object exploration in presence of cloth mother.

Fig. 13. Response in the open-field test in the absence of the mother surrogate.

Fig. 14. Response in the open-field test in the absence of the mother surrogate.

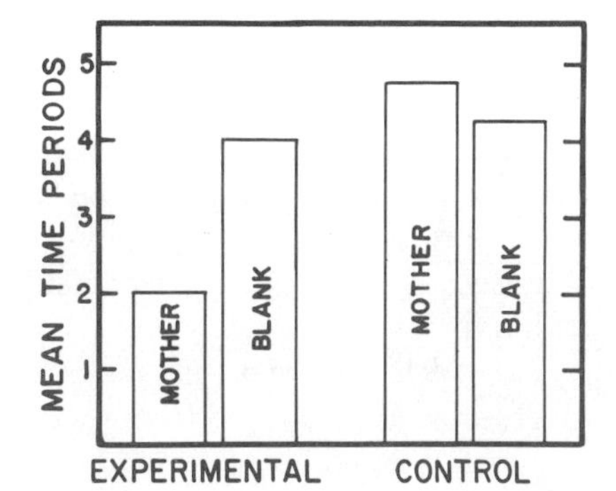

Fig. 15. Emotionality index with and without the presence of the cloth mother.

Fig. 16. Visual exploration apparatus.

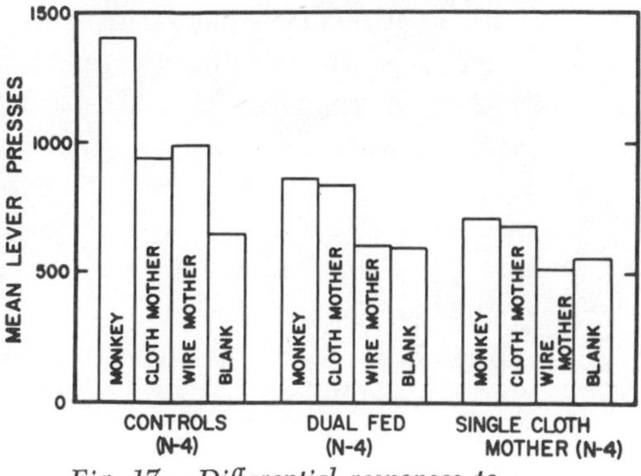

Fig. 17. Differential responses to visual exploration.

independent of the kind of mother that lactated, cloth or wire. The same results are found for a control group raised, but not fed, on a single cloth mother; these data appear in the graph on the right. Contrariwise, the graph on the left shows no differential responsiveness to cloth and wire mothers by a second control group, which was not raised on any mother surrogate. We can be certain that not all love is blind.

24 The first four infant monkeys in the dual mother-surrogate group were separated from their mothers between 165 and 170 days of age and tested for retention during the following 9 days and then at 30-day intervals for six successive months. Affectional retention as measured by the modified Butler box is given in Figure 18. In keeping with the data obtained on adult monkeys by Butler, we find a high rate of responding to any stimulus, even the empty box. But throughout the entire 185-day retention period there is a consistent and significant difference in response frequency to the cloth mother contrasted with either the wire mother or the empty box, and no consistent difference between wire mother and empty box.

25 Affectional retention was also tested in the open field during the first 9 days after separation and then at 30-day intervals, and each test condition was run twice at each retention interval. The infants' behavior differed from that observed during the period preceding separation. When the cloth mother was present in the post-separation period, the babies rushed to her, climbed up, clung tightly to her, and rubbed their heads and faces against her body. After this initial embrace and reunion, they played on the mother, including biting and tearing at her cloth cover; but they rarely made any attempt to leave her during the test period, nor did they manipulate or play with the objects in the room, in contrast with their behavior before maternal separation. The only exception was the occasional monkey that left the mother surrogate momentarily, grasped the folded piece of paper (one of the standard stimuli in the field), and brought it quickly back to the mother. It appeared that deprivation had enhanced the tie to the mother and rendered the contact-comfort need so prepotent that need for the mother overwhelmed the exploratory motives during the brief, three-minute test sessions. No change in these behaviors was observed throughout the 185-day period. When the mother was absent from the open field, the behavior of the infants was similar in the initial retention test to that during the preseparation tests; but they tended to show gradual adaptation to the open-field situation with repeated testing and, consequently, a reduction in their emotionality scores.

26 In the last five retention test periods, an additional test was introduced in which the surrogate mother was placed in the center of the room and covered with a clear Plexiglas box. The monkeys were initially disturbed and frustrated when their explorations and manipulations of the box failed to provide contact with the mother. However, all animals adapted to the situation rather rapidly. Soon they used the box as a place of orientation for exploratory and play behavior, made frequent contacts with the objects in the field, and very often brought these objects to the Plexiglas box. The emotionality index was slightly higher than in the condition of the available cloth mothers, but it in no way approached the emotionality level displayed when the cloth mother was absent. Obviously, the infant monkeys gained emotional security by the presence of the mother even though contact was denied.

27 Affectional retention has also been measured by tests in which the monkey must unfasten a three-device mechanical puzzle to obtain entrance into a compartment containing the mother surrogate. All the trials are initiated by allowing the infant to go through an unlocked door, and in half the trials it finds the mother present and in half, an empty compartment. The door is then locked and a ten-minute test conducted. In tests given prior to separation from the surrogate mothers, some of the infants had solved this puzzle and others had failed. The data of Figure 19 show that on the last test before separation there were no differences in total manipulation under mother-present and mother-absent conditions, but striking differences exist between the two conditions throughout the post-separation test periods. Again, there is no interaction with conditions of feeding.

28 The over-all picture obtained from surveying the retention data is unequivocal. There is little, if any, waning of responsiveness to the mother throughout this five-month period as indicated by any measure. It becomes perfectly obvious that this affectional bond is highly resistant to forgetting and that it can be retained for very long periods of time by relatively infrequent contact reinforcement. During the next year, retention tests will be conducted at 90-day intervals, and further plans are dependent upon the results obtained. It would appear that affectional responses may show as much resistance to extinction as has been previously demonstrated for learned fears and learned pain, and such data would be in keeping with those of common human observation.

29 The infants' responses to the mother surrogate in the fear tests, the open-field situation, and the baby Butler box and the re-

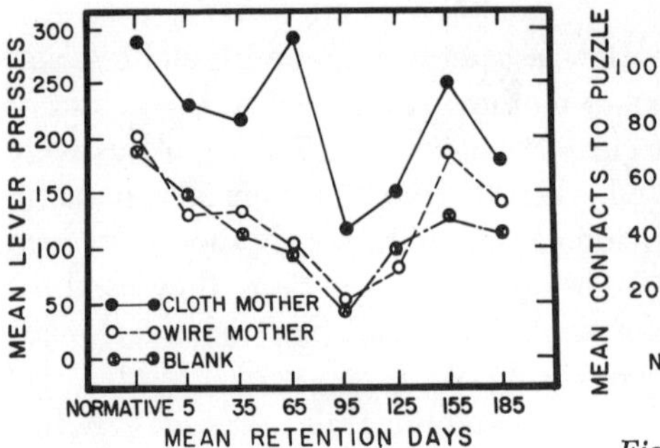

Fig. 18. Retention of differential visual-exploration responses.

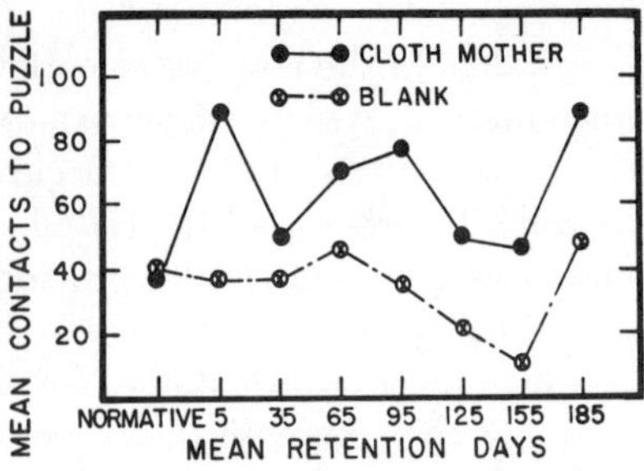

Fig. 19. Retention of puzzle manipulation responsiveness.

sponses on the retention tests cannot be described adequately with words. For supplementary information we turn to the motion picture record. (At this point a 20-minute film was presented illustrating and supplementing the behaviors described thus far in the address.)

30 We have already described the group of four control infants that had never lived in the presence of any mother surrogate and had demonstrated no sign of affection or security in the presence of the cloth mothers introduced in test sessions. When these infants reached the age of 250 days, cubicles containing both a cloth mother and a wire mother were attached to their cages. There was no lactation in these mothers, for the monkeys were on a solid-food diet. The initial reaction of the monkeys to the alterations was one of extreme disturbance. All the infants screamed violently and made repeated attempts to escape the cage whenever the door was opened. They kept a maximum distance from the mother surrogates and exhibited a considerable amount of rocking and crouching behavior, indicative of emotionality. Our first thought was that the critical period for the development of maternally directed affection had passed and that these macaque children were doomed to live as affectional orphans. Fortunately, these behaviors continued for only 12 to 48 hours and then gradually ebbed, changing from indifference to active contact on, and exploration of, the surrogates. The home-cage behavior of these control monkeys slowly became similar to that of the animals raised with the mother surrogates from birth. Their manipulation and play on the cloth mother became progressively more vigorous to the point of actual mutilation, particularly during the morning after the cloth mother had been given her daily change of terry covering. The control subjects were now actively running to the cloth mother when frightened and had to be coaxed from her to be taken from the cage for formal testing.

31 Objective evidence of these changing behaviors is given in Figure 20, which plots the amount of time these infants spent on the mother surrogates. Within 10 days mean contact time is approximately nine hours, and this measure remains relatively constant throughout the next 30 days. Consistent with the results on the subjects reared from birth with dual mothers, these late-adopted infants spent less than one and one-half hours per day in contact with the wire mothers, and this activity level was relatively constant throughout the test sessions. Although the maximum time that the control monkeys spent on the cloth mother was only about half that spent by the original dual mother-surrogate group, we cannot be sure that this discrepancy is a function of differential early experience. The control monkeys were about three months older when the mothers were attached to their cages than the experimental animals had been when their mothers were removed and the retention tests begun. Thus, we do not know what the amount of contact would be for a 250-day-old animal raised from birth with surrogate mothers. Nevertheless, the magnitude of the differences and the fact that the contact-time curves for the mothered-from-birth infants had remained constant for almost 150 days suggest that early experience with the mother is a variable of measurable importance.

32 The control group has also been tested for differential visual exploration after the introduction of the cloth and wire mothers; these behaviors are plotted in Figure 21. By the second test session a high level of exploratory behavior had developed, and the responsiveness to the wire mother and the empty box is significantly greater than that to the cloth mother. This is probably not an artifact since there is every reason to believe that the face of the cloth mother is a fear stimulus to

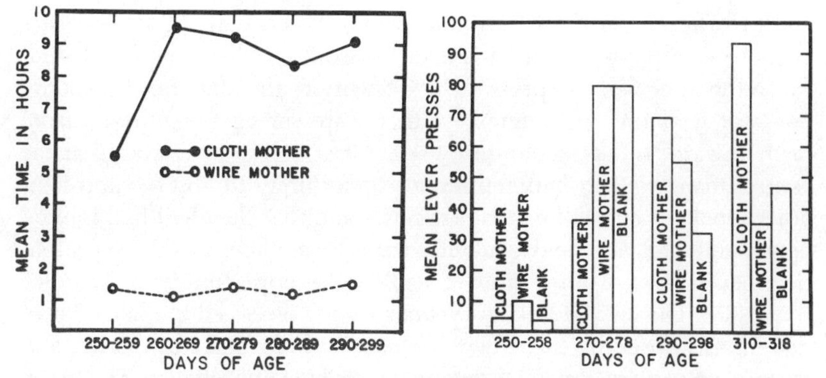

Fig. 20. Differential time spent on cloth and wire mother surrogates by monkeys started at 250 days of age.

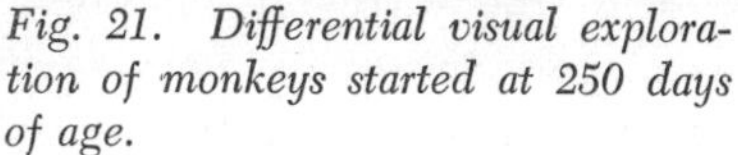

Fig. 21. Differential visual exploration of monkeys started at 250 days of age.

most monkeys that have not had extensive experience with this object during the first 40 to 60 days of life. Within the third test session a sharp change in trend occurs, and the cloth mother is then more frequently viewed than the wire mother or the blank box; this trend continues during the fourth session, producing a significant preference for the cloth mother.

33 Before the introduction of the mother surrogate into the home-cage situation, only one of the four control monkeys had ever contacted the cloth mother in the open-field tests. In general, the surrogate mother not only gave the infants no security, but instead appeared to serve as a fear stimulus. The emotionality scores of these control subjects were slightly higher during the mother-present test sessions than during the mother-absent test sessions. These behaviors were changed radically by the fourth post-introduction test approximately 60 days later. In the absence of the cloth mothers the emotionality index in this fourth test remains near the earlier level, but the score is reduced by half when the mother is present, a result strikingly similar to that found for infants raised with the dual mother-surrogates from birth. The control infants now show increasing object exploration and play behavior, and they begin to use the mother as a base of operations, as did the infants raised from birth with the mother surrogates. However, there are still definite differences in the behavior of the two groups. The control infants do not rush directly to the mother and clutch her violently; but instead they go toward, and orient around, her, usually after an initial period during which they frequently show disturbed behavior, exploratory behavior, or both.

34 That the control monkeys develop affection or love for the cloth mother when she is introduced into the cage at 250 days of age cannot be questioned. There is every reason to believe, however, that this interval of delay depresses the intensity of the affectional response below that of the infant monkeys that were surrogate-mothered from birth onward. In interpreting these data it is well to remember that the control monkeys had had continuous opportunity to observe and hear other monkeys housed in adjacent cages and that they had had limited opportunity to view and contact surrogate mothers in the test situations, even though they did not exploit the opportunities.

35 During the last two years we have observed the behavior of two infants raised by their own mothers. Love for the real mother and love for the surrogate mother appear to be very similar. The baby macaque spends many hours a day clinging to its real mother. If away from the mother when frightened, it rushes to her and in her presence shows comfort and composure. As far as we can observe, the infant monkey's affection for the real mother is strong, but no stronger than that of the experimental monkey for the surrogate cloth mother, and the security that the infant gains from the presence of the real mother is no greater than the security it gains from a cloth surrogate. Next year we hope to put this problem to final, definitive, experimental test. But, whether the mother is real or a cloth surrogate, there does develop a deep and abiding bond between mother and child. In one case it may be the call of the wild and in the other the McCall of civilization, but in both cases there is "togetherness."

36 In spite of the importance of contact comfort, there is reason to believe that other variables of measurable importance will be discovered. Postural support may be such a variable, and it has been suggested that, when we build arms into the mother surrogate, 10 is the minimal number required to provide adequate child care. Rocking motion may be such a variable, and we are comparing rocking and stationary mother surrogates and inclined planes. The differential responsiveness to cloth mother and cloth-covered inclined plane suggests that clinging as well as contact is an affectional variable of importance. Sounds, particularly natural, maternal sounds, may operate as either unlearned or learned affectional variables. Visual responsiveness may be such a variable, and it is possible that some semblance of visual imprinting may develop in the neonatal monkey. There are indications that this becomes a variable of importance during the course of infancy through some maturational process.

37 John Bowlby has suggested that there is an affectional variable which he calls "primary object following," characterized by visual and oral search of the mother's face. Our surrogate-mother-raised baby monkeys are at first inattentive to her face, as are human neonates to human mother faces. But by 30 days of age ever-increasing responsiveness to the mother's face appears—whether through learning, maturation, or both—and we have reason to believe that the face becomes an object of special attention.

38 Our first surrogate-mother-raised baby had a mother whose head was just a ball of wood since the baby was a month early and we had not had time to design a more esthetic head and face. This baby had contact with the blank-faced mother for 180 days and was then placed with two cloth mothers, one motionless and one rocking, both being endowed with painted, ornamented faces. To our surprise the animal would compulsively rotate both faces 180 degrees so that it viewed only a round, smooth face and never the painted, ornamented face. Furthermore, it would do this as long as the patience of the experimenter in reorienting the faces persisted. The monkey showed no sign of fear or anxiety, but it showed unlimited persistence. Subsequently it improved its technique, compulsively removing the heads and rolling them into its cage as fast as they were returned. We are intrigued by this observation, and we plan to examine systematically the role of the mother face in the development of infant-monkey affections. Indeed, these observations suggest the need for a series of ethnological-type researches on the two-faced female.

39 Although we have made no attempts thus far to study the generalization of infant-macaque affection or love, the techniques which we have developed offer promise in this uncharted field. Beyond this, there are few if any technical difficulties in studying the affection of the actual, living mother for the child, and the techniques developed can be utilized and expanded for the analysis and developmental study of father-infant and infant-infant affection.

40 Since we can measure neonatal and infant affectional responses to mother surrogates, and since we know they are strong and persisting, we are in a position to assess the effects of feeding and contactual schedules; consistency and inconsistency in the mother surrogates; and early, intermediate, and late maternal deprivation. Again, we have here a family of problems of fundamental interest and theoretical importance.

41 If the researches completed and proposed make a contribution, I shall be grateful: but I have also given full thought to possible practical applications. The socioeconomic demands of the present and the threatened socioeconomic demands of the future have led the American woman to displace, or threaten to displace, the American man in science and industry. If this process continues, the problem of proper child-rearing practices faces us with startling clarity. It is cheering in view of this trend to realize that the American male is physically endowed with all the really essential equipment to compete with the American female on equal terms in one essential activity: the rearing of infants. We now know that women in the working classes are not needed in the home because of their primary mammalian capabilities; and it is possible that in the foreseeable future neonatal nursing will not be regarded as a necessity, but as a luxury—to use Veblen's term—a form of conspicuous consumption limited perhaps to the upper classes. But whatever course history may take, it is comforting to know that we are now in contact with the nature of love.

PART THREE

SPEAKING TO PERSUADE

In Chapters 3 and 4, we identified the constraints imposed on the choices a speaker makes whenever he seeks to enlighten his audience either by imparting established knowledge or by augmenting it through careful inquiry and interpretation. In the following four chapters we will focus our attention on the constraints governing a speaker's choices when he seeks to persuade an audience.

Speaking to inform and speaking to persuade involve different modes of operation. The informative speaker attempts to ascertain the truth by inquiry; the advocate attempts to establish a proposition to the satisfaction of another. The informative speaker tries to interpret truth in order that others may understand; the advocate tries to win converts to his point of view. The informative speaker seeks to present an accurate, complete, and unified view of a body of knowledge or a clear conception of the processes of inquiry by which his discoveries were made; the advocate selects telling facts and data that best prove his point to a given audience. The informative speaker enlightens; the advocate persuades.

When the college speech student first encounters the term persuasion, it may call to his mind the Vance Packard conception of packaged sex, politics, and values; of advertising men exploiting our hidden urges and desires to merchandize a product—"Now it's Pepsi for those who think young"; of political hucksters catering to the irrationality of man in seeking to influence voting behavior—"In your heart, you know he's right"; of motivational analysts manipulating human values for profit—"Don't miss the fun of smoking." While these examples of persuasion may not be consistent with the highest tenets of advocacy in a free society, we would be unrealistic if we failed to recognize their existence. While many institutions and speakers in a free society employ persuasion as a means of enlisting popular support on behalf of truth, wisdom, and justice, others seek to exploit human ignorance and irrationality. In advocacy, as in all other forms of human behavior, a man commits himself to certain values and courses of action. As in other forms of human behavior, his choices are not always free. While in certain instances the advocate may speak in support of propositions based on his own inquiry and investigation, in others his choices may be less free—a lawyer, for example, may be called upon to defend a client whose innocence he has cause to doubt; a statesman may be asked to justify a violation of national sovereignty over air space when he believes such sovereignty to be inviolate; or a public relations counsel may be assigned to promote the use of tobacco when he considers it injurious to personal health. While these circumstances may or may not justify the commitments that the advocate makes, they do demonstrate the moral complexity of his choices. They demonstrate, as well, the difficulty of the critic's task in judging ethical responsibility.

Once the advocate espouses a cause, the virtue of which each man must judge, it becomes his responsibility to give that cause the best representation possible within the ethical constraints imposed by the truth as he knows it or believes it to be.

He should not deliberately do less. The conduct of the advocate who intentionally distorts or suppresses the truth under whatever banner should be carefully scrutinized by the members of his audience.

Advocates seek to gain popular approval of propositions of fact, value, problem, *or* policy, *on the assurance that they are true, just, significant, or wise. Since these varying types of propositions create different constraints on the speaker's behavior, the next four chapters will treat, in the following order, speeches that affirm propositions of fact, speeches that affirm propositions of value, speeches that create concern for problems, and speeches that affirm propositions of policy.*

Chapter Five

SPEECHES THAT AFFIRM PROPOSITIONS OF FACT

There are instances of persuasive discourse in which a speaker seeks to prove to the satisfaction of his audience that a given proposition of fact is, in reality, true. Such speeches are concerned with *existence, occurrence,* or *causality.* While the preceding chapters were concerned with the art of interpreting established knowledge or original inquiry *for the enlightenment of an audience,* the present chapter is devoted to the principles involved in establishing an alleged truth *in order to win common agreement.* Earlier, the primary task for the speaker was to help his audience understand an event, fact, process, concept, or inquiry; in this chapter the speaker's efforts are directed, either explicitly or implicitly, toward seeking approval of the facts he presents. In the previous speech forms, the speaker might publicly analyze these questions: "What is extremism?" "Why is the United States committed to space exploration?" "What are the economic implications of disarmament?" In the present chapter the speaker seeks to gain acceptance of conclusions: "Extremism," he might say, "is contrary to the American democratic tradition." "The American program of space exploration is without military significance." Or "Disarmament would lead to economic disaster in the American economy."

It should be apparent to the reader that while some propositions of fact may be the product of exhaustive and exact inquiry on the part of the speaker, others may be defined by society (as in the case of legal proceedings), or may evolve from a speaker's intuitive perception of fact, or from his blind adherence to an authority he venerates. Whatever the source of his proposition, the speaker who seeks to gain popular acceptance of a probable fact is governed by certain distinctive constraints on the choices he may make.

CONSTRAINTS IMPOSED BY SPEECH PURPOSE

The social environments that produce speeches affirming factual propositions are diverse. A district attorney may seek to establish the guilt of a labor leader charged with misuse of union funds. A historian may allege that recent major wars have caused recurring trends in the methods of writing history. The president of a liberal arts college may try to convince his board of regents that fraternities interfere with a student's academic life. A state legislator may attempt to prove to his constituency that the condition of state highways will deter expansion of the tourist industry. While in certain instances the affirmation of a proposition of fact is the sole purpose of a persuasive speech, at other times a speaker may affirm a fact as a means of building social unity, creating concern for a problem, or in gaining acceptance for a course of action.

Whatever the circumstances may be in which men speak to affirm factual propositions, the audience is asked to render a favorable judgment on the speaker's assessment of reality. In order that they may do so, the speaker must *present knowledge* about the facts or events to be judged, *delineate the standards,* explicitly or implicitly, by which the judgment is to be made, and *apply the standards* in appraising the case at hand. He must present—and if necessary defend—the tests or criteria to be used in assessing the alleged facts, and he must clearly and convincingly demonstrate that they meet or fail to meet these qualifications. He must do so not because of ethical dictates, but because these are the orders of knowledge that his audience must have if they are to agree with his appraisal of fact.

The nature of the speaker's choices within these constraints may be better understood by looking at the types of factual propositions that men seek to establish.

In treating those situations in which audiences function as judges of facts and events, Aristotle was concerned with legal judgments and discussed them under the heading of *forensic discourse.* Although there are many other circumstances that give rise to persuasive speeches on propositions of fact, now, as then, *propositions of legal fact* are socially prevalent. In complying with the constraints we have just identified, the legal advocate, for example, who is attempting to prove the guilt of a labor leader charged with the misuse of union funds must get an affirmative response to three essential issues in his case: (1) union funds were spent on non-union activities; (2) a test of available evidence reveals who was responsible for these expenditures; (3) the labor leader in question used union funds for non-union activities.

Another important type of factual proposition concerns controversial claims about past events. In seeking to establish the validity of *propositions of past fact,* whether of existence or causality, the speaker must again be concerned with presenting knowledge of the fact or event to be judged, knowledge of the standards by which the judgment is to be made, and the applicability of these standards of judgment to the particular case in question. In complying with these constraints on his behavior, the historian who alleges that recent major wars have caused recurring trends in the writing of history must affirm three vital issues: (1) that following recent major wars distinctive trends in historical writing have recurred; (2) that the relationship between these phenomena can be measured by tests of causality; (3) that the application of tests of causality demonstrate the influence of major wars on the recurring trends in historical writing.

A third type of factual proposition concerns the speaker's appraisal of present circumstances. Here, as before, the same constraints apply. In presenting a *proposition of present fact,* the president of a liberal arts college who hopes to persuade the board of regents that fraternities interfere with a student's academic development must affirm three essential contentions: (1) that certain patterns of behavior may be attributed to members of fraternities; (2) that standards of judgment exist by which interference with a student's academic development can be measured; (3) that the specific patterns of behavior in question are sufficient to warrant the generalization of interference with academic development.

The final order of factual propositions may be called *propositions of prediction.* Concerned with future occurrences or events, these propositions may be established only by observing the same previous constraints. The state legislator, for example, who hopes to prove that the condition of his state's highways will deter expansion of the tourist industry must obtain the following popular affirmations: (1) that the highways of the state are in a poor condition; (2) that the condition of highways has significant effect on the tourist industry; (3) that the condition of the highways in question is sufficient to justify the inference that the state's tourist industry will suffer.

In seeking to gain audience acceptance of these propositions, the speaker must select those rhetorical means that best define and clarify the details of that which is to be judged. He will employ the technique of imparting knowledge to make his proposition vivid, clear, and meaningful. He will clarify the standards to be used in judgment and the applicability of these standards to the immediate fact at issue. He will present those factual examples, statistics, and expert testimony that logically affirm his proposition.

CONSTRAINTS IMPOSED BY A PARTICULAR AUDIENCE

Most theorists in rhetoric pay tribute to the rational persuader who seeks to gain acceptance of a proposition on intellectually sound and logically adequate grounds. Most theorists also abhor the overzealous advocate who seeks to exploit the unthinking response. "That persuasion is best," so the theory goes, "which is most fully committed to reason." While such veneration of reason may be commendable as an abstract ideal, it is impracticable when applied to the dictates of actual public discourse. The speaker who seeks to affirm a proposition of fact must recognize that the correlation between acceptance of fact and logical demonstration of fact is, at best, not a perfect one. Audiences have sometimes rejected propositions of fact that were demonstrated to be true beyond a reasonable doubt. Audiences have also been known to accept propositions founded on whim and fancy as the truth. If an advocate is to elicit a favorable response concerning the probability of a fact, he must not underestimate the influence of emotions, tastes, and desires on the judgments of audiences. While he should seek to enlist commitments on rational grounds, he must adapt to the nonrational facets of his audience's behavior in order to be given a fair hearing.

Just as is the case in imparting and augmenting knowledge, the speaker who seeks to affirm a proposition of fact must consider the *interest* and the *meaning* his subject holds for his audience. The political candidate who demonstrates for an urban audience that the administration's farm policy has led to a reduction of farm income has erred in one respect. The nuclear physicist who employs technical jargon to establish the effects of atmospheric testing for a League of Women Voters meeting has erred in another.

A third constraint of this speech form concerns the audience's perception of the *credibility of the speaker*. When a speaker leaves the area of established fact and enters the area of the controversial, the reaction of his listeners becomes increasingly dependent on their appraisal of his judgment. Aristotle, in exploring the importance of speaker ethos, wrote, "As a rule we trust men of probity more, and more quickly, about things in general, while on points outside the realm of exact knowledge, where opinion is divided, we trust them absolutely."

A speaker who seeks to affirm a proposition of fact must recognize that audiences tend to believe statements made by speakers they admire and respect. A college professor of economics wishing to persuade audiences that misrepresentation in American advertising is prevalent may be considered an "expert" by an audience of high school sophomores, as a "starry-eyed idealist" by an audience of businessmen, and a "liberal democrat" by a Congressional investigating committee. That he should consider these different reactions in his choice of rhetorical devices is clear. The nature of his choices is not.

While most authors agree that the speaker who is considered highly credible has an advantage over the speaker whose ethos is low, they do not always agree on the factors determining speaker prestige. Aristotle said that ethos is derived from wisdom, sound character, and an attitude of good will toward the audience. Hance, Ralph, and Wiksell list *competence,* which "grows out of a combination of mental ability, know-how, intelligence, understanding, experience with the subject, and knowledge"; *good character,* which "is made up of honesty, integrity, sincerity, fairness, and similar qualities that meet the standards of the listeners"; *good will,* which "consists of friendliness, likeableness, rapport, warmth, and being 'in' with the audience."[1] Minnick includes confidence and poise, physical energy and tone, sincerity and conviction, mental alertness, intelligence and knowledge, fairness and justice, self-discipline, even temper and restraint, sympathy and understanding, decisiveness, and color, eccentricity, and uniqueness.[2]

The final order of audience constraints relevant to this speech form concerns the *standards of validity* that an audience uses in appraising the truth of an alleged fact. Since the data, events, and ideas presented to an audience for acceptance are interpreted by each member in the light of some standard or criterion, it is important for the speaker to understand the particular basis for judgment that the members of his audience are likely to use. These standards may include the existing law, statistical theories of probability, principles of sound historical research, accepted tests of evidence, or standard tests of

[1] Kenneth G. Hance, David C. Ralph, and Milton J. Wiksell, *Principles of Public Speaking* (Belmont, Calif.: Wadsworth Publishing Co., 1962), pp. 38–39.

[2] Wayne C. Minnick, *The Art of Persuasion* (Boston: Houghton Mifflin Co., 1957), pp. 113–121.

causal relationships. But whatever the measure of validity may be, the speaker who seeks to affirm a proposition of fact must convince his audience of his ability to judge.

CONCLUSION

In certain instances of persuasive discourse, speakers seek to prove to the satisfaction of their audiences that given propositions of fact are really true. Whether such propositions are the product of exhaustive inquiry or of social commitment or evolve from the speaker's own, and sometimes blind, intuition, certain constraints govern his behavior. In order that he may achieve this social purpose, he must *present knowledge* about the facts or events to be judged; he must *delineate the standards* by which the judgment is to be made; and he must *apply the standards* in appraising the case at hand. He must also be aware of the constraints audiences impose because of their *interest* in the subject, their ability to grasp the *meaning* of the message, their perception of *speaker credibility,* and the *standards of validity* that they use in appraising the probability of a fact.

In the speeches comprising the rest of this chapter, the student may examine the choices others have made in affirming propositions of fact within the constraints that speech purpose and particular audiences impose. In "How Separate Should Government and God Be?" Howard C. Wilkinson alleges that historically government and religion in the United States have not been separate. Carolyn Kay Geiman in "Are They Really 'Unteachable'?" seeks to persuade her audience that culturally deprived children can be taught. In "The Bill of Rights," Hugo L. Black, Supreme Court Justice, alleges that there are absolutes in our Constitution's Bill of Rights and that their framers put them there on purpose. These absolutes balance the right to petition and the freedoms of religion, speech, press, and assembly against the needs of a powerful central government.

For Further Reading

Anderson, Kenneth, and Theodore Clevenger, Jr., "A Summary of Experimental Research in Ethos," *Speech Monographs,* Vol. 30 (June 1963), pp. 59–78.

Berlo, David, *The Process of Communication,* Holt, Rinehart and Winston, 1960, pp. 217–234, 250–271. Analyzes the process of reporting observations (knowledge), seeking judgments, and making inferences.

Buehler, E. C., and Wil A. Linkugel, *Speech: A First Course,* Harper & Row, 1962. Chapter 2 probes the nature and importance of the speaker's image in speech communication.

Ehninger, Douglas, and Wayne Brockriede, *Decision by Debate,* Dodd, Mead and Co., 1963, pp. 98–107, 134–162, 190–222. Touches on propositions of fact, outlines the nature and sources of belief, and explains the valid use of statistics, expert testimony, examples, parallel cases, and reasoning (Toulmin approach).

Freeley, Austin J., *Argumentation and Debate,* Wadsworth Publishing Co., 1961. Chapters 5, 6, and 7 succinctly explore the nature of evidence, tests of evidence, and sound reasoning.

Graves, Harold F., and Bernard S. Oldsey, *From Fact to Judgment,* The Macmillan Co., 2nd ed., 1963. Chapter 4 discusses questions of probability and the nature of inferences.

Hance, Kenneth G., David C. Ralph, and Milton J. Wiksell, *Principles of Speaking,* Wadsworth Publishing Co., 1962. Chapter 3 examines the nature and role of personal proof.

Huber, Robert, *Influencing through Argument,* David McKay Co., 1963, pp. 41–44, 92–142, 177–205, 295–299. Discusses propositions of fact and explains the sound use of evidence, induction, analogy, and causal reasoning.

Mills, Glenn, *Reason in Controversy,* Allyn and Bacon, 1964, pp. 43–44, 62–65, 97–119, 125–145. Explains how questions of fact, legality, and value all involve criteria and application; discusses the use of evidence and reasoning (Toulmin approach).

Walter, Otis, and Robert L. Scott, *Thinking and Speaking,* The Macmillan Co., 1962, pp. 33–51, 134–147. Discusses thinking and speaking about causal relationships; explains the use of statistics, examples, analogies, and expert testimony.

HOW SEPARATE SHOULD GOVERNMENT AND GOD BE?

Howard C. Wilkinson

Howard C. Wilkinson, Chaplain at Duke University in Durham, North Carolina, delivered this speech before the Charlotte Executive Club in Charlotte, North Carolina on January 22, 1963. He alleges that historically government and religion in the United States have not been clearly separate. To give credibility to this claim he documents it with expert opinions and historical examples. Since evidence is of primary importance in a speech affirming a proposition of fact, you will want to evaluate the sufficiency of evidence, its validity, and the skill with which Wilkinson uses it in demonstrating his point.

Next to evidence, the speaker's ethos is perhaps the most important factor in this speech. Consider in what ways the speaker tries to utilize personal proof to give credibility to the fact he wants the audience to accept.

This speech is reprinted by permission from Vital Speeches of the Day *(March 15, 1963), pp. 337–340.*

1 The basic assumption which underlies this address is that there is a kind of separation which should exist between government and God. But there is a problem involved in our effort to stake out the boundaries of this separation.

2 The problem arises out of the total impossibility of neutrality. It is not at all possible for a government to be completely neutral toward religion. The concept of a government which is religiously colorless is a mirage. It occurs only in the abstract imagination, not in existential history.

3 I base that statement not only upon the teaching of Jesus of Nazareth that neutrality regarding religion is non-existent (Matthew 12:30; Luke 11:23-26), but upon empirical observation of history and modern life. Suppose the founders of the American government had recognized that some people believe in God and that some others do not, and had therefore concluded that they did not want the government to take sides in the matter. Suppose, further, that they had determined they would fashion our government in a completely neutral way, with no reference whatever to a Supreme Being.

4 This very attempt to avoid taking sides would have placed them squarely on the side *against* the God of the Judeo-Christian religion! This is the case because one of the basic teachings of the Judeo-Christian faith is that God is relevant to every area of life. The founders would have been *denying* this claim by saying that God is *not* relevant to the area of government. Indeed, they would have been boldly affirming the basic doctrine of secularism, which is that, if there is a God, He does not need to be taken into account when we make plans.

5 Communist Russia, Communist China and Communist Cuba realize the impossibility of religious neutrality in government, and they

have openly set their governments against God and religion. This does not mean that no religious life exists in Russia, China or Cuba, but it means that their governments are officially against it. The reverse is true in America. We can easily find atheism and secularism in our land, but our government is officially on the side of God. The same is true of Israel, Britain, and the Moslem nations—to mention only a few.

6 Since there is no such thing as neutrality as a government contemplates religion, what are the possible postures which government may take with regard to it. Dr. James A. Pike, who for five years was a professor of Constitutional Law in the Columbia University Law School, and who now is Episcopal Bishop of California, told the Senate Judiciary Committee last August that there are three possibilities. One is for the government deliberately to secularize all public life, to deny the relevance of religion to the affairs of state. This position sometimes is advocated in a mild form, with claims of neither friendship nor hostility toward religion. It occasionally is advocated in a threatening form, with elaborate plans being made to eradicate religion. However separate government and God should be in America, I am one who believes they should not be *that* separate!

7 A second posture which government may take with regard to religion, said Bishop Pike, is to go to the opposite extreme, not only professing faith in God but officially choosing a particular, organized expression of religion as the state church. We today call this "the established church" plan. Under this arrangement, the government usually appoints the church's ministers, pays their salaries by tax money, builds and repairs the houses of worship from taxes, and in some instances requires under penalty that all office-holders give verbal assent to the theological beliefs of that particular church.

8 It is worth our pausing here long enough to note that this is the plan which the first part of the First Amendment to the Constitution specifically forbids. Here are the words: "Congress shall make no law respecting an establishment of religion . . ." Now there are some people in our country today who are attempting to make those words mean an entirely different thing from what they were intended to mean by those who wrote them and who ratified them. These persons would have you and me believe that this part of the First Amendment was intended to prevent the government from professing faith in God, confessing its reliance upon God, allowing prayers to be said in public institutions, permitting baccalaureate services to be held in public schools, or anything of the kind. The most charitable thing which can be said about such people is that they are ignorant at this point; they have not read the pertinent portions of American history and therefore do not know what they are talking about.

9 For a number of years I have studied this question and have read extensively in the relevant sections of American history. It has become crystal clear to me that the phrase in the First Amendment, "an establishment of religion," meant one thing, and only one thing, at the time of its adoption. It referred to what we today would call "an established church."

10 At the time of the American Revolution, eight of the American colonies had established churches. England had then, and has now, an established church, the Anglican Church. The Evangelical-Lutheran Church is the state church of Norway. Our founding fathers did not like this plan, and the first portion of the First Amendment was designed to prevent its adoption in the United States.

11 The founding fathers sometimes referred to this scheme by the words we use, that is, "an established church," but more frequently by the phrase, "an establishment of religion." George Mason drafted the Bill of Rights which was adopted by the Virginia Convention in 1776, and it is conceded by historians that this Bill of Rights was the most influential document in all subsequent Bills of Rights, including the one in the U.S. Constitution. The Library of Congress has preserved Mason's original, hand-written draft of this Bill of Rights. The way the "First Amendment" reads in Mason's Bill of Rights is as follows: ". . . no particular religious *Sect* or *Society* of Christians ought to be favored or established by Law, in preference to others." In other words, "no established denomination," "no state church."

12 Perhaps the personal influence of Thomas Jefferson was greater than the personal influence of any other in this whole area of religious freedom, in those early days. I have read everything I can find which Jefferson wrote on the subject of religion, both in his published works and in his private letters. It is clear from these writings that he understood "an establishment of religion" to mean what we mean by "an established church."

13 A conclusive example is given in a book of *Notes* which he published in 1787, only two years before Congress voted to adopt the First Amendment. There is a section in that book which describes what he therein called "an establishment of religion." Here are a few representative descriptions: He wrote of "poor Quakers (who) were flying from persecutions in England"; he said that "heresy was a capital offence, punishable by burning; its definition (being) left to the ecclesiastical judges." He wrote of "laws giving salaries to the clergy"; and he recited how that ". . . if a person . . . denies the being of a God, or the Trinity, or asserts there are more gods than one, or denies the Christian religion to be true, or the scriptures to be of divine authority, he is punishable . . . by three years of imprisonment without bail." This was Jefferson's concept of "an establishment of religion." With that in mind, it should be easier for us to remember that when Jefferson referred in a private letter to the First Amendment as erecting "a wall of separation," he had made it clear that this "wall" would separate *church* and state, not religion and government.

14 This plan of the established church is not for us to use in America. The First Amendment forbids it, and we would not want to employ it even if there were no Constitutional prohibition. Government and God should be separated to the extent that no religious organizations or denomination should be chosen by the state as being God's favored representative to the state.

15 The third posture which Bishop Pike said that government can take with regard to religion is what he called the middle way, or the American way. In our nation every branch of the government has affirmed its faith in God, its reliance upon God, and the relevance of God's power, wisdom and justice to our national survival and welfare. This has been done without any suggestion that any private citizen must make this his own personal creed. Complete freedom to believe or not to believe is guaranteed every citizen. The rights of atheists, agnostics, deists, theists and polytheists are alike respected. Moreover, all of them are free to propagate their beliefs as they wish. But the American government has always proclaimed the nation's faith in God and prayed for the blessing of His wisdom and protection in our national life.

16 Let me take a few minutes to remind you of some of the historical, legal and Constitutional reasons why this is true. It might be said that the first government which our forebears formed on this land was constituted by the Mayflower Compact, signed November 11, 1620. It provided for a form of democratic government, and then within the body of the Compact, the Pilgrims plainly stated that they had established that government in the Name of God, by the Grace of God, in the Presence of God, and for the Glory of God.

17 A century and a half later, the same religious basis was claimed for a new venture in American government, called the Declaration of Independence. In announcing to the world America's independent, national existence, the framers of the Declaration openly affirmed the new nation's dependence upon God and named Him as the author of our "inalienable rights."

18 A few years later, when the Constitution was adopted, two items in it showed the religious orientation of the government which it brought into being, and by which we are governed today. In Article I, Section 7, paragraph 2, there is a specification that the President shall have ten days in which to return a bill to Congress, but an exception is noted. Sundays shall not be counted when computing the ten-day limit! Why? Here one could haggle for hours over technicalities, but most historians would agree that the reason why this item was placed in the U.S. Constitution was that Sunday had been observed from the earliest colonization of this land as a day of worship. The Constitution provides that even the urgent legislative business of Congress must not be permitted to crowd out the President's day of worship.

19 The second religious guidepost in the U.S. Constitution appears at the end of the document. In Article VII, second paragraph, we read the following: "Done in convention, by the unanimous consent of the states present, the seventeenth day of September, in the year of our Lord one thousand seven hundred and eighty-seven, and of the independence of the United States of America the twelfth." If it were said, as one college professor has said, that the phrase, "in the year of our Lord" was merely a meaningless formality, I would reply by pointing out two things: First, there is no historical evidence that those who toiled over that Constitution were engaged in meaningless formalities of any sort. They, at least, would vehemently have denied the charge! Second, I would ask which atheistic society anywhere in the world has dated its constitution by such a "meaningless formality" as "in the year of our Lord."

20 As we move to a slightly different field to harvest evidence of the religious character of our government, it would be well to note a point made by Dr. W. B. Munro, who was professor of history and government at California Institute of Technology at the time he wrote the textbook entitled THE GOVERNMENT OF THE UNITED STATES. Dr. Munro made it clear (Chapter 6) that the official, basic nature of the American government is to be ascertained not only by reference to the printed words of the Constitution, but equally as much by the acts of Congress, the decisions of the Presidents, and the enactment of the various state legislatures which have been allowed by the Supreme Court to stand.

21 Consider, then, some of these official actions. Let us begin with the Presidents. The first President proclaimed the first day of national Thanksgiving under the Constitution with the following words in a presidential proclamation:

> Whereas it is the duty of all *nations* to acknowledge the providence of the Almighty God, to obey His will, to be grateful for His benefits, and humbly to implore His protection and favor, and whereas both Houses of Congress have by their joint Committee requested me to 'recommend to the People of the United States a day of public thanksgiving and prayer to be observed by acknowledging with grateful hearts the many signal favors of Almighty God, especially for their safety and happiness.' Now therefore I do recommend and assign Thursday the 26th day of November . . .

22 Without a single exception, every President from Washington to Kennedy has acknowledged either in his inaugural address or in his message to Congress (or both) that he relied upon a personal God. Every President has taken the oath of his office upon the Holy Bible. Lest some one should think these presidential confessions of faith are more pronounced in the past than in the present, let me quote a sentence from the inaugural address of President John F. Kennedy: ". . . the same revolutionary beliefs for which our forebears fought are still at issue around the globe—the belief that the rights of man come not from the generosity of the state, but from the hand of God." Parenthetically, I might add that these very American words could have been spoken by a Methodist, a Baptist, an Episcopalian or a Jew. They happen to have been spoken by a Roman Catholic.

23 Let us turn now to the official actions of the Congress, and we shall discover the same unequivocal religious faith as a part of the official nature of our government. The very first Congress which was elected and brought together under the U.S. Constitution convened on March 4, 1789, and recessed on September 29, less than seven months later. During that short but important period, the members organized the Congress and fixed many historic policies which continue to this day. One of the first actions of this initial Congress was to make provision for the appointment of two Congressional Chaplains, among whose duties would be that of leading the houses of Congress in prayer to Almighty God each day, an official practice which continues to this moment.

24 A second significant achievement of that first Congress was that, by joint action of both houses, plans were carried out to the effect that, as soon as Washington took his oath of office as the first President of the United States, he, together with all the officials of the government and all members of both houses of Congress went directly to St. Paul's Chapel to attend divine services, conducted by a Congressional Chaplain. (This was on April 30, 1789).

25 A few days before that first Congress recessed, the members reflected back upon the perilous journey through which the new nation had passed. They thought of their strong enemies who had tried to keep them in subjection from without, and they thought of the anarchy and dissension within. And then they realized that, despite all these and other perils, they nevertheless were the stockholders of a free nation, in which there could be liberty and justice for all. So what did they then do? Did they pat themselves on the back and get drunk? Not at all! Elias Boudinot, of New Jersey, introduced a resolution calling upon President Washington to proclaim a day of national thanksgiving to Almighty God.

26 When this resolution was introduced, a Mr. T. T. Tucker, from South Carolina, arose and spoke against it, giving some of the arguments which we have heard the secularists of today use. He declared that the Congress and the President should not call upon the people of the United States to set aside a day of Thanksgiving to God because, said he, it might be that not all of the people will *want* to give thanks. Whether this is the case or not, he continued, it is no business of Congress to call people to prayer, for this is a religious matter. Finally, he said, if a day of thanksgiving must take place, let some one else call it.

27 The members of the Congress heard all that Tucker had to say, but they did not agree with him. They decided it *was* the business of the Congress and the President to invite people to pray. And so, by an overwhelming vote, they did just that.

28 Since that time, the Congress has not only been paying Congressional Chaplains to lead the houses in prayer, but Congress has been voting money to put chaplains in all the divisions of every branch of the armed forces, and they have built chapels for worship with tax money, but without choosing any religious organization as the nation's church. In 1864, Congress declared our national motto to be "In God We Trust," and ordered that this should appear on our coins. It is even inscribed on the wall of the chamber of the U.S. Senate. The Congress voted that "The Star-Spangled Banner" is our national anthem. The fourth stanza of that anthem contains these lines: "Blest with victory and peace, may the heav'n rescued land/Praise the Pow'r that hath made and preserved us a nation." Also by official action of Congress, our Pledge of Allegiance to the flag contains the descriptive phrase, "one Nation under God."

29 We move now from the Executive and the Legislative branches of the government, to the Judicial branch. The Supreme Court is opened with prayer at each and every session it holds. The crier offers this petition: "God save the United States and this Honorable Court."

30 On February 29, 1892, the Supreme Court handed down a decision in the case of THE CHURCH OF THE HOLY TRINITY VS. THE UNITED STATES, and along with the decision gave an opinion which proclaimed that the United States is officially a Christian nation. The opinion was quite lengthy and recited many reasons why this government is of a religious nature.

31 Eleven years ago, in 1952, in the so-called "released time" decision, the Supreme Court declared that when the government encourages or cooperates with religion "it follows the best of our traditions," and it further declared that "We are a religious people whose institutions presuppose a Supreme Being."

32 The religious orientation of our judiciary continues down through the inferior courts, in which witnesses are sworn to tell the truth with their hands placed upon the Holy Bible. To realize the significance of this, try imagining a witness being sworn to tell the truth with his hand upon the dictionary, or the almanac, or the Communist Manifesto!

33 If Professor Will Herberg is right in his statement that institutions are best understood when they are understood historically, then the American government has to be declared a religious one; with faith in God, reliance upon Him, and with thanksgiving for His many favors.

34 To be sure, there is a significant number of determined people in America today who are trying to sweep all these references I have given under the rug of history, and they would make it appear that our government is religiously barren and colorless, without any faith commitment worth mentioning. They are seeking to permeate our educational system. They are pounding loudly upon the door of the Supreme Court. They are attempting to distort history by twisting the First Amendment to mean something it never meant. They would abolish prayer and all religious observances in every kind of state institution. In direct violation of the second portion of the First Amendment, which clearly specifies that "Congress shall make no law . . . prohibiting the free exercise (of religion)," they would prohibit the free exercise of religion in schools, in Congress, in the state legislatures, and in every public institution. If they can get their way, they will fashion the public institutions of this land in such form that only a godless secularist could feel at home in them. I am one who does not believe that the founders of American democracy intended this. I am one who believes we Americans in the Twentieth Century should not permit this to occur.

35 The question might be asked as to why it is, if what I have been saying is true, so many people are unsure of it. The answer is twofold. First, the major part of the materials I have here presented have not been in general circulation, and the average American has not read history to the extent necessary to know for himself. Second, a great deal of misinformation has been in general circulation in recent years, calculated to propagandize the American public to believe that secularized institutions are somehow required by the system under which we live.

36 Consider an illustration of this mis-information. Last July 13, *Time* magazine printed the following statement which had been sent to it by one Albert B. Norwalk: ". . . George Washington wrote, 'The government of the United States of America is not in any sense founded on the Christian Religion.' . . ." Well, *Time* not only nodded: its editors were soundly asleep when this was printed, because Mr. Norwalk not only sent the quotation but included the reference where it could be located. *Time's* editors could easily have checked it for authenticity. Instead, they printed it without comment, and very likely millions of *Time's* readers today believe George Washington wrote those words. I know of one very distinguished university professor who read this quote in *Time* and circulated it as representing the position of the early American government regarding religion. But alas! The entire statement is a complete fraud! Our State Department historians have indicated that the statement was a figment of the imagination of an obscure and inept clerk in the American consulate in Tripoli, many years ago. State Department historians are at a total loss to explain why this clerk fabricated the statement and wrongfully attributed it to Washington.

37 It not only is true that Washington never wrote those words. Actually, they present the reverse of his views. In his famous Farewell Address to the American people, which has been termed "one of the world's most remarkable documents," Washington stated plainly and convincingly that he did not believe the nation would be able to maintain enough character and integrity to survive without religion.

These views of his should be re-emphasized in 1963. Former President Dwight D. Eisenhower agreed with Washington as he spoke these words of equal significance: "You can't explain free government in any other terms than religious."

38 How separate should government and God be? Organizationally, they must be entirely separate. In terms of values, morality, and the goals of life, they must not be separate. As the Supreme Court wisely ruled in 1962, it is not the business of government either to write the prayers which the citizens are to pray, nor to require that the citizens *must* pray at all. The government certainly must not interfere with the free exercise of religion. As Justice Stewart of the U.S. Supreme Court wrote last June, ". . . to deny the wish of . . . school children to join in reciting . . . prayer is to deny them the opportunity of sharing in the spiritual heritage of our nation." When the government encourages and cooperates with religion it follows the best of our traditions.

39 There must be no state church and no required religion. But good religion supports legitimate government, and good government is on the side of ethical religion.

ARE THEY REALLY "UNTEACHABLE"?

Carolyn Kay Geiman

Carolyn Kay Geiman, a sophomore at the University of Kansas, delivered this speech to fulfill an assignment in a speech class during the 1964 spring semester. She alleges a present and continuing fact—that culturally deprived children are teachable. Although she cites authorities to support her point, she also uses hypothetical and factual examples. In reading this speech, evaluate the clarity, vividness, and interest of her description of the "culturally deprived child and his environment" and determine whether this description functions primarily as proof or as illustration. What are the standards of judgment Miss Geiman is asking the audience to use in appraising her proposition of fact? Is she primarily establishing existence or causality?

Speeches concerning propositions of fact frequently are uninteresting and unemotional. This failure tends to stem from a heavy em-

phasis upon logical documentation. This speech, however, has specific interest factors, demonstrating that a speech which alleges a fact need not be dull. What are the factors of interest you find in this speech? Does the speaker's style in any way contribute to the level of interest? How effective are her introduction and conclusion as interest devices?

This speech is printed by permission of Miss Geiman.

1 In Charles Schulz's popular cartoon depiction of happiness, one of his definitions has special significance for the American school system. The drawing shows Linus, with his eyes closed in a state of supreme bliss, a broad smile across two-thirds of his face and holding a report card upon which is a big bold "A." The caption reads: "Happiness is finding out you're not so dumb after all." For once, happiness is not defined as a function of material possessions, yet even this happiness is practically unattainable for the "unteachables" of the city slums. Are these children intellectually inferior? Are they unable to learn? Are they not worth the time and the effort to teach? Unfortunately, too many people have answered "yes" to these questions and promptly dismissed the issue.

2 If we base our answers on the results of IQ tests, "yes" answers may seem justified. In the largest American metropolitan areas, the students in the top school of the wealthiest suburbs have an average IQ of 120; those in the bottom school of the worst slums have an average IQ of 85. Valid factual proof, right?

3 In a city-wide group testing program in the New York City schools, IQ scores showed a lower and slower rate of increase with grade advancement in the large, low socio-economic districts than in the median for the city as a whole. In the third grade, there was a ten-point difference in IQ's; in the sixth grade, a seventeen-point difference; and in the eighth grade, a twenty-point difference. Valid factual proof again, right?

4 No, wrong! The fallacy of these "facts" lies in the IQ test itself. The very fact that IQ test results vary over a given span of time indicates, as many educators today are realizing, that these are in truth tests of cultural experience and not of native ability. These children of the slums are underdeveloped culturally, but are not innately unintelligent, and this deficiency can and should be corrected.

5 Horace Mann Bond, Dean of the School of Education at Atlanta University, in his lecture entitled "The Search for Talent,"

points out that the almost universal reliance upon the results of standardized testing is allowing an enormous leakage of human resources in our society. The results of such tests, he argues, tend to follow the lines of social class and cultural opportunity and thus tend to mask the real intellectual ability of children in slum areas. There are two specific problems which limit the educational development of these children. The first is that many of them arrive at school-age possessing very little skill in communication as a result of the stifling environment of the slum. Secondly, children in slum areas, and often their parents as well, show little interest in education.

6 Let's take a look at the culturally deprived child and his environment. First of all, what he calls home may be one poorly-lit room on the sixth floor of a large apartment building—a room which he shares with eleven other people. On either side loom identical buildings. The noise and filth are inescapable. Look around. There are no pencils, no paper, no books, maybe a few scattered toys. To gain even a semblance of privacy in the midst of the clatter, he must train himself to shut out the noise so that he hears only what he wants to hear. He has learned to communicate by pulling or pointing, by grunts or groans. In the "living unit," which can hardly be called a home, a question such as, "How are we going to eat?" is valid, but there is no time for questions like "Where do the stars come from?" or "What causes rain?" When the child talks baby talk, his parents are either too harrassed or not articulate enough themselves to correct him. This child may not even know that things have names, that he himself is a somebody with a name. He may seem to have trouble looking at things, but the fault lies not in his eyes, but in his experiences. He can't see differences in size, shape, color, and texture because he hasn't been taught to look for them. So what happens when he starts to school? He is branded as "unteachable" by teachers who cannot or will not understand this background or its effect on the child.

7 Dr. Martin Deutsch, the Director of the Institution for Developmental Studies of New York Medical College's Department of Psychiatry, became interested in the plight of the culturally deprived child in the public schools and studied the problem for five years. Following his theory that "intelligence is not inherited, but a dynamic process that can be stunted or stimulated by experience," he inaugurated the first scientific and concerted attempt by any public school system to confront the problem of the education of the poor pre-school age child. Ninety-six four year olds in New York City were given the advantage of this progressive program. Let's see what methods were used.

8 First, each child was taught that he had a name of his own, that he was somebody special, a unique person. Every work of art was signed. Parents were urged to make a fuss over the child's work, even if it was poorly done. "If a child doesn't feel pride, he can't learn."

9 Secondly, each child was urged to express his thoughts and wishes in words. Teachers were instructed not to respond to tuggings at their skirts or mumbled noises. The formation of a thought into a complete sentence, with subject, verb, and predicate was lauded as a major accomplishment.

10 Rhoda was one of the subjects of this experiment. In the classroom she stands, "clutching her favorite toys—a Negro doll and a toy baby bottle. The only game she knows is caring for the baby—bathing it, feeding it, rocking it. Fatherless Rhoda lives with her mother, who bore her at fifteen, her thirty-eight year old grandmother, two younger sisters, and eight uncles and aunts ranging in age from two months to ten years. After eleven weeks in school, Rhoda still hasn't spoken or smiled. Scowling fiercely now, she reaches out for some wax grapes and puts them in a frying pan on the stove." Hearing a noise behind her, the teacher turned around to discover Rhoda struggling with a pan. She heard Rhoda speak her first whole sentence: "Dem goddam peaches is burnin'." It's poor English, it's profane, but it is a complete thought, and this is a major achievement. Rhoda was rewarded with a big hug from her teacher, not scolded for her profanity.

11 Projects such as this one indicate that with care, understanding, and attention children in slum areas can be helped in mastering the basic skill of communication so vital to their educational process. What then of the indifference so prevalent in slum areas? Frank Reissman, a noted educator who has spent much of the last twenty years dealing with problems in the education of underprivileged children, is quick to point out that a distinction must be made in talking about indifference to education. Children and parents in slum areas, he says, are apathetic, and even antagonistic, not toward education, but rather toward the school system which writes them off as hopeless. Parents see the teacher as a middle-class citizen uninterested in their or their childrens' problems. The children who sense their rejection strongly, begin to simply tune the teacher out. The results of this neglect are that the streets that used to be their playgrounds become their hangouts. They roam the streets. They join the ranks of the unemployed. Instead of becoming constructive citizens of the community, they become anti-social and rebellious. But this need not be. Dr. Riessman points out that time and time again projects in our major cities have established that interest in the schools can be achieved simply by demonstrating the school's interest in the underprivileged child. Parents called in for conferences, not because Johnny played hookey, but because the teacher wanted to discuss his progress have responded gratefully. Children treated with respect and interest have blossomed.

12 When we understand that these two major stumbling blocks to the educational progress of the underprivileged child can be eliminated—that they can be encouraged to communicate and that apathy and antagonism can be conquered—we realize that we need not write these children off as a lost cause. We need not lose these valuable human resources. We can help the "unteachables" to discover the magic of learning and achieving. We can help them to understand Schulz's definition: "Happiness is finding out you're not so dumb after all."

THE BILL OF RIGHTS

Hugo L. Black

Hugo L. Black, Associate Justice of the United States Supreme Court since 1937, delivered this address as the first James Madison Lecture at the New York University School of Law on February 17, 1960. To support his thesis that the Bill of Rights contains absolutes and that their framers put them there on purpose, Justice Black examines each amendment and relates pertinent historical documentation to it. In effect Black is saying to his audience that we must measure the proposition by what historical documents and historical incidents tell us. In evaluating an argument based on documents, it is vital to analyze not only the merit of the documents as evidence but also the speaker's interpretation of them. To help understand the flow of Black's argument, outline the speech and then analyze the use of documentation in relation to each point. Justice Black relies heavily on the testimony of James Madison in demonstrating his thesis. Why would Madison be an especially useful source of evidence on this occasion? How does Black qualify Madison as a credible source of evidence?

It is obvious that Justice Black is addressing an interested audience with high intellectual capability. Perhaps, as a consequence, the speech contains few common interest factors; the speaker merely seeks to document his thesis. What changes would be necessary to gain the interest of a lay audience?

The text of this speech is from the New York University Law Review, *Vol. 35 (April 1960), pp. 865–881. It is reprinted with permission of New York University, copyright owner.*

1 I am honored to be the first speaker in your new annual series of James Madison lectures. The title of the series suggested the title of my talk: The Bill of Rights. Madison lived in the stirring times between 1750 and 1836, during which the Colonies declared, fought for, and won their independence from England. They then set up a new national government dedicated to Liberty and Justice. Madison's role in creating that government was such a major one that he has since been generally referred to as the Father of our Constitution. He was a most influential member of the Philadelphia Convention that submitted the Constitution to the people of the states; he alone kept a comprehensive report of the daily proceedings of the Convention; he was an active member of the Virginia Convention that adopted the Constitution after a bitter fight; finally, as a member of the First Congress, he offered and sponsored through that body proposals that became the first ten amendments, generally thought of as our Bill of Rights. For these and many other reasons, Madison's words are an authentic source to help us understand the Constitution and its Bill of Rights. In the course of my discussion I shall have occasion to refer to some of the many things Madison said about the meaning of the Constitution and the first ten amendments. In doing so, I shall refer to statements made by him during the Bill of Rights debates as reported in the *Annals of Congress.* There has been doubt cast upon the accuracy of the reports of Congressional debates and transactions in the *Annals.* I am assured by Mr. Irving Brant, the eminent biographer of Madison, that Madison's discussions of the Bill of Rights as reported in the *Annals* are shown to be correct by Madison's own manuscripts on file in the Library of Congress.[1]

[1] See also Brant, The Madison Heritage, 35 N.Y.U.L. Rev. 882 (1960).

2 What is a bill of rights? In the popular sense it is any document setting forth the liberties of the people. I prefer to think of our Bill of Rights as including all provisions of the original Constitution and Amendments that protect individual liberty by barring government from acting in a particular area or from acting except under certain prescribed procedures. I have in mind such clauses in the body of the Constitution itself as those which safeguard the right of habeas corpus, forbid bills of attainder and ex post facto laws, guarantee trial by jury, and strictly define treason and limit the way it can be tried and punished. I would certainly add to this list the last constitutional prohibition in Article Six that "no religious Test shall ever be required as a Qualification to any Office or public Trust under the United States."

3 I shall speak to you about the Bill of Rights only as it bears on powers of the Federal Government. Originally, the first ten amendments were not intended to apply to the states but, as the Supreme Court held in 1833 in *Barron v. Baltimore,*[2] were adopted to quiet fears extensively entertained that the powers of the big new national government "might be exercised in a manner dangerous to liberty." I believe that by virtue of the Fourteenth Amendment, the first ten amendments are now applicable to the states, a view I stated in *Adamson v. California.*[3] I adhere to that view. In this talk, however, I want to discuss only the extent to which the Bill of Rights limits the Federal Government.

4 In applying the Bill of Rights to the Federal Government there is today a sharp difference of views as to how far its provisions should be held to limit the lawmaking power of Congress. How this difference is finally resolved will, in my judgment, have far-reaching consequences upon our liberties. I shall first summarize what those different views are.

5 Some people regard the prohibitions of the Constitution, even its most unequivocal commands, as mere admonitions which Congress need not always observe. This viewpoint finds many different verbal expressions. For example, it is sometimes said that Congress may abridge a constitutional right if there is a clear and present danger that the free exercise of the right will bring about a substantive evil that Congress has authority to prevent. Or it is said that a right may be abridged where its exercise would cause so much injury to the public that this injury would outweigh the injury to the individual who is

[2] 32 U.S. (7 Pet.) 242, 249 (1833).

[3] 332 U.S. 46, 71–72 (1947) (dissenting opinion).

deprived of the right. Again, it is sometimes said that the Bill of Rights' guarantees must "compete" for survival against general powers expressly granted to Congress and that the individual's right must, if outweighed by the public interest, be subordinated to the Government's competing interest in denying the right. All of these formulations, and more with which you are doubtless familiar, rest, at least in part, on the premise that there are no "absolute" prohibitions in the Constitution, and that all constitutional problems are questions of reasonableness, proximity, and degree. This view comes close to the English doctrine of legislative omnipotence, qualified only by the possibility of a judicial veto if the Supreme Court finds that a congressional choice between "competing" policies has no reasonable basis.

6 I cannot accept this approach to the Bill of Rights. It is my belief that there *are* "absolutes" in our Bill of Rights, and that they were put there on purpose by men who knew what words meant, and meant their prohibitions to be "absolutes." The whole history and background of the Constitution and Bill of Rights, as I understand it, belies the assumption or conclusion that our ultimate constitutional freedoms are no more than our English ancestors had when they came to this new land to get new freedoms. The historical and practical purposes of a Bill of Rights, the very use of a written constitution, indigenous to America, the language the Framers used, the kind of three-department government they took pains to set up, all point to the creation of a government which was denied all power to do some things under any and all circumstances, and all power to do other things except precisely in the manner prescribed. In this talk I will state some of the reasons why I hold this view. In doing so, however, I shall not attempt to discuss the wholly different and complex problem of the marginal scope of each individual amendment as applied to the particular facts of particular cases. For example, there is a question as to whether the First Amendment was intended to protect speech that courts find "obscene." I shall not stress this or similar differences of construction, nor shall I add anything to the views I expressed in the recent case of *Smith v. California*.[4] I am primarily discussing here whether liberties *admittedly* covered by the Bill of Rights can nevertheless be abridged on the ground that a superior public interest justifies the abridgment. I think the Bill of Rights made its safeguards superior.

7 Today most Americans seem to have forgotten the ancient evils which forced their ancestors to flee to this new country and to

[4] 361 U.S. 147, 155 (1959) (concurring opinion).

form a government stripped of old powers used to oppress them. But the Americans who supported the Revolution and the adoption of our Constitution knew firsthand the dangers of tyrannical governments. They were familiar with the long existing practice of English persecutions of people wholly because of their religious or political beliefs. They knew that many accused of such offenses had stood, helpless to defend themselves, before biased legislators and judges.

8 John Lilburne, a Puritan dissenter, is a conspicuous example.[5] He found out the hard way that a citizen of England could not get a court and jury trial under English law if Parliament wanted to try and punish him in some kind of summary and unfair method of its own. Time and time again, when his religious or political activities resulted in criminal charges against him, he had demanded jury trials under the "law of the land" but had been refused. Due to "trials" either by Parliament, its legislative committees, or courts subservient to the King or to Parliament, against all of which he vigorously protested as contrary to "due process" or "the law of the land," Lilburne had been whipped, put in the pillory, sent to prison, heavily fined and banished from England, all its islands and dominions, under penalty of death should he return. This last sentence was imposed by a simple Act of Parliament without any semblance of a trial. Upon his defiant return he was arrested and subjected to an unfair trial for his life. His chief defense was that the Parliamentary conviction was a nullity, as a denial of "due process of law," which he claimed was guaranteed under Magna Charta, the 1628 Petition of Right, and statutes passed to carry them out. He also challenged the power of Parliament to enact bills of attainder on the same grounds—due process of law. Lilburne repeatedly and vehemently contended that he was entitled to notice, an indictment, and court trial by jury under the known laws of England; that he had a right to be represented by counsel; that he had a right to have witnesses summoned in his behalf and be confronted by the witnesses against him; that he could not be compelled to testify against himself. When Lilburne finally secured a jury, it courageously acquitted him, after which the jury itself was severely punished by the court.

9 Prompted largely by the desire to save Englishmen from such legislative mockeries of fair trials, Lilburne and others strongly advocated adoption of an "Agreement of the People" which contained

[5] See The Trial of John Lilburne and John Wharton (Star Chamber 1637) in 3 How. St. Tr. 1315 (1816).

most of the provisions of our present Bill of Rights. That Agreement would have done away with Parliamentary omnipotence. Lilburne pointed out that the basic defect of Magna Charta and statutes complementing it was that they were not binding on Parliament since "that which is done by one Parliament, as a Parliament, may be undone by the next Parliament: but an Agreement of the People begun and ended amongst the People can never come justly within the Parliament's cognizance to destroy."[6] The proposed "Agreement of the People," Lilburne argued, could be changed only by the people and would bind Parliament as the supreme "law of the land." This same idea was picked up before the adoption of our Federal Constitution by Massachusetts and New Hampshire, which adopted their constitutions only after popular referendums. Our Federal Constitution is largely attributable to the same current of thinking.

10 Unfortunately, our own colonial history also provided ample reasons for people to be afraid to vest too much power in the national government. There had been bills of attainder here; women had been convicted and sentenced to death as "witches"; Quakers, Baptists and various Protestant sects had been persecuted from time to time. Roger Williams left Massachusetts to breathe the free air of new Rhode Island. Catholics were barred from holding office in many places. Test oaths were required in some of the colonies to bar any but Christians from holding office. In New England Quakers suffered death for their faith. Baptists were sent to jail in Virginia for preaching, which caused Madison, while a very young man, to deplore what he called that "diabolical hell-conceived principle of persecution."[7]

11 In the light of history, therefore, it is not surprising that when our Constitution was adopted without specific provisions to safeguard cherished individual rights from invasion by the legislative, as well as the executive and judicial departments of the National Government, a loud and irresistible clamor went up throughout the country. These protests were so strong that the Constitution was ratified by the very narrowest of votes in some of the states. It has been said, and I think correctly, that had there been no general agreement that a supplementary Bill of Rights would be adopted as soon as possible after Congress met, the Constitution would not have been ratified. It seems clear that this widespread demand for a Bill of Rights was due to a common fear of political and religious persecution should

[6] Leveller Manifestoes of the Puritan Revolution 423 (Wolfe ed. 1944).

[7] 1 Rives, History of the Life and Times of James Madison 44 (1859).

the national legislative power be left unrestrained as it was in England.

12 The form of government which was ordained and established in 1789 contains certain unique features which reflected the Framers' fear of arbitrary government and which clearly indicate an intention absolutely to limit what Congress could do. The first of these features is that our Constitution is written in a single document. Such constitutions are familiar today and it is not always remembered that our country was the first to have one. Certainly one purpose of a written constitution is to define and therefore more specifically limit government powers. An all-powerful government that can act as it pleases wants no such constitution—unless to fool the people. England had no written constitution and this once proved a source of tyranny, as our ancestors well knew. Jefferson said about this departure from the English type of government: "Our peculiar security is in the possession of a written Constitution. Let us not make it a blank paper by construction."[8]

13 A second unique feature of our Government is a Constitution supreme over the legislature. In England, statutes, Magna Charta and later declarations of rights had for centuries limited the power of the King, but they did not limit the power of Parliament. Although commonly referred to as a constitution, they were never the "supreme law of the land" in the way in which our Constitution is, much to the regret of statesmen like Pitt the elder. Parliament could change this English "Constitution"; Congress cannot change ours. Ours can only be changed by amendments ratified by three-fourths of the states. It was one of the great achievements of our Constitution that it ended legislative omnipotence here and placed all departments and agencies of government under one supreme law.

14 A third feature of our Government expressly designed to limit its powers was the division of authority into three coordinate branches none of which was to have supremacy over the others. This separation of powers with the checks and balances which each branch was given over the others was designed to prevent any branch, including the legislative, from infringing individual liberties safeguarded by the Constitution.

15 Finally, our Constitution was the first to provide a really independent judiciary. Moreover, as the Supreme Court held in *Mar-*

[8] 4 Jefferson, Writings 506 (Washington ed. 1859).

bury v. Madison,[9] correctly I believe, this judiciary has the power to hold legislative enactments void that are repugnant to the Constitution and the Bill of Rights. In this country the judiciary was made independent because it has, I believe, the primary responsibility and duty of giving force and effect to constitutional liberties and limitations upon the executive and legislative branches. Judges in England were not always independent and they could not hold Parliamentary acts void. Consequently, English courts could not be counted on to protect the liberties of the people against invasion by the Parliament, as many unfortunate Englishmen found out, such as Sir Walter Raleigh, who was executed as the result of an unfair trial, and a lawyer named William Prynne, whose ears were first cut off by court order and who subsequently, by another court order, had his remaining ear stumps gouged out while he was on a pillory. Prynne's offenses were writing books and pamphlets.

16 All of the unique features of our Constitution show an underlying purpose to create a new kind of limited government. Central to all of the Framers of the Bill of Rights was the idea that since government, particularly the national government newly created, is a powerful institution, its officials—all of them—must be compelled to exercise their powers within strictly defined boundaries. As Madison told Congress, the Bill of Rights' limitations point "sometimes against the abuse of the Executive power, sometimes against the Legislative, and in some cases against the community itself; or, in other words, against the majority in favor of the minority."[10] Madison also explained that his proposed amendments were intended "to limit and qualify the powers of Government, by excepting out of the grant of power those cases in which the Government ought not to act, or to act only in a particular mode."[11] In the light of this purpose let us now turn to the language of the first ten amendments to consider whether their provisions were written as mere admonitions to Congress or as absolute commands, proceeding for convenience from the last to the first.

17 The last two Amendments, the Ninth and Tenth, are general in character, but both emphasize the limited nature of the Federal Government. Number Ten restricts federal power to what the Constitution delegates to the central government, reserving all other powers to

[9] 5 U.S. (1 Cranch) 137 (1803).

[10] 1 Annals of Cong. 437 (1789).

[11] Ibid.

the states or to the people. Number Nine attempts to make certain that enumeration of some rights must "not be construed to deny or disparage others retained by the people." The use of the words, "the people," in both these Amendments strongly emphasizes the desire of the Framers to protect individual liberty.

18 The Seventh Amendment states that "In Suits at common law, where the value in controversy shall exceed twenty dollars, the right of trial by jury shall be preserved. . . ." This language clearly requires that jury trials must be afforded in the type of cases the Amendment describes. The Amendment goes on in equally unequivocal words to command that "no fact tried by a jury, shall be otherwise re-examined in any Court of the United States, than according to the rules of the common law."

19 Amendments Five, Six, and Eight relate chiefly to the procedures that government must follow when bringing its powers to bear against any person with a view to depriving him of his life, liberty, or property.

20 The Eighth Amendment forbids "excessive bail," "excessive fines," or the infliction of "cruel or unusual punishments." This is one of the less precise provisions. The courts are required to determine the meaning of such general terms as "excessive" and "unusual." But surely that does not mean that admittedly "excessive bail," "excessive fines," or "cruel punishments" could be justified on the ground of a "competing" public interest in carrying out some generally granted power like that given Congress to regulate commerce.

21 Amendment Six provides that in a criminal prosecution an accused shall have a "speedy and public trial, by an impartial jury of the State and district wherein the crime shall have been committed, which district shall have been previously ascertained by law, and to be informed of the nature and cause of the accusation; to be confronted with the witnesses against him; to have compulsory process for obtaining witnesses in his favor, and have the Assistance of Counsel for his defence." All of these requirements are cast in terms both definite and absolute. Trial by jury was also guaranteed in the original Constitution. The additions here, doubtless prompted by English trials of Americans away from their homes, are that a trial must be "speedy and public," "by an impartial jury," and in a district which "shall have been previously ascertained by law." If there is any one thing that is certain it is that the Framers intended both in the original Constitution and in the Sixth Amendment that persons charged with crime by the Federal Government have a right to be tried by jury. Suppose juries began acquitting people Congress thought should be convicted. Could Congress then provide some other form of trial, say by an administrative agency, or the military, where convictions could be more readily and certainly obtained, if it thought the safety of the nation so required? How about secret trials? By *partial* juries? Can it be that these are not absolute prohibitions?

22 The Sixth Amendment requires notice of the cause of an accusation, confrontation by witnesses, compulsory process and assistance of counsel. The experience of centuries has demonstrated the value of these procedures to one on trial for crime. And this Amendment purports to guarantee them by clear language. But if there are no absolutes in the Bill of Rights, these guarantees too can be taken away by Congress on findings that a competing public interest requires that defendants be tried without notice, without witnesses, without confrontation, and without counsel.

23 The Fifth Amendment provides:

> No person shall be held to answer for a capital, or otherwise infamous crime, unless on a presentment or indictment of a Grand Jury, except in cases arising in the land or naval forces, or in the Militia, when in actual service in time of War or public danger; nor shall any person be subject for the same offence to be twice put in jeopardy of life or limb; nor shall be compelled in any criminal case to be a witness against himself, nor be deprived of life, liberty, or property, without due process of law; nor shall private property be taken for public use, without just compensation.

24 Most of these Fifth Amendment prohibitions are both definite and unequivocal. There has been much controversy about the meaning of "due process of law." Whatever its meaning, however, there can be no doubt that it must be granted. Moreover, few doubt that it has an historical meaning which denies Government the right to take away life, liberty, or property without trials properly conducted according to the Constitution and laws validly made in accordance with it. This, at least, was the meaning of "due process of law" when used in Magna Charta and other old English Statutes where it was referred to as "the law of the land."

25 The Fourth Amendment provides:

> The right of the people to be secure in their persons, houses, papers, and effects, against unreasonable searches and seizures, shall not be violated, and no Warrants shall issue, but upon probable cause, supported by Oath or affirmation, and particularly

> describing the place to be searched, and the persons or things to be seized.

26 The use of the word "unreasonable" in this Amendment means, of course, that not *all* searches and seizures are prohibited. Only those which are *unreasonable* are unlawful. There may be much difference of opinion about whether a particular search or seizure is unreasonable and therefore forbidden by this Amendment. But if it *is* unreasonable, it is absolutely prohibited.

27 Likewise, the provision which forbids warrants for arrest, search or seizure without "probable cause" is itself an absolute prohibition.

28 The Third Amendment provides that:

> No Soldier shall, in time of peace be quartered in any house, without the consent of the Owner, nor in time of war, but in a manner to be prescribed by law.

29 Americans had recently suffered from the quartering of British troops in their homes, and so this Amendment is written in language that apparently no one has ever thought could be violated on the basis of an overweighing public interest.

30 Amendment Two provides that:

> A well regulated Militia, being necessary to the security of a free State, the right of the people to keep and bear Arms, shall not be infringed.

Although the Supreme Court has held this Amendment to include only arms necessary to a well-regulated militia, as so construed, its prohibition is absolute.

31 This brings us to the First Amendment. It reads:

> Congress shall make no law respecting an establishment of religion, or prohibiting the free exercise thereof; or abridging the freedom of speech, or of the press; or the right of the people peaceably to assemble, and to petition the Government for a redress of grievances.

The phrase "Congress shall make no law" is composed of plain words, easily understood. The Framers knew this. The language used by Madison in his proposal was different, but no less emphatic and unequivocal. That proposal is worth reading:

The civil rights of none shall be abridged on account of religious belief or worship, nor shall any national religion be established, nor shall the full and equal rights of conscience be in any manner, or on any pretext, infringed.
The people shall not be deprived or abridged of their right to speak, to write, or to publish their sentiments; and the freedom of the press, as one of the great bulwarks of liberty, shall be inviolable.
The people shall not be restrained from peaceably assembling and consulting for their common good; nor from applying to the Legislature by petitions, or remonstrances, for redress of their grievances.[12]

32 Neither as offered nor as adopted is the language of this Amendment anything less than absolute. Madison was emphatic about this. He told the Congress that under it "The right of freedom of speech is secured; the liberty of the press is expressly declared to be *beyond the reach of this Government. . . .*"[13] (Emphasis added in all quotations.) Some years later Madison wrote that "it would seem scarcely possible to doubt that *no power whatever* over the press was supposed to be delegated by the Constitution, as it originally stood, and that the amendment was intended as a *positive and absolute reservation of it.*"[14] With reference to the positive nature of the First Amendment's command against infringement of religious liberty, Madison later said that "there is not a shadow of right in the general government to intermeddle with religion,"[15] and that "this subject is, for the honor of America, perfectly free and unshackled. The *government has no jurisdiction over it.*"[16]

33 To my way of thinking, at least, the history and language of the Constitution and the Bill of Rights, which I have discussed with you, make it plain that one of the primary purposes of the Constitution with its amendments was to withdraw from the Government all power to act in certain areas—whatever the scope of those areas may be. If I am right in this then there is, at least in those areas, no justification whatever for "balancing" a particular right against some expressly granted power of Congress. If the Constitution withdraws from Gov-

[12] 1 Annals of Cong. 434 (1789).

[13] 1 Annals of Cong. 738 (1789).

[14] 6 Madison, Writings 391 (Hunt ed. 1906).

[15] 5 Madison, Writings 176 (Hunt ed. 1904).

[16] Id. at 132.

ernment all power over subject matter in an area, such as religion, speech, press, assembly, and petition, there is nothing over which authority may be exerted.

34 The Framers were well aware that the individual rights they sought to protect might be easily nullified if subordinated to the general powers granted to Congress. One of the reasons for adoption of the Bill of Rights was to prevent just that. Specifically the people feared that the "necessary and proper" clause could be used to project the generally granted Congressional powers into the protected areas of individual rights. One need only read the debates in the various states to find out that this is true. But if these debates leave any doubt, Mr. Madison's words to Congress should remove it. In speaking of the "necessary and proper" clause and its possible effect on freedom of religion he said, as reported in the *Annals of Congress:*

> Whether the words are necessary or not, he did not mean to say, but they had been required by some of the State Conventions, who seemed to entertain an opinion that under the clause of the Constitution, which gave power to Congress to make all laws *necessary and proper* to carry into execution the Constitution, and the laws made under it, enabled them to make laws of such a nature as might infringe the rights of conscience, and establish a national religion; to prevent these effects he presumed the amendment was intended, and he thought it as well expressed as the nature of the language would admit.[17]

35 It seems obvious to me that Congress, in exercising its general powers, is expressly forbidden to use means prohibited by the Bill of Rights. Whatever else the phrase "necessary and proper" may mean, it must be that Congress may only adopt such means to carry out its powers as are "proper," that is, not specifically prohibited.

36 It has also been argued that since freedom of speech, press, and religion in England were narrow freedoms at best, and since there were many English laws infringing those freedoms, our First Amendment should not be thought to bar similar infringements by Congress. Again one needs only to look to the debates in Congress over the First Amendment to find that the First Amendment cannot be treated as a mere codification of English law. Mr. Madison made a clear explanation to Congress that it was the purpose of the First Amendment to grant greater protection than England afforded its citizens. He said:

[17] 1 Annals of Cong. 730 (1789). (Emphasis added.)

In the declaration of rights which that country has established, the truth is, they have gone no farther than to raise a barrier against the power of the Crown; the power of the Legislature is left altogether indefinite. Although I know whenever the great rights, the trial by jury, freedom of the press, or liberty of conscience, come in question in that body, the invasion of them is resisted by able advocates, yet their Magna Charta does not contain any one provision for the security of those rights, respecting which the people of America are most alarmed. The freedom of the press and rights of conscience, those choicest privileges of the people, are unguarded in the British Constitution.

But although the case may be widely different, and it may not be thought necessary to provide limits for the legislative power in that country, yet a different opinion prevails in the United States.[18]

37 It was the desire to give the people of America greater protection against the powerful Federal Government than the English had had against their government that caused the Framers to put these freedoms of expression, again in the words of Madison, "beyond the reach of this Government."

38 When closely analyzed the idea that there can be no "absolute" constitutional guarantees in the Bill of Rights is frightening to contemplate even as to individual safeguards in the original Constitution. Take, for instance, the last clause in Article Six that "no religious Test shall ever be required" for a person to hold office in the United States. Suppose Congress should find that some religious sect was dangerous because of its foreign affiliations. Such was the belief on which English test oaths rested for a long time and some of the states had test oaths on that assumption at the time, and after, our Constitution was adopted in 1789. Could Congress, or the Supreme Court, or both, put this precious privilege to be free from test oaths on scales, find it outweighed by some other public interest, and therefore make United States officials and employees swear they did not and never had belonged to or associated with a particular religious group suspected of disloyalty? Can Congress, in the name of overbalancing necessity, suspend habeas corpus in peacetime? Are there circumstances under which Congress could, after nothing more than a legislative bill of attainder, take away a man's life, liberty, or property? Hostility of the Framers toward bills of attainder was so great that they took the unusual step of barring such legislative punishments by the States as

[18] 1 Annals of Cong. 436 (1789).

well as the Federal Government. They wanted to remove any possibility of such proceedings anywhere in this country. This is not strange in view of the fact that they were much closer than we are to the great Act of Attainder by the Irish Parliament, in 1688, which condemned between two and three thousand men, women, and children to exile or death without anything that even resembled a trial.[19]

39 Perhaps I can show you the consequences of the balancing approach to the Bill of Rights liberties by a practical demonstration of how it might work. The last clause of the Fifth Amendment is: "nor shall private property be taken for public use, without just compensation." On its face this command looks absolute, but if one believes that it should be weighed against the powers granted to Congress, there might be some circumstances in which this right would have to give way, just as there are some circumstances in which it is said the right of freedom of religion, speech, press, assembly and petition can be balanced away. Let us see how the balancing concept would apply to the just compensation provision of the Bill of Rights in the following wholly imaginary judicial opinion of Judge X:

> This case presents an important question of constitutional law. The United States is engaged in a stupendous national defense undertaking which requires the acquisition of much valuable land throughout the country. The plaintiff here owns 500 acres of land. The location of the land gives it a peculiarly strategic value for carrying out the defense program. Due to the great national emergency that exists, Congress concluded that the United States could not afford at this time to pay compensation for the lands which it needed to acquire. For this reason an act was passed authorizing seizure without compensation of all the lands required for the defense establishment.
>
> In reaching a judgment on this case, I cannot shut my eyes to the fact that the United States is in a desperate condition at this time. Nor can I, under established canons of constitutional construction, invalidate a Congressional enactment if there are any rational grounds upon which Congress could have passed it. I think there are such grounds here. Highly important among the powers granted Congress by the Constitution are the powers to declare war, maintain a navy, and raise and support armies. This, of course, means the power to conduct war successfully. To make sure that Congress is not unduly restricted in the exercise of these constitutional powers, the Constitution also gives Congress power to make all laws 'necessary and proper to carry

[19] See Joint Anti-Fascist Refugee Comm. v. McGrath, 341 U.S. 123, 146–49 (1951) (appendix to concurring opinion of Black, J.).

into execution the foregoing powers. . . .' This 'necessary and proper' clause applies to the powers to make war and support armies as it does to all the other granted powers.

Plaintiff contends, however, that the Fifth Amendment's provision about compensation is so absolute a command that Congress is wholly without authority to violate it, however great this nation's emergency and peril may be. I must reject this contention. We must never forget that it is a constitution we are expounding. And a constitution, unlike ordinary statutes, must endure for ages; it must be adapted to changing conditions and the needs of changing communities. Without such capacity for change, our Constitution would soon be outmoded and become a dead letter. Therefore its words must never be read as rigid absolutes. The Bill of Rights' commands, no more than any others, can stay the hands of Congress from doing that which the general welfare imperatively demands. When two great constitutional provisions like these conflict—as here the power to make war conflicts with the requirements for just compensation—it becomes the duty of courts to weigh the constitutional right of an individual to compensation against the power of Congress to wage a successful war.

While the question is not without doubt, I have no hesitation in finding the challenged Congressional act valid. Driven by the absolute necessity to protect the nation from foreign aggression, the national debt has risen to billions of dollars. The Government's credit is such that interest rates have soared. Under these circumstances, Congress was rationally entitled to find that if it paid for all the lands it needs it might bankrupt the nation and render it helpless in its hour of greatest need. Weighing as I must the loss the individual will suffer because he has to surrender his land to the nation without compensation against the great public interest in conducting war, I hold the act valid. A decree will be entered accordingly.

40 Of course, I would not decide this case this way nor do I think any other judge would so decide it today. My reason for refusing this approach would be that I think the Fifth Amendment's command is absolute and not to be overcome without constitutional amendment even in times of grave emergency. But I think this wholly fictitious opinion fairly illustrates the possibilities of the balancing approach, not only as to the just compensation clause, but as to other provisions of the Bill of Rights as well. The great danger of the judiciary balancing process is that in times of emergency and stress it gives Government the power to do what it thinks necessary to protect itself, regardless of the rights of individuals. If the need is great, the right of Government can always be said to outweigh the rights of the individual. If "balancing" is accepted as the test, it would be hard for any conscientious judge to hold otherwise in times of dire need. And laws adopted in times of dire need are often very hasty and oppressive laws, especially when, as often happens, they are carried over and accepted as normal. Furthermore, the balancing approach to basic individual liberties assumes to legislators and judges more power than either the Framers or I myself believe should be entrusted, without limitation, to any man or any group of men.

41 It seems to me that the "balancing" approach also disregards all of the unique features of our Constitution which I described earlier. In reality this approach returns us to the state of legislative supremacy which existed in England and which the Framers were so determined to change once and for all. On the one hand, it denies the judiciary its constitutional power to measure acts of Congress by the standards set down in the Bill of Rights. On the other hand, though apparently reducing judicial powers by saying that acts of Congress may be held unconstitutional only when they are found to have no rational legislative basis, this approach really gives the Court, along with Congress, a greater power, that of overriding the plain commands of the Bill of Rights on a finding of weighty public interest. In effect, it changes the direction of our form of government from a government of limited powers to a government in which Congress may do anything that Courts believe to be "reasonable."

42 Of course the decision to provide a constitutional safeguard for a particular right, such as the fair trial requirements of the Fifth and Sixth Amendments and the right of free speech protection of the First, involves a balancing of conflicting interests. Strict procedures may release guilty men; protecting speech and press may involve dangers to a particular government. I believe, however, that the Framers themselves did this balancing when they wrote the Constitution and the Bill of Rights. They appreciated the risks involved and they decided that certain rights should be guaranteed regardless of these risks. Courts have neither the right nor the power to review this original decision of the Framers and to attempt to make a different evaluation of the importance of the rights granted in the Constitution. Where conflicting values exist in the field of individual liberties protected by the Constitution, that document settles the conflict, and its policy should not be changed without constitutional amendments by the people in the manner provided by the people.

43 Misuse of government power, particularly in times of stress, has brought suffering to humanity in all ages about which we have authentic history. Some of the world's noblest and finest men have suffered ignominy and death for no crime—unless unorthodoxy is a crime. Even enlightened Athens had its victims such as Socrates. Because of the same kind of bigotry, Jesus, the great Dissenter, was put to death on a wooden cross. The flames of inquisitions all over the world have warned that men endowed with unlimited government power, even earnest men, consecrated to a cause, are dangerous.

44 For my own part, I believe that our Constitution, with its absolute guarantees of individual rights, is the best hope for the aspirations of freedom which men share everywhere. I cannot agree with those who think of the Bill of Rights as an 18th Century straitjacket, unsuited for this age. It is old but not all old things are bad. The evils it guards against are not only old, they are with us now, they exist today. Almost any morning you open your daily paper you can see where some person somewhere in the world is on trial or has just been convicted of supposed disloyalty to a new group controlling the government which has set out to purge its suspected enemies and all those who had dared to be against its successful march to power. Nearly always you see that these political heretics are being tried by military tribunals or some other summary and sure method for disposition of the accused. Now and then we even see the convicted victims as they march to their execution.

45 Experience all over the world has demonstrated, I fear, that the distance between stable, orderly government and one that has been taken over by force is not so great as we have assumed. Our own free system to live and progress has to have intelligent citizens, citizens who cannot only think and speak and write to influence people, but citizens who are free to do that without fear of governmental censorship or reprisal.

46 The provisions of the Bill of Rights that safeguard fair legal procedures came about largely to protect the weak and the oppressed from punishment by the strong and the powerful who wanted to stifle the voices of discontent raised in protest against oppression and injustice in public affairs. Nothing that I have read in the Congressional debates on the Bill of Rights indicates that there was any belief that the First Amendment contained any qualifications. The only arguments that tended to look in this direction at all were those that said "that all paper barriers against the power of the community are too weak to be worthy of attention."[20] Suggestions were also made in and out of

[20] 1 Annals of Cong. 437 (1789).

Congress that a Bill of Rights would be a futile gesture since there would be no way to enforce the safeguards for freedom it provided. Mr. Madison answered this argument in these words:

> If they [the Bill of Rights amendments] are incorporated into the Constitution, independent tribunals of justice will consider themselves in a peculiar manner the guardians of those rights; they will be an impenetrable bulwark against any assumption of power in the Legislative or Executive; they will be naturally led to resist every encroachment upon rights expressly stipulated for in the Constitution by the declaration of rights.[21]

I fail to see how courts can escape this sacred trust.

47 Since the earliest days philosophers have dreamed of a country where the mind and spirit of man would be free; where there would be no limits to inquiry; where men would be free to explore the unknown and to challenge the most deeply rooted beliefs and principles. Our First Amendment was a bold effort to adopt this principle—to establish a country with no legal restrictions of any kind upon the subjects people could investigate, discuss and deny. The Framers knew, better perhaps than we do today, the risks they were taking. They knew that free speech might be the friend of change and revolution. But they also knew that it is always the deadliest enemy of tyranny. With this knowledge they still believed that the ultimate happiness and security of a nation lies in its ability to explore, to change, to grow and ceaselessly to adapt itself to new knowledge born of inquiry free from any kind of governmental control over the mind and spirit of man. Loyalty comes from love of good government, not fear of a bad one.

48 The First Amendment is truly the heart of the Bill of Rights. The Framers balanced its freedoms of religion, speech, press, assembly and petition against the needs of a powerful central government, and decided that in those freedoms lies this nation's only true security. They were not afraid for men to be free. We should not be. We should be as confident as Jefferson was when he said in his First Inaugural Address:

> If there be any among us who would wish to dissolve this Union or to change its republican form, let them stand undisturbed as monuments of the safety with which error of opinion may be tolerated where reason is left free to combat it.[22]

[21] 1 Annals of Cong. 439 (1789).

[22] 8 Jefferson, Writings 2–3 (Washington ed. 1859).

Chapter Six

SPEECHES THAT AFFIRM PROPOSITIONS OF VALUE

Regardless of the simplicity or complexity of a society, its future is largely determined by the personal and social values its members hold. Landis has written:

> In order to understand the guiding principles of a social order and to see the underlying factors which tend to shape social behavior one needs to search into the nature of the cultural values predominating in an age. The acts of every individual as well as those of the masses fall under the shadow of these values. In fact in their broadest sense they constitute the most general yet the most pervasive elements of social control in that they permeate all groups and all classes. . . . They are the mass motivating ideas of a society having their origin in historical experience.[1]

Values not only shape goals and means of collective human action; they also guide personal thought and behavior. Thus concern for personal and social values is of central importance in public dialogue. No matter what the speaker's social purpose for speaking, he must realize that his audience's behavior depends on its members' values. Focusing on values, then, is often a means of creating concern for a problem or for gaining acceptance of a policy. But there are times when a speaker's sole purpose is to affirm to the satisfaction of his audience that a proposition of value has merit.

Often on these occasions, the speaker needs only to intensify or reinforce those values his audience already holds. In 431 B.C., Pericles, in an oration immortalized by the historian Thucydides, gave compelling expression to the values of Athenian democracy. This June, thou-

[1] Paul H. Landis, *Social Control*, rev. ed. (Philadelphia: J. B. Lippincott, 1956), p. 93.

sands of commencement speakers, in speeches that will not be immortalized, will seek to revitalize the tenets of the American democratic ethic. At other times, speakers address audiences whose special values are yet to be defined. In 1899, Theodore Roosevelt, addressing the Hamilton Club of Chicago, extolled the doctrine of the strenuous life. Next September, countless college presidents speaking to convocations of incoming freshmen will attempt to establish the social role of the American scholar. On still other occasions, speakers address audiences whose values run counter to their own. In the 1932 Presidential campaign, Franklin D. Roosevelt, speaking to the conservative businessmen of the Commonwealth Club of San Francisco, offered a striking reappraisal of the traditional business ethic in light of the need for greater governmental supervision. This year, prominent evangelists will be asking audiences to alter their values concerning their spiritual lives.

Whether the speaker seeks to intensify, formulate, or change values, his behavior is governed by the distinctive constraints imposed by the proposition that affirms the justice or injustice, rightness or wrongness, goodness or badness, sagacity or foolishness of a person, institution, action, or way of life.

CONSTRAINTS IMPOSED BY SPEECH PURPOSE

Whenever a speaker seeks to affirm (or reaffirm) a proposition of value, he asks the members of his audience to accept as their own the evaluative judgments he has formulated. In so doing, he must, either explicitly or implicitly, *identify criteria of value* and *relate these criteria to the subject at hand* for the purpose of enlisting popular acceptance. At those times when he wishes to gain acceptance of a set of values, he must link them with the higher values held by his audience. For example, a speaker may espouse certain characteristics of leadership as desirable because they promote the "sane" society. At other moments, he may use value criteria for the purpose of making a critical judgment. For example, he may hold that the life of Eleanor Roosevelt epitomizes the best of America's womanhood or that the style of contemporary political speaking is inferior to that of the nineteenth century. Whatever the subject of his message or the criteria of his evaluation, the speaker's task is to deepen existing values, to formulate new values where none now exists, and to change or reorient those values contrary to his own.

CONSTRAINTS IMPOSED BY A PARTICULAR AUDIENCE

Often the speaker who seeks to affirm propositions of value may be speaking to a highly sympathetic audience. A Negro minister addresses a civil-rights rally in Washington, D.C., on the value of commitment to the cause of freedom; a famous general addresses West Point cadets on the value of leadership, courage, and patriotism; a noted evangelist addresses the faithful and the near-faithful in the Los Angeles Coliseum on the value of Christian commitment. But at other times and in less dramatic places, speakers seeking to affirm propositions of value may find that their subjects hold little natural *interest* for their audience. At these times, the speaker must overcome apathy by selecting those rhetorical means that give life and vitality to his message.

A second constraint applicable to this speech form concerns the *meaning* a given proposition of value holds for a specific audience. Before the members of an audience can approve or disapprove of the goodness, morality, excellence, or beauty of a person, institution, action, idea, or way of life, they must first understand the fundamental bases on which such judgment rests. The speaker must choose those speech devices that permit the widest popular understanding: definition, example, analogy, description, illustration, or metaphor.

A third constraint an audience imposes on the speaker in his choice of devices is its perception of his *credibility as a source* of evaluative propositions. General Douglas MacArthur, returning to West Point to receive the Sylvanus Thayer Award for service to his nation, was a highly credible source to his audience of cadets as he sought to reinforce their feelings for "duty, honor, country." That he recognized the importance of his ethos is demonstrated by his opening remarks:

> As I was leaving the hotel this morning, a door-man asked me, "Where are you bound for, General?" And when I replied, "West Point," he remarked, "Beautiful place. Have you ever been there before?"

In a less ideal moment Henry Ward Beecher, addressing a crowd of pro-South Englishmen at Liverpool in 1863, sought to counter the hostility his unsolicited journey had aroused so that his cause might receive a fair hearing. In adapting to this constraint, Beecher said:

> . . . if you do permit me to speak here tonight you will hear very plain talking. [Applause and hisses.] You will not find me to be a man that dared to speak about Great Britain three thousand miles off, and then is afraid to speak to Great Britain when he stands on her shores. [Immense applause and hisses.] And if I do not mistake the tone and temper of Englishmen, they had rather have a man who opposes them in a manly way [applause from all parts of the hall] than a sneak that agrees with them in an unmanly way. [Applause and "Bravo!"] Now, if I can carry you with me by sound convictions, I shall be immensely glad [applause]; but if I cannot carry you with me by facts and sound arguments, I do not wish you to go with me at all; and all that I ask is simply *fair play.* [Applause, and a voice: "You shall have it too."]

Though these two examples illustrate extreme reactions to the speaker as an authority, they should suggest the importance of his need to adapt to this particular constraint.

The final order of constraints imposed on the speaker who seeks to affirm propositions of value refers to the ideals and values that determine an audience's standards of judgment. The *validity* an audience assigns to a speaker's proposition of value will depend on the degree that the proposition appears to coincide or conflict with his audience's ideals and values. Since values tend to be deep-rooted, saturated with emotion, and wrapped in tradition, the speaker who would succeed in changing values hostile to his own must carefully avoid antagonizing audience members by scoffing at their beliefs or by coming into *direct* conflict with them. To gain acceptance, the speaker normally must mesh the value judgment he is presenting with those his audience holds. That a speaker need not fail when his values run counter to his audience's may be demonstrated by example. When, in 1932, Franklin D. Roosevelt spoke to San Francisco's Commonwealth Club, a group of businessmen with conservative economic values, he began his speech with a careful historical review of the values that produced industrial America; he pointed out that these values had served our nation well but were no longer consistent with our best national interests. In 1886, Southerner Henry W. Grady, in an address to members of the New England Society, sought to erase their long-standing hostility to the South by eulogizing the spirit of Lincoln and by urging commitment to national values, rather than to regional loyalties. Other speakers have demonstrated that socially undesirable consequences will result from adherence to old values or that favorable consequences will emerge from a fuller commitment to new ones.

CONCLUSION

Since human values play such an important role in decisions related to individual and social well-being, the constraints imposed upon a speaker seeking to affirm propositions of value are especially important. Whenever a speaker affirms the justice or injustice, rightness or wrongness, goodness or badness, sagacity or foolishness of a person, institution, action, or way of life, he must *identify criteria of value* and *relate them to the subject at hand.* Since an audience's acceptance of values presupposes a willingness to listen and an ability to understand, the speaker must also give *interest* and *meaning* to his message. The final two constraints that an audience imposes on a speaker is its willingness to assign *credibility to the speaker* and *validity to his message.* While operating within these constraints, the speaker seeks to intensify audience values when they are consistent with his own, to formulate values when his audience is uncommitted, and to alter audience values when they are hostile to his own.

In the following speeches, the student may examine the choices speakers have made in affirming propositions of value. The first speech by General Douglas MacArthur, "Farewell to the Cadets," seeks to reinforce cadet acceptance of the value symbols "duty, honor, country" as a meaningful code for the West Point soldier. Martin Luther King's "I Have a Dream" restates and intensifies values concerning the Negro movement. John F. Kennedy's Inaugural Address advances the basic operational values of his incoming administration and then outlines the need for adherence to international values consistent with world peace. Grayson Kirk, President of Columbia University, sets forth the "Responsibilities of the Educated Man." Bishop Bryan McEntegart presents "A Totality of Outlook" concerning the Second Vatican Council. The Bishop identifies those questions he thinks modern man must ask himself in order to achieve the proper spiritual outlook. Ralph T. Eubanks' "Leadership and the 'Sane Society'" advocates value standards for sound leadership. Lastly, Gerald J. Lynch seeks to alter audience values by contending that "The Pursuit of Security" is often undesirable and that man instead should welcome opportunity and risk.

For Further Reading

Baier, Kurt, *The Moral Point of View: A Rational Basis of Ethics,* Cornell University Press, 1958. Chapter Two presents a discussion of the nature and process of value judgments.

Buck, Philo M., Jr., *Literary Criticism: A Study of Values in Literature,* Harper & Row, 1930. Chapters 1, 6–8, and 16 analyze the process of literary criticism as one of judgment based on standards of value.

Chase, Stuart, *American Credos,* Harper & Row, 1962. Chapter 12 briefly summarizes the basic American beliefs, attitudes, and values reflected in contemporary public opinion.

Graves, Harold F., and Bernard S. Oldsey, *From Fact to Judgment,* The Macmillan Co., 2nd ed., 1963. Chapter 5 discusses questions of value. It takes up critical evaluation, criteria for evaluation, and means of support.

Hourani, George F., *Ethical Value,* Allen and Unwin, 1956. Chapters 1 and 4–11 probe in detail the concepts of value, such as "good" and "right," as they relate to human conduct and character.

Kluckhohn, Clyde, "Have There Been Discernible Shifts in American Values in the Past Generation?" in *The American Style,* ed. Elting Morison, Harper & Row, 1958, pp. 145–217. Surveys and discusses social-science research bearing on shifts in the American system of values.

Minnick, Wayne C., *The Art of Persuasion,* Houghton Mifflin Co., 1957, pp. 207–214. Outlines and categorizes basic American values.

Walter, Otis, and Robert L. Scott, *Thinking and Speaking,* The Macmillan Co., 1962, pp. 158–162, 173–176. Defines and discusses thinking and speaking about values.

Williams, Robin M., *American Society: A Sociological Interpretation,* Knopf, 2nd Rev. Ed., 1961, pp. 367–470. Surveys the components of the contemporary American value system.

Yeager, Willard H., *Effective Speaking for Every Occasion,* 2nd ed., Prentice-Hall, 1951. Chapters 4, 6, 8, and 9 discuss the various types of speeches of praise and censure, all of which involve value judgments.

FAREWELL TO THE CADETS

Douglas MacArthur

General Douglas MacArthur became a national hero during World War II as the Supreme Allied commander in the Pacific. Perhaps his greatest moment was when he successfully returned to Manila after the Japanese early in the war had driven American forces from the Philippines. Upon leaving Manila, MacArthur had vowed, "I shall return." At the close of the war, he commanded the Allied occupational forces in Japan and his skillful supervision of the restoration of the Japanese nation was widely acclaimed, even by the Japanese. When President Truman ordered American forces into Korea in 1950 to stop the invasion of the South by the North, General MacArthur was again placed in command of the expedition. However, he became an outspoken critic of the administration's Korean policy and, as a consequence, President Truman relieved General MacArthur of his command in 1951. MacArthur returned to America to a hero's welcome. He accepted an invitation to address a joint session of Congress, and his concluding remarks concerning the ballad of the "Old Soldier" captured the imagination of the American people. He died April 5, 1964.

Two years before his death, General MacArthur, himself an honor graduate of the institution, went to the United States Military Academy at West Point to receive the Sylvanus Thayer award for service to his nation. The Old Soldier, then 82, accepted the award and, despite failing health, made a moving and inspirational farewell speech to the cadets of the academy, an institution he had served earlier as superintendent. Speaking without text or notes, he sought to reinforce the cadets' feelings for the values of "duty, honor, country," the motto inscribed on the academy coat of arms. Although he was originally gifted with an exceptionally rich and resonant voice, it was now hoarse and often faint. He spoke slowly and deliberately, gaining intensity when he reached phrases such as "faint bugles blowing reveille" and "the strange, mournful mutter of the battlefield."

As you analyze this speech, we suggest you focus upon two important rhetorical factors. The first is credibility of source. MacArthur, a legendary war hero, doubtless enjoyed high ethos with the cadets. Moreover, the text of the speech reveals that MacArthur was fully aware of ethos factors. Analyze and evaluate the speaker's use of his credibility as a source. Second, MacArthur was a conscious speech stylist, a fact that is readily apparent in this address; imagery, metaphor, and elegance of language are pronounced. Evaluate MacArthur's style critically. What special stylistic principles can you develop from this speech?

Considering the nature of the audience, we can easily classify this speech as one designed to reinforce values. The cadets probably would not willingly accept the rigors of West Point and stay at the academy, if they were not already committed to "duty, honor, country." However, in peacetime, some people tend to be critical of the military. Since MacArthur provides a rationale that reinforces the cadets' motto against attack, he is not only intensifying values but also defending them. To what higher values does MacArthur relate "duty, honor, country" in order to demonstrate the "worth" of the cadets' motto?

The text of this speech was taken from a recording of the address and is reprinted by permission of the MacArthur Memorial Foundation.

1 As I was leaving the hotel this morning, a doorman asked me, "Where are you bound for, General?" And when I replied, "West Point," he remarked, "Beautiful place. Have you ever been there before?"

2 No human being could fail to be deeply moved by such a tribute as this, coming from a profession I have served so long and a people I have loved so well.

3 It fills me with an emotion I cannot express. But this award is not intended primarily to honor a personality, but to symbolize a great moral code—the code of conduct and chivalry of those who guard this beloved land of culture and ancient descent. That is the animation of this medallion. For all eyes and for all time it is an expression of the ethics of the American soldier. That I should be integrated in this way with so noble an ideal arouses a sense of pride and yet of humility, which will be with me always.

4 Duty, honor, country: those three hallowed words reverently dictate what you want to be, what you can be, what you will be. They are your rallying point to build courage when courage seems to fail, to regain faith when there seems to be little cause for faith, to create hope when hope becomes forlorn.

5 Unhappily, I possess neither that eloquence of diction, that poetry of imagination, nor that brilliance of metaphor to tell you all that they mean.

6 The unbelievers will say they are but words, but a slogan, but a flamboyant phrase. Every pedant, every demagogue, every cynic, every hypocrite, every troublemaker, and, I am sorry to say, some others of an entirely different character, will try to downgrade them even to the extent of mockery and ridicule.

7 But these are some of the things they do. They build your basic character. They mold you for your future roles as the custodians of the nation's defense. They make you strong enough to know when you are weak and brave enough to face yourself when you are afraid.

8 They teach you to be proud and unbending in honest failure, but humble and gentle in success; not to substitute words for action; not to seek the path of comfort, but to face the stress and spur of

difficulty and challenge; to learn to stand up in the storm, but to have compassion on those who fall; to master yourself before you seek to master others; to have a heart that is clean, a goal that is high; to learn to laugh, yet never forget how to weep; to reach into the future, yet never neglect the past; to be serious, yet never take yourself too seriously; to be modest so that you will remember the simplicity of true greatness, the open mind of true wisdom, the meekness of true strength.

9 They give you a temper of the will, a quality of the imagination, a vigor of the emotions, a freshness of the deep springs of life, a temperamental predominance of courage over timidity, of an appetite for adventure over love of ease.

10 They create in your heart the sense of wonder, the unfailing hope of what next, and the joy and inspiration of life. They teach you in this way to be an officer and a gentleman.

11 And what sort of soldiers are those you are to lead? Are they reliable? Are they brave? Are they capable of victory? Their story is known to all of you. It is the story of the American man-at-arms. My estimate of him was formed on the battlefields many, many years ago, and has never changed. I regarded him then, as I regard him now, as one of the world's noblest figures—not only as one of the finest military characters but also as one of the most stainless.

12 His name and fame are the birthright of every American citizen. In his youth and strength, his love and loyalty, he gave all that mortality can give. He needs no eulogy from me or from any other man. He has written his own history and written it in red on his enemy's breast.

13 But when I think of his patience under adversity, of his courage under fire, and his modesty in victory, I am filled with an emotion of admiration I cannot put into words. He belongs to history as furnishing one of the greatest examples of successful patriotism. He belongs to posterity as the instructor of future generations in the principles of liberty and freedom. He belongs to the present—to us—by his virtues and by his achievements.

14 In 20 campaigns, on a 100 battlefields, around a 1,000 campfires, I have witnessed that enduring fortitude, that patriotic self-abnegation, and that invincible determination which has carved his statue in the hearts of his people.

15 From one end of the world to the other, he has drained deep the chalice of courage. As I listened to those songs, in memory's eye I could see those staggering columns of the First World War, bending under soggy packs on many a weary march, from dripping dusk to drizzling dawn, slogging ankle-deep through the mire of shell-pocked roads; to form grimly for the attack, blue-lipped, covered with sludge and mud, chilled by the wind and rain, driving home to their objective, and, for many, to the judgment seat of God.

16 I do not know the dignity of their birth, but I do know the glory of their death. They died unquestioning, uncomplaining, with faith in their hearts, and on their lips the hope that we would go on to victory.

17 Always for them: duty, honor, country. Always their blood, and sweat, and tears, as we saw the way and the light and the truth. And 20 years after, on the other side of the globe, again the filth of dirty foxholes, the stench of ghostly trenches, the slime of dripping dugouts, those boiling suns of relentless heat, those torrential rains of devastating storms, the loneliness and utter desolation of jungle trails, the bitterness of long separation from those they loved and cherished, the deadly pestilence of tropical disease, the horror of stricken areas of war.

18 Their resolute and determined defense, their swift and sure attack, their indomitable purpose, their complete and decisive victory—always victory, always through the bloody haze of their last reverberating shot, the vision of gaunt, ghastly men, reverently following your password of duty, honor, country.

19 The code which those words perpetuate embraces the highest moral law and will stand the test of any ethics or philosophies ever promulgated for the uplift of mankind. Its requirements are for the things that are right and its restraints are from the things that are wrong. The soldier, above all other men, is required to practice the greatest act of religious training—sacrifice. In battle and in the face of danger and death he discloses those divine attributes which his Maker gave when he created man in his own image. No physical courage and no brute instinct can take the place of the divine help, which alone can sustain him. However horrible the incidents of war may be, the soldier who is called upon to offer and to give his life for his country is the noblest development of mankind.

20 You now face a new world, a world of change. The thrust into outer space of the satellite spheres and missiles marks a beginning of another epoch in the long story of mankind. In the five-or-more billions of years the scientists tell us it has taken to form the earth, in the three-or-more billion years of development of the human race, there has never been a more abrupt or staggering evolution.

21 We deal now, not with things of this world alone, but with the illimitable distances and as yet unfathomed mysteries of the universe. We are reaching out for a new and boundless frontier. We speak in strange terms of harnessing the cosmic energy; of making winds and tides work for us; of creating synthetic materials to supplement or even replace our old standard basics; to purify sea water for our drink; of mining ocean floors for new fields of wealth and food; of disease preventatives to expand life into the hundreds of years; of controlling the weather for a more equitable distribution of heat and cold, of rain and shine; of space ships to the moon; of the primary target in war no longer limited to the armed forces of an enemy, but instead to include his civil populations; of ultimate conflicts between a united human race and the sinister forces of some other planetary galaxy; of such dreams and fantasies as to make life the most exciting of all times.

22 And through all this welter of change and development your mission remains fixed, determined, inviolable. It is to win our wars. Everything else in your professional career is but corollary to this vital dedication. All other public purposes, all other public projects, all other public needs, great or small, will find others for their accomplishments; but you are the ones who are trained to fight.

23 Yours is the profession of arms, the will to win, the sure knowledge that in war there is no substitute for victory, that if you lose the nation will be destroyed, that the very obsession of your public service must be duty, honor, country.

24 Others will debate the controversial issues, national and international, which divide men's minds. But serene, calm, aloof, you stand as the nation's war guardians, as its lifeguards from the raging tides of international conflict, as its gladiators in the arena of battle. For a century-and-a-half you have defended, guarded, and protected its hallowed traditions of liberty and freedom, of right and justice.

25 Let civilian voices argue the merits or demerits of our processes of government: whether our strength is being sapped by deficit financing indulged in too long; by federal paternalism grown too mighty; by power groups grown too arrogant; by politics grown too corrupt; by crime grown too rampant; by morals grown too low; by taxes grown too high; by extremists grown too violent; whether our personal liberties are as firm and complete as they should be.

26 These great national problems are not for your professional participation or military solution. Your guidepost stands out like a tenfold beacon in the night: duty, honor, country.

27 You are the lever which binds together the entire fabric of our national system of defense. From your ranks come the great captains who hold the nation's destiny in their hands the moment the war tocsin sounds.

28 The long, gray line has never failed us. Were you to do so, a million ghosts in olive drab, in brown khaki, in blue and gray, would rise from their white crosses, thundering those magic words: duty, honor, country.

29 This does not mean that you are warmongers. On the contrary, the soldier above all other people prays for peace, for he must suffer and bear the deepest wounds and scars of war. But always in our ears ring the ominous words of Plato, that wisest of all philosophers: "Only the dead have seen the end of war."

30 The shadows are lengthening for me. The twilight is here. My days of old have vanished—tone and tints. They have gone glimmering through the dreams of things that were. Their memory is one of wondrous beauty watered by tears and coaxed and caressed by the smiles of yesterday. I listen vainly, but with thirsty ear, for the witching melody of faint bugles blowing reveille, of far drums beating the long roll.

31 In my dreams I hear again the crash of guns, the rattle of musketry, the strange, mournful mutter of the battlefield. But in the evening of my memory always I come back to West Point. Always there echoes and re-echoes: duty, honor, country.

32 Today marks my final roll call with you. But I want you to know that when I cross the river, my last conscious thoughts will be of the Corps, and the Corps, and the Corps.

33 I bid you farewell.

I HAVE A DREAM

Martin Luther King, Jr.

Late in August 1963, more than 200,000 Negroes and whites held a peaceful demonstration in the nation's capital to focus attention on Negro demands for equality in jobs and civil rights. The marchers assembled at the Washington Monument on the morning of the 28th and filed in two columns down to the Lincoln Memorial. A little later, ten civil-rights leaders met with President Kennedy at the White House and subsequently returned to the Lincoln Memorial, where each of them addressed the assembled throng. As measured by crowd reaction, this speech by Martin Luther King was the high point of the day.

The occasion of this speech was wrought with passion. An important but difficult question to answer is "What constitutes message validity in such a highly emotional audience situation?" How would the standards differ from those of other audiences? How important do you think Dr. King's ethos was to the acceptance of his message by the Washington audience?

Dr. King, wishing to intensify the values of the Negro movement, spoke in an elevated inspirational style. Does his style seem genuine and inspired by the subject or does it seem artificial? Especially evaluate his use of metaphor. Can you identify metaphors that effectively stem from the subject matter? Are there any that seem superimposed?

Repetition, refrain, and parallelism produce a strong rhythmical effect. Do these devices, as used by Dr. King, serve purposes other than rhythmical? How effectively does Dr. King use these factors?

This speech is reprinted by permission from Rhetoric of Racial Revolt, *ed. Roy L. Hill (Denver, Colo.: Golden Bell Press, 1964), pp. 371–375.*

1 Five score years ago, a great American, in whose symbolic shadow we stand today, signed the Emancipation Proclamation. This momentous decree came as a great beacon of light of hope to millions of Negro slaves who had been seared in the flames of withering injustice. It came as a joyous daybreak to end the long night of their captivity.

2 But one hundred years later, the Negro still is not free. One hundred years later, the life of the Negro is still sadly crippled by the manacles of segregation and the chains of discrimination.

3 One hundred years later, the Negro lives on a lonely island of poverty in the midst of a vast ocean of material prosperity. One hundred years later, the Negro is still languished in the corners of American society and finds himself an exile in his own land. So we have come here today to dramatize a shameful condition.

4 In a sense we have come to our nation's capital to cash a check. When the architects of our republic wrote the magnificent words of the Constitution and the Declaration of Independence, they were signing a promissory note to which every American was to fall heir.

This note was a promise that all men, yes, black men as well as white men, would be granted the unalienable rights of life, liberty, and the pursuit of happiness.

5 It is obvious today that America has defaulted on this promissory note insofar as her citizens of color are concerned. Instead of honoring this sacred obligation, America has given the Negro people a bad check; which has come back marked "insufficient funds."

6 But we refuse to believe that the bank of justice is bankrupt. We refuse to believe that there are insufficient funds in the great vaults of opportunity of this nation. So we have come to cash this check——a check that will give us upon demand the riches of freedom and the security of justice.

7 We have also come to this hallowed spot to remind America of the fierce urgency of now. This is no time to engage in the luxury of cooling off or to take the tranquilizing drug of gradualism. Now is the time to make real the promises of democracy. Now is the time to rise from the dark and desolate valley of segregation to the sunlit path of racial justice. Now is the time to lift our nation from the quick sands of racial injustice to the solid rock of brotherhood. Now is the time to make justice a reality for all of God's children.

8 It would be fatal for the nation to overlook the urgency of the movement and to underestimate the determination of the Negro. This sweltering summer of the Negro's legitimate discontent will not pass until there is an invigorating autumn of freedom and equality. 1963 is not an end but a beginning. Those who hope that the Negro needed to blow off steam and will now be content will have a rude awakening if the nation returns to business as usual.

9 There will be neither rest nor tranquility in America until the Negro is granted his citizenship rights. The whirlwinds of revolt will continue to shake the foundations of our nation until the bright day of justice emerges.

10 But there is something that I must say to my people who stand on the warm threshold which leads into the palace of justice. In the process of gaining our rightful place we must not be guilty of wrongful deeds.

11 Let us not seek to satisfy our thirst for freedom by drinking from the cup of bitterness and hatred. We must forever conduct our struggle on the high plane of dignity and discipline. We must not allow our creative protest to degenerate into physical violence. Again and again we must rise to the majestic heights of meeting physical force with soul force.

12 The marvelous new militancy which has engulfed the Negro community must not lead us to a distrust of all white people, for many of our white brothers, as evidenced by their presence here today, have come to realize that their destiny is tied up with our destiny and they have come to realize that their freedom is inextricably bound to our freedom. This offense we share mounted to storm the battlements of injustice must be carried forth by a bi-racial army. We cannot walk alone.

13 And as we walk, we must make the pledge that we shall always march ahead. We cannot turn back. There are those who are asking the devotees of civil rights, "When will you be satisfied?" We can never be satisfied as long as the Negro is the victim of the unspeakable horrors of police brutality.

14 We can never be satisfied as long as our bodies, heavy with the fatigue of travel, cannot gain lodging in the motels of the highways and the hotels of the cities. We cannot be satisfied as long as the Negro's basic mobility is from a smaller ghetto to a larger one.

15 We can never be satisfied as long as our children are stripped of their selfhood and robbed of their dignity by signs stating "for whites only." We cannot be satisfied as long as a Negro in Mississippi cannot vote and a Negro in New York believes he has nothing for which to vote. No, we are not satisfied, and we will not be satisfied until justice rolls down like waters and righteousness like a mighty stream.

16 I am not unmindful that some of you have come here out of excessive trials and tribulation. Some of you have come fresh from narrow jail cells. Some of you have come from areas where your quest for freedom left you battered by the storms of persecution and staggered by the winds of police brutality. You have been the veterans of creative suffering. Continue to work with the faith that unearned suffering is redemptive.

17 Go back to Mississippi; go back to Alabama; go back to South Carolina; go back to Georgia; go back to Louisiana; go back to the slums and ghettos of the Northern cities, knowing that somehow this situation can, and will be changed. Let us not wallow in the valley of despair.

18 So I say to you, my friends, that even though we must face the difficulties of today and tomorrow, I still have a dream. It is a dream deeply rooted in the American dream that one day this nation will rise up and live out the true meaning of its creed—we hold these truths to be self evident, that all men are created equal.

19 I have a dream that one day on the red hills of Georgia, sons of former slaves and sons of former slave-owners will be able to sit down together at the table of brotherhood.

20 I have a dream that one day, even the state of Mississippi, a state sweltering with the heat of injustice, sweltering with the heat of oppression, will be transformed into an oasis of freedom and justice.

21 I have a dream my four little children will one day live in a nation where they will not be judged by the color of their skin but by content of their character. I have a dream today!

22 I have a dream that one day, down in Alabama, with its vicious racists, with its governor having his lips dripping with the words of interposition and nullification, that one day, right there in Alabama, little black boys and black girls will be able to join hands with little white boys and white girls as sisters and brothers. I have a dream today!

23 I have a dream that one day every valley shall be exalted, every hill and mountain shall be made low, the rough places shall be made plain, and the crooked places shall be made straight and the glory of the Lord will be revealed and all flesh shall see it together.

24 This is our hope. This is the faith that I go back to the South with.

25 With this faith we will be able to hew out of the mountain of despair a stone of hope. With this faith we will be able to transform the jangling discords of our nation into a beautiful symphony of brotherhood.

26 With this faith we will be able to work together, to pray together, to struggle together, to go to jail together, to stand up for freedom together, knowing that we will be free one day. This will be the day when all of God's children will be able to sing with new meaning—"my country 'tis of thee; sweet land of liberty; of thee I sing; land where my fathers died, land of the pilgrim's pride; from every mountain side, let freedom ring"—and if America is to be a great nation, this must become true.

27 So let freedom ring from the prodigious hilltops of New Hampshire.

28 Let freedom ring from the mighty mountains of New York.

29 Let freedom ring from the heightening Alleghenies of Pennsylvania.

30 Let freedom ring from the snow-capped Rockies of Colorado.

31 Let freedom ring from the curvaceous slopes of California.

32 But not only that.

33 Let freedom ring from Stone Mountain of Georgia.

34 Let freedom ring from Lookout Mountain of Tennessee.

35 Let freedom ring from every hill and molehill of Mississippi, from every mountainside, let freedom ring.

36 And when we allow freedom to ring, when we let it ring from every village and hamlet, from every state and city, we will be able to speed up that day when all of God's children—black men and white men, Jews and Gentiles, Catholics and Protestants—will be able to join hands and to sing in the words of the old Negro spiritual. "Free at last, free at last; thank God Almighty, we are free at last."

INAUGURAL ADDRESS

John F. Kennedy

On January 20, 1961, the late John Fitzgerald Kennedy delivered his Presidential inaugural address to a large outdoor audience before the nation's Capitol on a cold, clear day. In contrast to his rapid-fire delivery on the campaign trail, Kennedy spoke slowly, giving careful emphasis to special phrases and the cadence of his prose. The newly installed President first made a declaration of values people could expect from his incoming administration; then he pleaded for citizens of the world to begin anew their search for those values that lead to human brotherhood and lasting peace. Consequently, Kennedy was actually addressing several audiences: the inaugural crowd, Americans everywhere, world heads-of-state, and the people of the world.

It was quickly apparent that this speech contained memorable quotations. The passage most frequently quoted is "Ask not what your country can do for you—ask what you can do for your country." Examine the context in which this sentence was used. Does it appear to be a natural outgrowth from the flow of ideas in the speech? What makes this sentence memorable? What other lines of this speech are especially memorable?

Kennedy's address demonstrates that style is far more than a heavy use of figurative language. Perhaps the most important stylistic quality of his speech is his sentence construction. As you read the address, try to identify unusually striking sentences. What role does parallelism play in this speech? Rhythm? Energy and movement? Are there any balanced sentences?

The speeches by MacArthur, King, and Kennedy are all noted for stylistic embellishment. It is interesting to compare and contrast their styles. In which speech does style best implement the values expressed? In which speech does style seem the most genuine or natural? Is artifice too apparent in any of these speeches?

Speeches that intensify values seek social unity. Why is style especially important in this pursuit?

The text of this speech was taken from a recording of the address.

1 *Vice President Johnson, Mr. Speaker, Mr. Chief Justice, President Eisenhower, Vice President Nixon, President Truman, Reverend Clergy, Fellow Citizens:* We observe today not a victory of party but a celebration of freedom—symbolizing an end as well as a beginning—signifying renewal as well as change. For I have sworn before you and Almighty God the same solemn oath our forebears prescribed nearly a century and three quarters ago.

2 The world is very different now. For man holds in his mortal hands the power to abolish all forms of human poverty and all forms of human life. And yet the same revolutionary beliefs for which our forebears fought are still at issue around the globe—the belief that the rights of man come not from the generosity of the state but from the hand of God.

3 We dare not forget today that we are the heirs of that first revolution. Let the word go forth from this time and place, to friend and foe alike, that the torch has been passed to a new generation of Americans—born in this century, tempered by war, disciplined by a hard and bitter peace, proud of our ancient heritage—and unwilling to witness or permit the slow undoing of those human rights to which this nation has always been committed, and to which we are committed today, at home and around the world.

4 Let every nation know, whether it wishes us well or ill, that we shall pay any price, bear any burden, meet any hardship, support any friend or oppose any foe to assure the survival and the success of liberty.

5 This much we pledge—and more.

6 To those old allies whose cultural and spiritual origins we share, we pledge the loyalty of faithful friends. United, there is little we

cannot do in a host of cooperative ventures. Divided, there is little we can do—for we dare not meet a powerful challenge at odds and split asunder.

7 To those new states whom we welcome to the ranks of the free, we pledge our word that one form of colonial control shall not have passed away merely to be replaced by a far more iron tyranny. We shall not always expect to find them supporting our view.

8 But we shall always hope to find them strongly supporting their own freedom—and to remember that, in the past, those who foolishly sought power by riding the back of the tiger ended up inside.

9 To those people in the huts and villages of half the globe struggling to break the bonds of mass misery, we pledge our best efforts to help them help themselves, for whatever period is required—not because the Communists may be doing it, not because we seek their votes, but because it is right. If a free society cannot help the many who are poor, it cannot save the few who are rich.

10 To our sister republics south of our border, we offer a special pledge—to convert our good words into good deeds—in a new alliance for progress—to assist free men and free governments in casting off the chains of poverty. But this peaceful revolution of hope cannot become the prey of hostile powers. Let all our neighbors know that we shall join with them to oppose aggression or subversion anywhere in the Americas. And let every other power know that this hemisphere intends to remain the master of its own house.

11 To that world assembly of sovereign states, the United Nations, our last best hope in an age where the instruments of war have far outpaced the instruments of peace, we renew our pledge of support—to prevent it from becoming merely a forum for invective—to strengthen its shield of the new and the weak—and to enlarge the area in which its writ may run.

12 Finally, to those nations who would make themselves our adversary, we offer not a pledge but a request: That both sides begin anew the quest for peace, before the dark powers of destruction unleashed by science engulf all humanity in planned or accidental self-destruction.

13 We dare not tempt them with weakness. For only when our arms are sufficient beyond doubt can we be certain beyond doubt that they will never be employed.

14 But neither can two great and powerful groups of nations take comfort from our present course—both sides overburdened by the cost of modern weapons, both rightly alarmed by the steady spread of the deadly atom, yet both racing to alter that uncertain balance of terror that stays the hand of mankind's final war.

15 So let us begin anew—remembering on both sides that civility is not a sign of weakness, and sincerity is always subject to proof. Let us never negotiate out of fear. But let us never fear to negotiate.

16 Let both sides explore what problems unite us instead of belaboring those problems which divide us.

17 Let both sides, for the first time, formulate serious and precise proposals for the inspection and control of arms—and bring the absolute power to destroy other nations under the absolute control of all nations.

18 Let both sides seek to invoke the wonders of science instead of its terrors. Together let us explore the stars, conquer the deserts, eradicate disease, tap the ocean depths and encourage the arts and commerce.

19 Let both sides unite to heed in all corners of the earth the command of Isaiah—to "undo the heavy burdens . . . (and) let the oppressed go free."

20 And if a beachhead of cooperation may push back the jungle of suspicion, let both sides join in creating a new endeavor: not a new balance of power, but a new world of law, where the strong are just and the weak secure and the peace preserved.

21 All this will not be finished in the first one hundred days. Nor will it be finished in the first one thousand days, nor in the life of this administration, nor even perhaps in our lifetime on this planet. But let us begin.

22 In your hands, my fellow citizens, more than mine, will rest the final success or failure of our course. Since this country was founded, each generation of Americans has been summoned to give testimony to its national loyalty. The graves of young Americans who answered the call to service surround the globe.

23 Now the trumpet summons us again—not as a call to bear arms, though arms we need—not as a call to battle, though embattled we are—but a call to bear the burden of a long twilight struggle, year in and year out, "rejoicing in hope, patient in tribulation"—a struggle against the common enemies of man: Tyranny, poverty, disease and war itself.

24 Can we forge against these enemies a grand and global alliance, North and South, East and West, that can assure a more fruitful life for all mankind? Will you join in that historic effort?

25 In the long history of the world, only a few generations have been granted the role of defending freedom in its hour of maximum danger.

26 I do not shrink from this responsibility—I welcome it. I do not believe that any of us would exchange places with any other people or any other generation. The energy, the faith, the devotion which we bring to this endeavor will light our country and all who serve it—and the glow from that fire can truly light the world.

27 And so, my fellow Americans: Ask not what your country can do for you—ask what you can do for your country.

28 My fellow citizens of the world: Ask not what America will do for you, but what together we can do for the freedom of man.

29 Finally, whether you are citizens of America or citizens of the world, ask of us here the same high standards of strength and sacrifice which we ask of you. With a good conscience our only sure reward, with history the final judge of our deeds, let us go forth to lead the land we love, asking His blessing and His help, but knowing that here on earth God's work must truly be our own.

RESPONSIBILITIES OF THE EDUCATED MAN

Grayson Kirk

Dr. Kirk, President of Columbia University, delivered this address at a convocation celebrating the centennial of the University of Denver on April 9, 1964. Asked to speak upon the responsibilities of the educated man, he took the opportunity to cite the main values that a formal education should produce. Whether he influenced, as well as formulated, values depended, of course, upon his audience's prior attitudes.

Dr. Kirk affirms four specific responsibilities of the educated man. He then explains and gives reasons for the importance of these responsibilities, each of which can be considered a value criterion. These reasons are the standards of measurement Dr. Kirk is asking his audience to use in judging the values he is advocating. How successful is he in developing acceptable standards of measurement? Are his reasons for accepting the values he advances clear, logical, and impelling? What are the principal techniques he uses in developing his reasons for acceptance? Does his organizational technique aid in establishing his value criteria?

The introduction to this speech is long and chiefly devoted to the social niceties of the occasion. This approach is a common practice in speeches given on occasions like this. Do you think that Dr. Kirk is engaging in mere courtesy or does he hope to gain an early advantage by praising his audience and by making the "proper" references? Does the introduction enhance Dr. Kirk's ethos? Could he profitably have begun with stronger interest factors?

This speech is reprinted by permission from Vital Speeches of the Day *(May 15, 1964), pp. 471–474.*

1 It is a pleasure to be in Denver once more, to visit again this university where I taught one happy summer, and to have the opportunity to renew so many long-standing and precious friendships. Actually, I tend, in retrospect, to associate this institution with one of the major changes in the direction of my life. It was here that I enjoyed my last full-time teaching—though I did not know it at the time—because immediately after my return from that pleasant summer here I was invited to become the Provost of Columbia, a decision that, once made, brought my teaching days to a close. Now that I am here again, who knows but that when I go back to New York there might be a strong campus opinion developed in my absence in favor of my return to teaching. If this should be the case then, I think I ought to come back here and start where I left off in 1949.

2 Seriously, I am delighted to have the opportunity to have a very small part in the celebration of this University's Centennial Year. Ideally, one would not have selected the year, 1864, as the most auspicious time in which to launch any new venture in higher education, but the forward-looking Western spirit triumphed over war-time concerns, and in retrospect we can be grateful that they did. We can be grateful because of the hundred years of service that this institution has given to successive generations of young people. And we can be grateful because here as in all America, then as now, the greatness of our system of higher education depends for its fullest development upon a healthy dualism in which both publicly and privately supported institutions flourish in mutually beneficial juxtaposition with each other. Each helps to provide a separate and vital part of our total national need—one which the other can not do well or, usually, at all. How crippled our country would be if it were obliged to rely on either

one alone! How fortunate we are that the value of this principle has been recognized by our people, and that they have been willing to support both types of institutions so generously! Having the two, our country's future greatness is assured.

3 But a great anniversary observance is not merely a time in which one may pause and look back upon past accomplishments with such satisfaction as they may merit. It is also a time when one should look ahead, and with such wisdom as one may be able to summon, into the problems and prospects of the years ahead. For such an exercise, your centennial theme—"The Responsible Individual and a Free-Society in an Expanding Universe"—provides all the necessary latitude for the free play of one's imagination. Man, Society and The Universe—these great topics set no limit upon what your lecturers may discuss, and for such a gloriously free rein lecturers are always grateful. No one can say of us later that we did not deal with the subject.

4 Parenthetically, however, such great themes do place a burden upon those who guide and plan such an anniversary observance. I speak from experience because a decade ago I guided my own university through a year-long celebration devoted to the theme, "Man's Right to Knowledge and the Free Use Thereof." I do not know, Chancellor Alter, whether a bicentennial is twice as burdensome as a centennial, but I trust, for your sake, that this may be so. If not, it doesn't really matter because neither of us will ever have the opportunity to make a personal comparison, and for this we are, I know, properly grateful.

5 Tonight, I have been asked to talk with you about the responsibilities of the educated man. This, in itself, is no small canvas on which to sketch a few fragmentary ideas—and to do so in that span of time between this moment and that speaker's warning signal when the first stifled yawn in this audience is observed. Therefore, to reduce the canvas to a manageable size, let me say that I propose merely to talk about some of those responsibilities that ought to emerge from, and partially to be a product of an exposure to *formal* higher education. I say, "ought to emerge" because we all know that no formal education can guarantee that the graduate will in fact have all, or any, of the qualities I propose to mention. There are different kinds of responsibilities and different levels of responsibility, and some of our friends who hold an array of degrees appear to have managed with great skill to avoid both. Also, I have used the term, "formal education," because I would like to focus our thinking upon the task of the college and university in that brief segment of a student's life which it can

influence. When the student has become an alumnus, the University virtually has finished its effective effort toward his education. It may still be able to educate him about the virtues of philanthropy, but that is about the limit of what it can do in later years.

6 The first responsibility which I would impose on the educated man may seem surprising to some of you; it may appear to be a trifle pedestrian, something not quite worthy of this great theme. I do not mean it to be so, and, on reflection, I hope you will agree with me about its importance. It is this: a first responsibility of a university man is to endeavor to achieve clarity and precision in his spoken and written communication.

7 Thought-processes are linked intimately with expression. Clarity of thought and clarity of expression go hand in hand. In these days of mass-education, so many of our students are permitted to go through college, and beyond, without undergoing that discipline of expression that an educated man should have as the first weapon in his arsenal. A college graduate who has not learned to use his mother-tongue with grace, precision and clarity simply does not deserve the diploma of even a first degree. He is not an educated man, no matter how great the quantity of information that he may have stored away, hopefully, for some future use.

8 The uneducated man generally is lazy in his speech. When asked to describe something he says, "Oh, I guess it was kind of bluish." He is saying in reality that he has been unobservant or that he has not been trained to distinguish anything more than the primary colors. He relies upon such vague descriptive generalities as "that kind of thing" or "you know what I mean"—what my colleague, Jacques Barzun, has referred to as an "inelegant algebra." The imprecision of his speech merely reflects the imprecision of his observation and thought.

9 Our student should learn that precision is not pedantry. He must learn not to be impressed by the cult of vulgarity in speech as it is practised by writers for television and the advertisements that fill the pages of our mass-media with their pseudo-folksy barbarities of language. If he is to justify his education, and the time and money spent upon it, he ought to be proudly aware of the vast riches of the English language and strive as best he can to make use of this heritage which is his for the effort. No single investment of a student's time will pay greater dividends in his future life.

10 Our student also must learn that much scholarly language in its way is equally barbarous. To avoid the criticism of his peers about his value judgments, many a scholar will hedge his statement with so many qualifications that the tiny kernel of truth, if indeed there be one, is lost from sight. To impress his peers—and the laity—with the depth of his learning, many a scholar follows that ancient and deplorable rule: never use a simple word if you can think of one that is long and obscure. For the same reason, the scholar is, apparently, unimpressed by the virtues of a simple declarative sentence.

11 I realize, of course, that much scholarly jargon is a device whereby the writer communicates a precise thought to other scholars who have learned the same quasi-mathematical language. But I am equally, and uncomfortably, aware of the fact that our greatest scholars—and particularly many of those who write in English universities—somehow manage to combine the greatest precision of thought with a clarity, and even an elegance, of expression that is a blessing to the literate layman and a source of satisfactory enlightenment to one's scholarly colleagues. I repeat that confused and involved sentences, ponderous and dull exposition, unnecessary recourse to jargon words and terms—these are the characteristics of a pedantry that, in its way, is as intellectually irresponsible as the lazy vulgarity of colloquial speech. A properly educated man is aware of these traps and he avoids them valiantly.

12 The second responsibility is less easy to define and still less easy to acquire. If formal, higher education is to be meaningful to a man, it must have given him, somehow, somewhere, a sense of values and the courage with which to defend them. Such a sense of values derives from an ability to discriminate not only between right and wrong but also between the significant and the trivial, between that which is cheap and shoddy and that which has integrity and beauty. To put the matter in another way, an educated man should have a well-developed and refined "good taste" which he uses as a yardstick in making his moral, social and aesthetic judgments.

13 In the past, convention, tradition and authority set these standards of judgment, and the young individual, having been taught what his society approved and condemned, generally became the passive exemplar and exponent of the approved code of conduct and thought. But today the winds of change are blowing over our society and if we are indifferent to them, we may find too late that the wind has become a destructive hurricane. The plain, inescapable fact is that the family and the church, those traditional instruments for social and moral indoctrination, no longer exert their former influence upon our young people. The reasons for this decline are to be found in the whole complex process of social change and it is not my task tonight to undertake any searching analysis of them. But if we accept as true the conclusion that I have just stated, then we are obliged to say that, if the influence of church and family has declined, that of the school, college and university becomes potentially the greater.

14 At the college and university level, this new responsibility for character-building by default is awkward and even uncongenial. It is true that we do have many collegiate institutions that are closely church-related and are devoted to the indoctrination of a fixed set of social, moral and spiritual values. But such institutions are in a minority and their doctrinal zeal is frequently less intense than it was a generation ago. The norm today is that of the liberal arts college that proclaims its goal to be the search for truth, wherever it be found, and its procedure to be that of exposing the student to the whole spectrum of ideas and values that have influenced major segments of mankind in the long passage from savagery to the twentieth century.

15 Thus, the liberal arts college deliberately places the burden of conscious choice and decision upon the student. It can, and should, point out to him why certain moral and social values have been adopted as general and widely prevailing by civilized societies. It can, and should, point out to him that membership in a society, any society, places certain and obvious restrictions upon individual conduct. It can, and should, insist upon the observance of certain standards of conduct within the student community, and, insofar as possible, it should involve student opinion in the establishment and enforcement of those standards.

16 Beyond this, however, the college, by its nature and purpose, can do little by way of direct authority or precept. It cannot and must not attempt to fill the vacuum left by the lessened influence of the church and the abdication of responsibility by parents. Its social function is a different one, though no less important to the future of society. But what it can do, and what it must do, is to endeavor to instill in every student as a kind of residuum of the whole educational process, what I have called a developed sense of good taste, one that in its turn will cause the possessor consciously and responsibly to adopt certain codes of action and certain standards of value. If this effort is successful, the present confusion of moral and social standards will diminish. If this effort fails, one can only foresee trouble for our country. A valueless society is undisciplined and anarchic almost by definition. And, in these days, such a society would be obliged to struggle with the utmost difficulty for survival in face of competition from other societies that are disciplined and united. This is one reason why I conclude that the second responsibility of the educated man is to understand the importance of a set of social, moral and aesthetic values, to establish them for himself in full awareness of his social obligations, and finally, to be prepared to explain and defend them in every needful way.

17 My first responsibility was essentially pragmatic. My second was far more abstract and inherently more difficult to achieve. My third is no less important, but it is a little more difficult than the first and rather more *terre à terre* than the second. Perhaps it may be phrased in this fashion: it is the responsibility of the educated man to make every effort, honestly and objectively, not only to understand the nature and problems of our society, but to comprehend compassionately the differences that separate it from others.

18 Nationalism breeds a sense of superiority with respect to one's own institutions and a feeling of condescension or even contempt about others. The uneducated man assumes as a matter of course that his is the best society on earth, and that world progress will come only if and as other benighted societies undertake to remodel their institutions in the fashion of his own. It does not occur to him that every society grows out of its own geographical and historical roots, that each society is profoundly affected by the bounty or the parsimony of nature, and finally, that evolutionary social change is a slow and clumsy process.

19 It is this attitude which today is a great obstacle to our country in its new posture of world-wide interest and responsibility. It is an attitude that demands from our foreign policies quicker and more sweeping results than can possibly be achieved. It is an attitude that causes resentment among recipients of our aid program. It is a constant source of difficulty in our dealings with our allies.

20 Moreover, it is an attitude that is antagonistic to the success of our long-range policies and interests because it is emotional in content and because it provides the basis for a made-to-order argument for extremist critics of all kinds. It complicates still further the already impossibly complicated problems of any Secretary of State. He cannot demonstrate the readiness of others to follow our lead. And so, he is exposed to the emotion-filled argument that he is somehow ineffective, short-sighted or even downright subversive. And this cripples his general effectiveness in a world where other leaders watch carefully to estimate American popular support for or against an administration or a policy.

21 The educated man, on the contrary, ought to understand that we were merely naive when we supposed that the newly independent states of the world would, or could, promptly set up democratic institutions, copied from our own, and begin thereby immediately to enjoy the full blessings of liberty. He ought to have known that democracy demands literacy, a sense of fundamental unity that transcends momentary political differences, and a popularly-supported constitutional framework that is strong enough to tolerate that principle of the "loyal opposition" upon which the entire democratic party ideology is based. To suppose that such a sophisticated system could be applied—and quickly—to lands where there was no feeling of ethnic unity, no common languages, no familiarity with the principles of self-government, and no widespread degree of literacy—this was merely to demonstrate the fact that such assumptions were based on emotion and ignorance, and nothing more.

22 In one after another of these new countries, where early and unrealizable experiments in democracy have lapsed into authoritarianism, our national feeling has been that of betrayal, and we have assumed that communist agents must have engineered the disaster. Granting the probability that communist agents will be fishing actively in all politically troubled waters everywhere, we have failed to realize that these experiments would have failed anyhow because they were based on an impossible set of expectations.

23 May I cite one other brief illustration? We have today great national disillusionment over the relative failure of the much heralded "Alliance for Progress" in Latin America. It is true that the Administration promised too much and too soon from the effort, but our educated man ought to have known that, given the nature and structure of South American states and society, economic and political change would be extremely slow. He ought to have realized also that, in a particular country, if the Alliance effort were successful in raising rapidly the popular level of expectations, the net effect might be to expedite the process of political revolution—with the attendant dangers of Communism—rather than to avert it.

24 Perhaps all I have been saying about this third responsibility is that the educated man should not expect or demand the impossible from his government in its foreign dealings. This does not mean that he should fail to support the most vigorous prosecution of policies that are in the national interest. An improved understanding of a complicated situation does not necessarily lead to a supine policy toward it, nor necessarily to that state that the late Lord Birkett referred to in describing a well-known do-good political opponent. He said, "My opponent has such a warm heart that it has melted all his backbone." On the contrary, an improved understanding by educated citizens will strengthen the will of the state and provide that intelligent support for its policies that will make them respected all the more abroad. When a government knows that its people know that there are no simple solutions to complicated problems, it can devote its energies to the realities of a situation without being obliged to explain constantly why the simple solutions are, in fact, no solution at all.

25 A fourth responsibility is rather more general in nature. Like the third, it is an expression of an attitude, and not a positive or demonstrable accomplishment or skill. I do not know how to express this responsibility except in terms that might easily be labeled as trite or as a cliché. Accepting that risk, let me say that the educated man has the responsibility to look squarely at the world and its problems with courage and hope, and not with fear or rejection.

26 We hear overly much in these days about the fears of the younger generation. We are told that all the manifest troubles of our young people—cheating in college, the rising incidence of sexual promiscuity, the use of narcotics, the criminality that accompanies juvenile delinquency—can all be explained by the fact that they live in an atmosphere of fear caused by the threat of atomic annihilation. Why plan a career and work for it, why follow traditional standards of morality, when tomorrow all civilization may disappear under an atomic cloud?

27 I have listened to many such explanations from social psychologists and other people who profess to understand the well-springs of social action. I have spent many a recent evening in the theatre where I was told that society is decaying to the point that it is not worth saving, and that the only sensible thing for a young man to do is to reject the whole sorry mess and to have no part of it. I have read many a modern novel on the same theme, and I have read many a serious book devoted to an analysis of what is variously called either "the plight" or "the predicament" of modern man caught in the devitalizing, dehumanizing toils of the machine age. I am told that man has become a robot, a number in an IBM machine, a helpless and hapless pawn on a cosmic chess-board.

28 This, I am told, is the other reason—the first being the fear of atomic annihilation—why our young people are alternately so depressed over or so angry about the society into which they have been placed.

29 My first reaction, either about the danger of the thermonuclear bomb or about the horrors of the machine age, is one of incredulity. Are we actually talking about the same world? If so, then we are like the blind men feeling the elephant because we find such different things to report.

30 First, there is the matter of fear. It is true that ours is the first generation that has faced the fear of mass destruction on such a quasi-global scale, but sheer visceral fear is an emotion that a man has about himself and his family rather than about society. And men have always lived in the presence of fear. The fears symbolized by the horsemen of the Apocalypse are as old as mankind, but men never have given way to such fears. They have recognized them as hazards of a life that was so incomparably worth the risks that one could only accept the danger as a part of life.

31 What I am saying is that I believe the notion of fear of the bomb is little more than an excuse on the part of those who for other reasons are unable or unwilling to cope with the complexities of modern life. I simply cannot accept this notion at face value. I think it is as false as a counterfeit coin.

32 My feeling about the terrors of the machine age is about the same. In a material sense more men today live better lives than at any other time in human history. In a non-material sense, more men today live richer lives than in any previous era. Today the cultural riches of the world are at the doorstep of the average man. He has available, as his father did not, a wealth of music, cheap books, easy opportunities for travel and recreation, and unprecedented availability of knowledge about the world and its events. If this be the slavery of the machine, then I can only reply that those who so regard it are bemused by wholly romantic notions about how men really lived in past ages.

33 Today, therefore, the educated man has the responsibility, to be sure, of trying to make the world still better, to try to mitigate the hazards and the short-comings of our modern life—and every age will have them—but he has a right to take pride in what modern civilization has wrought, and he has the responsibility to do what his forbears have always done, which is to face the world with quiet courage, with determination, and above all with hope.

34 I have spoken tonight about four responsibilities of different degrees and kinds. If I have deliberately selected such different topics, from among the many which might have been chosen, it is in part because I wished to remind you that the educated man does in fact have a vast range of wholly disparate responsibilities. Society has done much for him; he owes much to society, and for so long as we have our splendid colleges and universities in this country, I, for one, have no fear that he will fail to be conscious of his obligations. The world of the future, the world of the next century of this institution, beckons to mankind with a new promise, and each man has a share in its fulfilment.

A TOTALITY OF OUTLOOK

Bryan McEntegart

Bryan McEntegart, Bishop of Brooklyn, New York, delivered this short address at the Cathedral Club dinner in Brooklyn on January 24, 1963. The Second Vatican Council has received widespread publicity for its deliberations, which have been of great importance to Roman Catholics throughout the world. Many of these deliberations have implications that extend beyond narrow denominational boundaries. In this speech, Bishop McEntegart sets forth what he considers to be an urgent lesson for mankind to learn from the Council.

Approximately one-half of this speech is introduction. Does the length in this case seem justified? Does the introduction have an integral bearing on the body of the speech or does the speaker have to strain to show a relationship?

Bishop McEntegart's speech is a clear example of the forecasting, or partitioning, method of speech organization. The speaker enumerates each main point at the close of his introduction and then proceeds to discuss them in that precise order. The conclusion then crystallizes the content of the speech. What special advantages and disadvantages does this method of organization offer in this address? Is this organizational approach better suited to certain speech subjects, occasions, and audiences than to others?

*You will note that each of the main points of this speech is in question form. This arrangement in a series is commonly called a parallel structure of main points—*parallel *because they are similar in form and significance. Is there any advantage in using questions as main points? Would parallel declarative sentences be equally effective in this case? What, if any, advantage is gained from using any form of parallelism?*

This speech is reprinted by permission from Vital Speeches of the Day *(February 1, 1963), pp. 299–300.*

1 Rarely in history has world-wide attention been concentrated so intensely on such a small section of the globe, as during the deliberations of the recent session of the Vatican Council.

2 In the few weeks since my return, I have been asked repeatedly what I thought was the Council's most meaningful contribution to the betterment of mankind. Tonight I would like to answer this question.

3 I believe that the Second Vatican Council will lead the way to our seeing much more clearly both the oneness of all mankind, and the purpose of man as an individual.

4 This unity of mankind with men of all lands was forcefully symbolized at the Council by the presence of 2700 Bishops from every corner of the world, each one representing thousands, or even millions, of people.

5 The 527 speeches made by these men, the discussions among non-Catholic observers in Rome, the writings in newspapers across the world echoed the same theme, namely, that whether he be Oriental or Occidental, black man or white man, Christian or Jew, man in this century must see the world as one, and must regard not just his own, but every man's rights, must understand and respect the sincerity of each man's belief.

6 But, there was an even more urgent lesson to be learned from the Council—more urgent because so little understood—and more urgent because of the modern need for man to think through the purpose of his existence. Never was this issue more vitally important than today, for today millions of men wander through life aimlessly, confusedly, without purpose, despite all our vaunted advancements.

7 It is indeed pathetic that modern man, in such large proportions, does not know where he is going; and it is absolutely tragic that he is unaware of having lost his way.

8 But, consider with me: today we have more wealth, and more wars; more technology, and more tragedy; more conveniences for the home, and more broken homes; more bank deposits, and more brooding dissatisfaction; more natural resources, and more neurotic restlessness; more intellectual prowess and more inhumane oppression.

9 Does this not explain why men of all countries, climes, colors and creeds look to the Vatican Council in the hope that it will inspire man to re-assess himself with a totality of outlook, to re-examine the purpose of his existence, and to re-determine where he must find his way once again?

10 The Fathers of the Council are very much aware of this aspect of their labors. Whether the subject under discussion concerned the Sacred Liturgy, or Christian Unity, or the relations of Scripture and Tradition, or Communications, or the Constitution of the Church, their mind was centered not on economic or political factors, but rather on the spiritual growth of men, their sanctification, and the salvation of their souls.

11 To achieve the proper spiritual outlook, modern man must ask himself four questions:—What is my purpose? What really counts? Why should I make the effort? How am I to go about it?

12 *What is my purpose in life?* Either I am an educated animal, whose existence is as meaningless and transient as an autumn leaf, or I am a child of an Almighty Father, an object of Divine Thought from all eternity, a man destined for immortality.

13 If, gentlemen, man did not come forth from God's Hand, if man is not each instant sustained by God's Power, if man is not capable of enjoying God's Presence through all eternity, then life has no meaning, faith is folly, and no man has any rights, for man's existence has no reason.

14 *What really counts in life?* In the total view, an honest man will measure himself, not by what he has done, but by what he has become. The character he has shaped through the years, this alone has lasting meaning. And this character is determined by the quality of his reverence for his God, his loyalty to his fellow-man, and his honesty with himself.

15 In these relationships, as in a crucible, is tested the fulfillment of a man's true destiny. Next to this, no achievement of popularity, prestige, or power can have lasting meaning.

16 *Why make the effort?* Because only spiritual values accompany man beyond the grave. What a man *is* lasts into eternity; what he has accumulated does not. How foolish to have wasted one's efforts on the perishable, to have thrown one's talents exclusively into the transient, to neglect the growth of one's mind and soul and spirit, for the graspings of power, or influence or wealth.

17 In life, gentlemen, each man goes around only once, and the greatest tragedy of all is to have missed its meaning.

18 *How, then, go about the achievement of man's purpose?* To maintain clarity of perspective, man must think; to sustain strength of character, man must develop self-mastery. Man must think in large terms if he is not to become stifled with little issues; man must control himself in small indulgences, if he is to generate strength for great resolves. For, without a modicum of daily thought and denial, man's vision becomes darkened, and his energy enervated.

19 Here, in my opinion, is the Second Vatican Council's greatest contribution—to inspire in men of every race and nation a totality of outlook, to create in them an awareness and understanding of man's spiritual purpose. To all mankind, to each individual man, no issue can possibly be more important.

20 For, each man must decide the goals that are worthy of his efforts, the purposes that deserve his resolves. And this decision, gentlemen, will determine not only the quality of his earthly deeds, but the question of his eternal destiny.

LEADERSHIP AND THE "SANE SOCIETY"

Ralph T. Eubanks

On March 24, 1963, Dr. Eubanks, Professor of Speech at the University of Arkansas, delivered this keynote address to the Annual Leadership Conference of the Arkansas Federation of Business and Professional Women's Clubs. This organization is a branch of a national federation that seeks to promote the interests, elevate the standards, and extend opportunities to business and professional women through education in industrial, scientific, and vocational activities.

This speech is carefully organized. The introduction discloses and clarifies the subject and ends with a forecast of the three main points of the speech. Each point of the body logically progresses into the next: the first one illuminates the challenge *or problem of the modern leader; the second* defines *the good modern leader; and the third* delineates the essential values *of this leader. How is the challenge of the modern leader made vivid? In the second point, what techniques does the speaker use for defining the ideal leader? The third main point is the essence of the speech. Dr. Eubanks forecasts its development by enumerating the three types of consciousness the Ideal Modern Leader must have. Do you think that he enumerates them because of their major importance to the speech? When he develops these types of consciousness, he discusses them in the reverse order. Is there any disadvantage in his discussing them this way? Dr. Eubanks judges these three types of consciousness to be important because they foster the "sane society," a lasting and noble democratic ideal. The reason he asks his audience to accept them and judge sound leadership in their light is because they will produce a* higher value—*the sane society. Dr. Eubanks' task, then, is to show that the values of leadership he champions are important and integral to the achievement of the higher good. How well does he perform this function?*

In developing his points, Dr. Eubanks uses many different kinds of materials. Reference to eminent individuals is especially prominent in this speech. When dealing with propositions of value, this device is a common persuasive strategy. What special effect does this type of allusion or reference have in a speech concerned with values?

This speech is reprinted by permission from Vital Speeches of the Day (*May 15, 1963*), *pp. 478–480.*

1 One of the traditions of the Phi Beta Kappa society is an annual reading of one more chapter in the biography of the American Scholar. I think the tradition a good one for it keeps the society alive to the meaning of scholarship for a changing world. In your annual conferences on leadership, I sense much of this same spirit—a spirit of inquiry into what light new times have shed upon the American Leader. I'm therefore pleased to be invited to make this venture with you. I'm the more pleased, too, because I believe your inquiry so intimately connected with the great moral question of our times—the baffling question of how to secure to ourselves a so-called "sane society." To be concerned with leadership is to be concerned with human excellence as it applies to our corporate lives. And I see the quest for human excellence as the first principle of faith in a society concerned with real cultural advance. Our ancient search for "the good life in the good society" is at last a search for human excellence, both private and public.

2 In general terms, then, our inquiry today concerns the uses and prospects of modern leadership. In more specific phrase, we shall be trying to form an image of what a modern leader should be. Just as we might ask, what is the good king, the good soldier, or the good politician, so we may ask: What is the good leader? In making this inquiry, I should first like to describe briefly the *challenge* of the modern leader. From an understanding of this challenge we can then shape a definition of the good modern leader. And finally, we can

complete the image by an analysis of the *kinds of awareness* the good modern leader should seek to develop.

3 Let me put the challenge of the leader of today in round terms. The modern leader must be able to help us advance toward the so-called "sane society." My own interpretation is that such a society can only be achieved by a people who are genuinely inspired to have what Albert Sweitzer has called "a living philosophy of the people." Such a society, I believe, is a society that concerns itself with the ethical ideals of civilization. And this is to say that it must know the ways of *teleology,* or the science of ends, as well as what the Greeks called *techne,* or the science of means and method.

4 We do not in the U.S.A. have today what can be called a healthy "public philosophy." We don't have because we have virtually abandoned what may be thought of as our ancient "search for wisdom." This great civilizing search has been religiously conducted in the Western world for some three thousand years. Its driving forces have been our Greco-Roman secular heritage and our Hebraic-Christian heritage. Together, these brilliant heritages have inspired Western man to a passionate search for the "sane society." But as so many Western thinkers have been pointing out for the last hundred years, we have been fast losing heart for this ancient quest. We do not carry forward in America today what Joseph Wood Krutch calls the great "Moral Discussion" of the West. If I may so phrase it, we are busy squandering the moral capital Western man has for long centuries so carefully accumulated. We have substituted for the great ethical ideals of our cultural heritage what Max Lerner, the American sociologist, has recently referred to as "sawdust goals." These goals have often been described as *success, money, power, prestige,* and *security.*

5 My conviction is that these "sawdust goals" have nothing to do with the creation of a "sane society." Why? In a nutshell, because they rest upon the "order of things" instead of the "order of persons." They find their justification in those curious modern views of man's nature which deny objective truth, that is, any truth which transcends what we can come by through our sensory organs of taste, smell, touch, etc. Like the sailors of Odysseus' voyage, Western man has eaten from the honey-sweet blossoms of the lotus tree. And he seems to desire always to dwell in the Lotus-Land of mere sense impressions, letting the memory of his former faiths slip away into soft forgetfulness. We must again learn how to conduct the ancient search for wisdom which has been carried forward by such leaders as Isaiah and St. Matthew and Socrates in the ancient world and by men and women like Ralph

Waldo Emerson, T. S. Eliot, Susanne K. Langer, Reinhold Niebuhr, Jacques Maritain and Albert Sweitzer in our modern age. In a word, we must aspire to a sound public philosophy based on the order of persons; which is to say, upon matters spiritual instead of matters mechanical. For a general guide, I can think of no better than that offered by Bertram Morris, the American philosopher, in his recent book, *Philosophical Aspects of Culture.* Morris holds that movement from a "less genuine to a more genuine culture," is measured in terms of "the achievement of ends and the care for persons in the process. Without achievement of ends [Morris explains] a society is impotent, and without caring for persons, achievement is suicidal."

6 How shall we overcome our loss of interest in the ancient search for great moral and ethical ends? How shall we recover from the numbing effects of the fruit of the lotus? How shall we rise out of what Sorokin has aptly called our "sensate culture," and put together a society based upon the order of persons?

7 We must, among other things, create a new leadership in America—a leadership not based on the phony drives of "status-seeking," "conformity," and "playing-it-safe," but rather upon *genuine cultural needs.* May I define this new leader in terms of the challenge presented by our present state of hopelessness, emptiness, cultural *in*sanity. The leader I shall define as one who can help his group conduct well the ancient search for the "good life in the good society." Put another way, a good leader for our times is one who can hold ever before the members of his group a truly human vision of themselves. In a little different terms, he is one who can help his group find their way to honorable, human goals and can teach them how to "care for persons" in the process. In still different terms, he is one who can help us live up to the ancient definition of ourselves as *Homo sapiens,* or Man the Wise. We might reasonably hope that he would jealously guard our sense of good and evil and help us to learn again how to choose between better and worse. Such a leader would keep us at a good safe distance from the fateful blossoms of the lotus tree.

8 Let us now consider briefly the kinds of consciousness this Ideal Modern Leader must have. I take them to be at base these three broad types: *rhetorical consciousness, empathic consciousness,* and *value consciousness.*

9 *Value consciousness* I shall define as an awareness of those ideas of the good upon which a "sane society" can be firmly based. This is an awareness of "ought," or the ethical dimension of life. With this awareness a leader will know how to tell the difference between a "less genuine" and "a more genuine" culture, between a good proposal and a bad one, between a desirable action and an undesirable one. This kind of consciousness may be called our new leader's moral "gyroscope." With this gyroscope he can show his group the way to order their lives around spiritual concerns instead of mere externals. He can help them to see the difference between something that's merely *desired* and something that's genuinely *desirable,* between deep human needs and shoddy wants.

10 A leader with a genuine value consciousness will have the courage that wells out of deep commitment. It is he who shall have earned the right to issue to us the modern existentialist call to "engage ourselves." We shall know him as the person who really *cares*—who cares about man, about life, and about the final mystery of things. He is the Robert Hutchins of education, the Margaret Chase Smith of politics, the Kenneth Burke of letters, the Gordon W. Allport of psychology, the Reinhold Niebuhr of religion, the Loren Eiseley of anthropology, the Henry Winthrop of sociology, the William Gaylord Simpson of biology, the Edith Hamilton of history and the Paul Arthur Schilpp of philosophy.

11 What values, let us ask, shall our modern leader call us to? Many answers could be given to this question. And, may I add: this is one of the most perplexing questions of modern scholarship. I would suggest as a modest beginning the four great values which form the basis of a searching recent book called *New Knowledge in Human Values.* In this book of essays, fifteen scholars from various fields of knowledge agreed on the highest human values as being those of *love, truth, beauty,* and *self-realization.* I think we should note that nothing new has been discovered here. Let us recall that these four master values taken together have provided a kind of "star in the East" by which Occidental man has conducted his search for wisdom. As our own culture advances and as it merges more and more with the great wisdom of the Orient, we shall doubtless create new human values. Yet for now, leadership could not go wrong in bestirring its consciousness anew with these four great cultural values.

12 The leader who can help us find our way to cultural sanity must also have what I shall here call *rhetorical consciousness.* This is the kind of consciousness that prepares us for the articulate discussion of things that matter in both private and public affairs. This kind of consciousness rests upon a command of the word, or what the Greeks called *logos.* And it is secured to us by a twofold training that includes the poetic as well as the logical resources of human speech. Rhetorical consciousness consists of two intimately connected parts: one, the desire to find truth and two, the desire to communicate it. The ideal in Western culture is caught up in one of Emerson's essays on the subject of eloquence. Emerson, a life-long student of rhetoric, defined the eloquent man as "a sane man with the power to communicate his sanity." Western man has yearned to *know*, but he has also felt a compulsion to *say* to others what he knows. It is this understanding of the character of Western man that prompted Robert Hutchins to describe Western culture as the "Civilization of the Dialogue."

13 *Rhetorical consciousness* is therefore the kind of consciousness that applies human values to man's private and corporate problems. We look at last for guidance to him who can help us find the alternative courses of action in a given case and can persuade us to take the one which seems best for us. "The business of rhetoric," said Francis Bacon, "is to make pictures of virtue and goodness, so that they may be seen." But as Bacon well knew, men and women can neither speak nor write impressively about virtue and goodness unless they have first of all discovered what virtue and goodness mean. Nor can they apply human values to the solution of vital public questions unless they can exercise reason. Rhetorical consciousness is therefore at bottom the power to think well. The ideal modern leader must therefore be more than a clear thinker in the technical matters of positive science and technology. He must be able to help us translate our cultural heritage for new patterns of living. His real work, as thinker and talker, will be to help us make sound *social* and *political* decisions. We shall continue to need his counsel on the whole gamut of tough cultural issues from the peaceful use of outer space, to college dropouts, and the fluoridation of city water. He shall not have to be a Demosthenes or a Charles James Fox or an F. D. R. or a Clare Booth Luce, but he shall have to possess some of their ability and spirit. As guardian of our general reason, he shall be guardian of our basic morality. For—as Pascal put it—the endeavor to think well constitutes the whole dignity of man. My own impression is that intellect in the Western sense is first, last, and always what I am here calling *rhetorical consciousness.* Jacques Barzun—a modern scholar whose writings have profoundly affected my life—puts the point well. "Intellect," says Barzun, "belongs largely to the Western tradition—the tradition of explicitness and energy, of inquiry and debate . . . What Intellect satisfies in us is the need for orderly and perspicuous expression, which may lead to common belief and concerted action." There is then a sense in which the shaping of "a living philosophy of the people" must at last await the vigorous rhetorical consciousness. We must learn again to associate the power of the word with leadership. Let us not be misled by the notion that rhetorical consciousness consists in the mere ability to spout endless unrelated facts in unimaginative phrases. Let us learn to be skeptical of the mentality which confuses *expertise* with wisdom, which perceives of the amassing of data as the legitimate end of human dialogue. If we would have an able leadership, we must at last inquire of a man as Emerson suggested in the case of the nineteenth century British orator, Disraeli: "What do you stand for?" We shall then be able to see the models of rhetorical consciousness as the Saint Augustines, the Edmund Burkes, the Abraham Lincolns, the Woodrow Wilsons, the Winston Churchills, the Edward Tellers and the Margaret Chase Smiths.

14 In addition to *value* consciousness and *rhetorical* consciousness, the leader must have what may be called *empathic consciousness.* This kind of consciousness enables us to "feel-in" with our fellowmen, to experience the joys, the fears, the sufferings and the aspirations of others. An empathic consciousness enables the leader to sense the profoundest needs of the group who looks to him for direction. It enables him to work toward significant ethical ends and to "care for persons in the process." Empathy is at bottom the capacity for creative love, the capacity to identify ourselves with other human beings in a universal sense. A genuine *empathic consciousness* is big enough to embrace in compassionate sympathy our ancestors of past ages, our neighbors here and now, and generations yet unborn. In one sense, it is *piety*—the deep sense of respect that says "yes" to the existence of things larger than and different from our own egos. Albert Sweitzer symbolizes to me the highest kind of empathic consciousness in his practice of the great philosophy of "Reverence for Life." He is the living modern exemplar of what Sorokin calls "creative, unselfish love." His life illuminates for us in modern social terms the prospect of a sane society grounded in humane feeling. You and I know well that when all is said, it is love and love alone that swings open the doors of genuine cultural progress. We sense in Dostoievski's words the deepest prophecy: "Humble love is the most effective force, the most terrific, the most powerful, unequalled by any other force in the world."

15 Only a leader with a genuine *empathic consciousness* can teach us how to harness this great force of cultural progress. He can show us by example and by precept what it means to identify oneself fully with the human race. On the modern scene his job will be no less than formidable. For he must somehow help us to see the difference between such hollow social forms as "belongingness" and "togetherness" on the one hand and the abiding sense of identity with humanity on the other hand that's suggested in the timeless call to be "our brother's keeper." We shall, I believe, find our models of *empathic consciousness* in such men and women as Albert Schweitzer, the German philosopher-physician, Paul Tournier, the Swiss psychiatrist, Arnold J. Toynbee, the English historian, Eleanor Roosevelt, the late American social leader, Joseph Wood Krutch, American man of letters, Walter Weisskopf, the American economist, and Reinhold Niebuhr, the American religious leader.

16 When we think of our prospects for a leadership that can show us the ways of cultural sanity, we are fronted immediately with a hard fact of human history. Simply put, it is just this: *Men organize their lives around their ideals, their images of the way things ought to be.* Whole epochs of history have been molded by such compelling images as the Christian Saint, the Armed Knight, the Southern Gentleman, the Self-Made Man, etc. But the harsh truth is that America does not today have any vivid images of human excellence by which to guide its corporate life. Our present image is astonishingly ambiguous. We are not sure whether the good American leader of today is Riesman's Other-Directed Man, Whyte's Organization Man, the psychologists' Cognitive Man, the universally admired Democratic Man or the scientists' creation, the Spaceman. We have no design for the mold in which family and school and community can form the character of the Ideal Man. Which is another way of saying we do not have a "living philosophy of the people."

17 My own conviction is that we shall have no bright image of the good leader until we fully recover our lost faith in true greatness, in heroism. One of the sad effects of our abandonment of the ancient search for wisdom is our contempt for heroism. We have celebrated the "common man"; we have treated the exceptional man meanly. Yet I believe we are beginning at last to sense the folly of our lotus-feast. Robert Oppenheimer spoke for many of us when he said in an AP interview recently: "We hunger for nobility: the rare words and acts that harmonize simplicity and truth." It matters very much that we kindle the three kinds of consciousness we have described today. For these are the very stuff of nobility and, at last, of cultural sanity. And if I may so put it, in this three-fold consciousness is contained the spirit of the West—the very spirit that enabled Western man to form an image of himself as "Man the Wise." Suburbia must find ways to reanimate this heroic image of man. For as Arthur M. Schlesinger, Jr. has put the issue: "If our society has lost its wish for heroes and its ability to produce them, it may well turn out to have lost everything else as well."

THE PURSUIT OF SECURITY

Gerald J. Lynch

Gerald J. Lynch, President and Chairman of the Board of Menasco Manufacturing Company, was awarded an honorary degree by the University of Dayton at graduation exercises on December 21, 1963. As the main speaker at the ceremonies, he challenged contemporary youth's overemphasis on security in selecting jobs after graduation. In the place of job security he stressed the value of job opportunity.

In this type of address speakers commonly use the strategy of making an old value seem throughly repugnant to an audience. How does Lynch try to make job security seem an undesirable primary value? How effective are his arguments in this respect? As a second step in their strategy to effect a change in their listeners, speakers link the new values they are proposing to worthy and higher values that, they say, will lead to a better life. With what values does Lynch identify the values of opportunity and risk? Is this identification sufficient to make one want to accept those values in preference to job security?

Much of this speech is delivered in the first tense. The introduction is personal and ends with a reference to Lynch's son; he also uses personal examples throughout the rest of his speech. Is the use of personal data a desirable speech technique? How effective is the subjective element in this speech?

Lynch also uses short quotations that succinctly express worthy ideals. Ralph Waldo Emerson once said, "I hate quotations." What do you think of using them for stylistic effect and for making ideas compelling?

Annually, thousands of commencement speeches are given to graduating classes all over the country, and, ordinarily, these speeches deal with human values. But as Lynch says in his opening paragraph, ". . . later on in life most graduates can't remember the commencement speaker's name—much less what he said." This fact may be attributed in part to the triteness of too many commencement addresses. Do you think it is possible for a speaker to meet the particular demands of a commencement audience and, at the same time, avoid platitudes? How well does Lynch succeed?

This speech is reprinted by permission from Vital Speeches of the Day *(June 1, 1964), pp. 504–506.*

1 Very Reverend President, distinguished guests, members of the faculty, graduates and friends: It is indeed an honor and privilege to be selected by this great university for an honorary degree. I welcome the opportunity to address you graduates on this important and joyous occasion. I must admit that when Father Roesch and Brother Lackner asked me to speak to you I had some misgivings about it, until one of my friends reminded me that later on in life most graduates can't remember the commencement speaker's name—much less what he said.

2 This is a very important day in the lives of you graduates. I extend my heartiest congratulations to each of you upon the completion of a major segment of your college career. I know it represents a well deserved step towards unlimited future opportunity. I want you to know that you are joining a growing and illustrious group of alumni of a university which is rapidly taking its place among the great universities in this land.

3 This graduating class represents an exciting hope for the future. Here are the future teachers, doctors and lawyers. Here are the scientists needed to light the way for generations to come. Here are the engineers who can translate the findings of science into productive machines and processes. Here are tomorrow's businessmen who will satisfy the growing demand for goods and services. Here, in short, are the men and women whose minds, skills and character will adapt the treasures of this earth to the service of mankind.

4 I must confess to a certain nostalgia on this great occasion. It was at this school over a generation ago that I had my first real contact with the world of ideas—with literature—with problem-solving—with philosophic thought. It was here that I enjoyed close contact with a faculty which had some of the most competent, stimulating and dedicated men it has ever been my privilege to know—men who have extended their own spiritual, intellectual and moral heritage and influence far into posterity.

5 As you may have inferred from the citation, it has been my privilege to have covered a broad spectrum of experience. One might be tempted to take advantage of this experience and offer you some direction and advice in your life's work. This would be unwise and futile—unwise because the world you face is vastly different, and futile because on the basis of experience with my oldest son, who will graduate next June, God willing, from a West Coast university, I know that youth would place less value on my advice than do I. Sometimes my son reminds me of the little Latin I have taught him—a line from Horace: "Senex, laudator temporis acti" which transalated means "The old man, champion of the past."

6 However, it might be appropriate on this occasion to reflect on a subject of some interest to me and to invite each of you to make your own application. This is the subject of security and what I believe to be the interrelated subjects of opportunity, risk, reward and failure in a free enterprise system.

7 Shortly after I was invited to speak to you a college graduate of your age group requested an opportunity to see me. He said he was considering an offer to join our company—he wanted to be certain he was making the right lifetime choice—and he felt he had a right to research this question up to the Chairman of the Board. He was intelligent, ambitious and personable. He appeared to have good potential for growth. In fact, I caught myself speculating as to whether or not he might run the company in twenty years.

8 However, his line of questioning was disappointing. It suggested that his goal was personal security and not opportunity. He was interested not in our problems and probable growth, but in our rate of employee turnover, in our fringe benefits, and in our pension plan—to a point where it became apparent to me that he wanted to spend his working days in an atmosphere of maximum personal security, and not in a dynamic environment of exploiting our opportunities.

9 I felt I had an obligation to place this matter in focus. He appeared shocked when I told him that I was sure he couldn't find security in our company because I had been looking for it for some time and couldn't find it myself. I told him that it was frequently necessary for us to make major strategic decisions with respect to product, key personnel, pricing, expansion and the like—and that despite our excellent staff, our sound product position and our financial strength, a major error could relegate all of our personal security programs to the ashcan. I reminded him, for example, that products can be obsoleted by research and invention conducted in some remote basement in the

world—which would have the effect of rendering unnecessary our plants, facilities, personnel, and even management. I also reminded him that this not only could happen, but has happened many times—and that the best evidence was the mortality table of businesses and the major shifts which have taken place in the relative position of the top 100 companies over the last 10-25-50 years.

10 I told him that there was no absolute security in our company or in any other company, except that which our personnel collectively earned from day to day and from year to year, and that, furthermore, there was no absolute security for him in our company unless he remained competitive in his work until the date of his retirement. Finally, I suggested that in planning his life work he place major emphasis on exploiting opportunities for growth, with their attendant successes and failures, rather than on personal security in and of itself. Unfortunately, he behaved like the young man reported in the Gospel who asked the Lord what he might do to gain eternal life—when he heard the answer, and considering it too hard he silently went away.

11 The idea of security seems to have grown so rapidly in recent years that the spirit of risk-taking—historically the dominant mark of youth—has become a little dulled. Last year I was disturbed to read an article in the *Saturday Evening Post* entitled "Youth—The Cool Generation." It was written by Dr. Gallup and Evan Hill and was based on 3,000 interviews with young people up to the age of 22. The article stated that the typical youth will settle for low success rather than risk high failure; that he has little spirit of adventure; that he wants little because he has so much, and is unwilling to risk what he has.

12 It would be natural and commendable for a person of middle or advanced years to give primary consideration to security. However, that security should loom so large with youth—particularly among college men and women who are most prepared to cope with the future—seems a bit at variance with those qualities which properly distinguish youth from age. Perhaps the greatest service I could render this class would be to reflect on the danger of over-emphasis on security as a life goal, and to re-examine the more heroic doctrine that life is an adventure with a higher purpose than insurance against risks.

13 Now I would not create the impression that there isn't a higher purpose to life than the attainment of economic security. On this subject I must yield to the many men here today who are more competent to develop this theme than I. However, I am sure they would tell you that there is only one place where security can be found—inside yourself. Here, and here alone, lies the real source of security. Ideals—not dollars; principles—not pensions; character—not convenience or expediency.

14 But getting back to my subject, I must remind you that you are entering a world which is difficult and complex. It is capricious in its rewards and often inexorable in exacting penalties for failures. Furthermore, this society—greater than at any time in history—is undergoing constant and breath-taking changes in its culture, its technology and its institutions. An intelligent man, in making an objective examination of this society—without courage and faith in himself—has reason to feel insecure and to attempt to discover some secure haven in that society.

15 It is my belief that it is difficult, if not impossible, to discover security. I believe that security must be attained—and when attained, that it must be maintained. I also believe that the probability of attaining security, when pursued as a life goal, is far less than if it is sought as a by-product of adventuresome and successful living.

16 Morbid emphasis on personal security generates a certain myopia, a dedication to the status quo, resistance to change and the rejection of opportunities for personal growth—with their associated risks and rewards—because there might be a finite chance to fail. I have learned over the years that preoccupation with security breeds insecurity, and that security, like happiness, most often eludes those who pursue it the most. Paradoxically, security most often comes to him who in life assumes the risks of insecurity.

17 A number of years ago I had a very modest part—as a member of a new management group—in reviving a very large company which in less than twenty years had lost one-half of its market to its principal competitor and had barely managed to break even in the process. Having come from the competitor, I was curious as to what kind of men would let this happen.

18 I met a group of executives who in the main were concerned primarily with the maintenance of their own personal positions rather than in undertaking programs for the company which, if successful, would have assured their own individual and corporate security. These men gloried in past accomplishments, worshiped tradition, were suspicious of change, and quite effectively insulated themselves against any suggestion that anyone had or could find a better way. These men had a Maginot Line concept of security which could not possibly survive in a competitive and free enterprise economy.

19 As against the discovery of our pursuit of security as a goal, I submit the more challenging and heroic—and, I believe, more realistic—view that your lives will abound in opportunities for growth and service—but also that the exploitation of these opportunities will entail risk, and the possibility of success, and the possibility of failure. Further, that if you pursue these opportunities with judgment, with courage, and with diligence, your lives will be marked by a pattern of successes and failures, but with a much higher probability of attaining security in fact than if you had established security as your only goal.

20 With respect to these opportunities I am reminded of a statement by Theodore Roosevelt: "Far better is it to dare mighty things, to win glorious triumphs, even though checkered by failure, than to take rank with those poor spirits who neither enjoy much or suffer much, because they live in the grey twilight that knows not victory nor defeat."

21 The society which you are entering is one of free enterprise in which you will have much freedom to succeed and much freedom to fail. Without freedom to fail you would have no freedom to succeed. Great opportunities are invariably accompanied by great risks. A Chinese friend of mine tells me that the Chinese word for crisis is a pictograph in two parts—one signifies great danger; the other great opportunity. I have noted that the venture which entails little risk usually holds out only a modest reward. I don't know of a major American business which wasn't founded at the risk of somebody's personal fortune. Every industry has a long obituary column of companies which failed to make the grade—but from the successes and failures has come our gigantic industrial complex and a resultant standard of living for the American people which is unparalleled in the history of the world.

22 In closing, let me read you a quotation from Dean Alfange, an eminent attorney, which epitomizes what I have been telling you today: "I want to take the calculated risk; to dream and to build, to fail and to succeed. I refuse to barter incentive for a dole. I prefer the challenges of life to the guaranteed existence; the thrill of fulfillment to the steel calm of utopia. I will not trade freedom for beneficence, nor my dignity for a handout. . . . It is my heritage to stand erect, proud and unafraid; to think and act for myself, to enjoy the benefits of my creations, and to face the world boldly and say, 'this I have done!' "

23 Good luck, and God bless you.

Chapter Seven

SPEECHES THAT CREATE CONCERN FOR A PROBLEM

Man's existence in society often gives rise to problems that threaten the perpetuation of the group and the welfare of its members. The ability of groups and individuals to perceive and understand the nature and importance of the problems confronting them is one measure of a society's maturity and strength. However, unless it is able to comprehend the significance of its problems, a society has little chance of ever solving them.

Consequently, speakers often address audiences for the purpose of creating a concern for problems. Whereas speeches that affirm propositions of value are designed to develop codes of conduct in the minds of listeners, speeches that aim to create concern for problems are directed toward specific social situations calling for remedial action. The mayor of a large city, for example, may seek to arouse popular concern over an increase in juvenile delinquency. A sociologist may attempt to create concern for indigent senior citizens. A politician may endeavor to arouse sympathy over the plight of the American Indian. Although sometimes a speaker's purpose is only to set the stage for private consideration or public discussion of the problem he is presenting, at other times his primary purpose is to interest his audience in the solution he wishes to propose. In either case, his behavior is influenced by definite constraints that creating concern for a problem produces.

CONSTRAINTS IMPOSED BY SPEECH PURPOSE

Whenever a speaker seeks to create concern for a problem, he must prepare his audience to search for and discover the best solution to it. To achieve this goal, he must explore the *nature of the problem* and *the reasons why it is of vital concern to his audience.*

Philosopher John Dewey emphasized the importance of the first of these two constraints when he wrote, "The essence of critical thinking is suspended judgment; and the essence of this suspense is inquiry to determine the nature of the problem before proceeding to attempts at its solution." In exploring the nature of the problem, the speaker must assume the role of the social informant. The success of his speech is governed, in large part, by the same constraints imposed on the speaker seeking to impart or augment knowledge or to affirm a proposition of fact. He must choose those supporting materials that best demonstrate the nature of the problem: analogy and illustration; expert testimony and factual example; description; definition; and narration. But this step is only a portion of his task. A problem is not really a problem to an audience until they perceive it as such. A situation may exist, and the audience may hear that it does, but in their eyes it may still be nothing more than a lifeless fact until they view it as something that may threaten or violate their needs and values. The members of an audience who have just been informed that many American Indians endure substandard economic lives may greet this knowledge with indifference. Although they may have accepted the situation as real, they have not perceived it as a problem for themselves, either as individuals or as members of society.

To make the plight of the American Indian important to his audience, a speaker may first stress a fact: "The national and state governments (and the peoples thereof) are not fulfilling their treaty obligations to provide for the economic well-being of Indian citizens"; he may secondly stress a value: "Whenever any American citizen, whatever his race or creed, is unable to provide adequately for his own economic needs, it is a matter of public concern."

In general, then, the speaker who would create popular concern for a problem must do more than explore the nature of the problem; he must give significance to it by relating it to the audience's value premises.

CONSTRAINTS IMPOSED BY A PARTICULAR AUDIENCE

As is the case in affirming propositions of fact or value, the speaker who wishes to create concern for a problem must use those rhetorical devices that enable his audience to find *interest* and *meaning* in his subject, to ascribe *credibility* to him as a source, and to assign *validity* to the problem at hand. When applied to this form of address, these constraints have special meanings, just as they did in each kind of speech studied earlier.

Speeches dealing with the significance of problems most often arise from the speaker's own personal involvement with his subject. Although the problem for diverse reasons may have become a central issue in his own life, it may often have little inherent *interest* for his listeners, who may receive his message with detachment. In recognition of this constraint, one college student, Ralph Zimmermann, speaking within the artificial confines imposed by contest oratory, began his speech, "Mingled Blood," with these words:

> I am a hemophiliac. To many of you, that word signifies little or nothing. A few may pause a moment and then remember that it has something to do with bleeding. Probably none of you can appreciate the gigantic impact of what those words mean to me.

While this speaker created an element of suspense and chose to make a direct statement of personal involvment to capture the interest of his audience, others have used quotations or rhetorical questions, vivid language, or analogy for this purpose.

A second constraint that audiences impose in this kind of speech is that the speaker must be able to translate his personal knowledge of a problem in such a way that it has *meaning* for his audience. Ralph Zimmermann, with tongue in cheek, began with the following description of his problem:

> What is this thing called hemophilia? Webster defines it as "a tendency, usually hereditary, to profuse bleeding even from slight wounds." Dr. Armand J. Quick, Professor of Biochemistry at Marquette University and recognized world authority on this topic, defines it as "a prothrombin consumption time of 8 to 13 seconds." Normal time is 15 seconds. Now do you know what hemophilia is?

He later gave real meaning to the term:

> What does it really mean to be a hemophiliac? The first indication comes in early childhood when a small scratch may bleed for hours. By the time the hemophiliac reaches school age, he begins to suffer from internal bleeding into muscles, joints, the stomach, the kidneys. This latter type is far more serious, for external wounds can usually be stopped in minutes with topical thromboplastin or a pressure bandage. But internal

> bleeding can be checked only by changes in the blood by means of transfusion or plasma injections. If internal bleeding into a muscle or joint goes unchecked repeatedly, muscle contraction and bone deformity inevitably result. . . . Childhood and early adolescence are the danger periods of a hemophiliac's life. As recently as November, 1950, *The Science Digest* reported that 85 percent of all hemophiliacs die during that period.

In this moment of persuasion, the speaker chose to use contrasting definitions, testimony, rhetorical questions, familiar terms, and statistics to give meaning to the problem he sought to dramatize. Others have made use of comparison, negation, and personification.

The third constraint on the choices a speaker may make in creating concern for a problem is related to the audience's perception of the speaker as a source of knowledge on his subject. It is quite clear that the choices the president of Americans for Democratic Action may make in discussing the medical needs of the aged will differ substantially from the choices the president of the American Medical Association may make when addressing the same audience on the same problem. In each case, the speaker must be conscious of his *credibility* as a source to his listeners. Since Ralph Zimmermann was unknown to most members of his audience he sought to demonstrate that he was a credible source of knowledge on hemophilia. In adapting to this constraint he said:

> I remember the three long years when I couldn't even walk because repeated hemorrhages had twisted my ankles and knees to pretzel-like forms. I remember being pulled to school in a wagon while other boys rode their bikes, and being pushed to my table. I remember sitting in the dark empty classroom by myself during recess while the others went out in the sun to run and to play. And I remember the first terrible day at the big high school when I came on crutches and built-up shoes carrying my books in a sack around my neck.

Ralph Zimmermann thus chose to use a compelling personal narrative in adapting to this constraint. Others have strengthened their credibility with expert testimony, detailed explanations of research methodology, and reference to prior training or experience.

The final constraint imposed on the speaker who seeks to create concern for a problem relates to the *measures of validity* his audience will use in assessing the significance of his problem. In some instances these measures are easily defined. A business executive speaking to his board of directors may assume that his audience will consider the problem of racial boycotts significant if he can demonstrate their effects on gross income. In other instances, a speaker may have greater difficulty determining the standards his audience will use to decide the importance of a problem. Ralph Zimmermann concluded that, for most listeners, it was sufficient *to show that the problem is a source of suffering for those who experience it.* Though the most hardened pragmatist might state that the problem is of little social importance since only 20,000 to 40,000 hemophiliacs exist in the United States, most Americans, motivated by the democratic ethic, would conclude with Mr. Zimmermann that "if society can keep a hemophiliac alive until after adolescence, society has saved a member."

But there are circumstances in which this standard of sufficiency is not enough. While the plight of white Christian Americans is traditionally of concern to white Christian Americans, the suffering and degradation of minority groups at home and most other groups abroad are met with much less interest. Not too many years ago, the Kingston Trio entertained numerous night club audiences with the knowledge that "they're rioting in Africa, tra la la la la la," and "starving in India, tra la la la la la." While this cheerful little ditty may tell us more about American humor than American values, it does suggest that the speaker who wishes to create concern for a problem is well advised to *demonstrate the relationship of the problem to his immediate audience.* While at times a speaker may find it sufficient to appeal to man's higher motives—"No man is an island unto himself"—at other times he must demonstrate the practical consequences that will occur should his problem remain unsolved—"Those who lack bread, see Red."

CONCLUSION

In our society, men often seek to inspire others to become concerned about problems, both great and small. At certain times the speaker's sole purpose is to set the stage for private thought or public discussion. At other times the speaker seeks to arouse interest in a problem for the purpose of preparing his audience to accept his solution. In either case, his behavior is governed by certain constraints, which necessitate his exploration of *the nature of the problem to be solved* and *the reasons why it is of impelling concern to his audience.* And since audiences differ in their interests and ability to learn, as well as in their perception of source credibility and message validity, he must also choose those rhetorical means that will help them to ascribe *interest, meaning, credibility,* and *validity* to his speech.

The following speeches provide concrete examples of the choices others have made in creating concern for problems. The first speech is "Mingled Blood" by Ralph Zimmermann. The second speech, "Culture and Communication," by Robert T. Oliver tries to create interest in intercultural communication problems. Daniel R. Crary's "Plague of People" warns us about the possible consequences of the population explosion. Sally Webb's "On Mousetraps" is a one-point speech illustrating the problem inherent in stereotyping. And last, Jenkin Lloyd Jones's "Who Is Tampering with the Soul of America?" focuses on a general breakdown in American moral values.

For Further Reading

Dewey, John, *How We Think,* D. C. Heath, 1910, pp. 72–74. Concisely explains the importance of understanding the nature of problems.

St. Onge, Keith R., *Creative Speech,* Wadsworth Publishing Co., 1964, pp. 203–213. Discusses in some detail the necessity and role of understanding society's problems.

Walter, Otis, and Robert L. Scott, *Thinking and Speaking,* The Macmillan Co., 1962, pp. 119–133. Focuses on suggestions for thinking and speaking about problems.

MINGLED BLOOD

Ralph Zimmermann

"Mingled Blood" won first place in the men's division of the 1955 Interstate Oratorical Contest. Later that year, Mr. Zimmermann graduated from Wisconsin State College at Eau Claire; in the fall, he entered law school at the University of Wisconsin in Madison; and the following spring, in March 1956, he died, a victim of hemophilia, the blood disease he describes so eloquently in this speech. That year's edition of Winning Orations *of the Interstate Oratorical Association made the inclusion of "Mingled Blood" especially poignant for it was dedicated to his memory. The speech was also printed and distributed by The National Hemophilia Foundation of New York City.*

In this speech Zimmermann relies upon compelling personal narrative, which he occasionally supports with scientific and historical data. In this way, he seeks to make the problems created by hemophilia real, painful, and tragic. Which portions of the speech do you find especially effective? Do you feel that Zimmermann's descriptions are so realistic at times that they might be too painful to a listener? Does the speaker's ethos derived from personal affliction mitigate this problem?

Zimmermann's conclusion is worth special attention. It brings the speech to an emotional climax and simultaneously creates admiration and respect for the speaker as a hemophiliac. Note those aspects of the conclusion that you think are instrumental in bringing the speech to such a moving end.

This speech is reprinted by permission from Winning Orations, 1956 (*Evanston, Ill.: The Interstate Oratorical Association, 1956*).

1 I am a hemophiliac. To many of you, that word signifies little or nothing. A few may pause a moment and then remember that it has something to do with bleeding. Probably none of you can appreciate the gigantic impact of what those words mean to me.

2 What is this thing called hemophilia? Webster defines it as "a tendency, usually hereditary, to profuse bleeding even from slight wounds." Dr. Armand J. Quick, Professor of Biochemistry at Marquette University and recognized world authority on this topic, defines it as "a prothrombin consumption time of 8 to 13 seconds." Normal time is 15 seconds. Now do you know what hemophilia is?

3 It is by no means a 20th century phenomenon. Ancient writings reveal the Jewish rabbis upon the death of first born sons from bleeding after circumcision, allowed the parents to dispense with this ceremony for any more sons. Family laws of ancient Egypt did not permit a woman to bear any more children if the first born should die of severe bleeding from a minor wound. How odd it seems to link the pyramids of the 4th dynasty with prothrombin consumption of 1955.

4 Hemophilia has had significant influence on the pages of history. Victoria, the queen of an empire on which the sun never set, was a transmitter of this dread ailment. Through her daughter, Alice, it was passed to the Russian royal family and Czarevitch Alexis, heir apparent to the throne of Nicholas II. Alexis, the hemophilic heir apparent, was so crippled by his ailment that the Bolshevik revolters had to carry him bodily to the cellar to execute him. And through Victoria's daughter, Beatrice, it was carried to the sons of the Spanish monarch, Alfonso XIII. While this good queen ruled her empire with an iron hand and unknowingly transmitted this mysterious affliction, my forebears, peasants of southern Germany, worked their fields, gave birth to their children, and buried their dead sons. Hemophilia shows no respect for class lines. It cares not whether your blood be red or blue.

5 For hemophilia is a hereditary disease. It afflicts only males, but paradoxically is transmitted only by females. The sons of a victim are not hemophiliacs, and do not pass it on. However, all of the daughters are transmitters. Of the transmitter daughter's children, half of the girls may be transmitters like their mother, and half of the sons may be hemophiliacs. Thus the net spreads out and on. Theoretically, it follows strict Mendelian principles. But because it is a recessive characteristic, it may lie dormant for generation after generation. As far back as my ancestral line can be traced, there is no evidence of hemophilia until my older brother Herbert and me. The same is true of 50 per cent of America's bleeders.

6 And there are many of us. Medical authorities estimate that there are some 20,000–40,000 hemophiliacs of all types in the United States. Clinically we divide into three groups: classic hemophilia AHG, and two other less common types of hemophilia, PTC and PTA. I am a classic hemophiliac—the real McCoy.

7 What does it really mean to be a hemophiliac? The first indication comes in early childhood when a small scratch may bleed for hours. By the time the hemophiliac reaches school age, he begins to suffer from internal bleeding into muscles, joints, the stomach, the kidneys. This latter type is far more serious, for external wounds can usually be stopped in minutes with topical thromboplastin or a pressure bandage. But internal bleeding can be checked only by changes in the blood by means of transfusion or plasma injections. If internal bleeding into a muscle or joint goes unchecked repeatedly, muscle contraction and bone deformity inevitably result. My crooked left arm, the built-up heel on my right shoe, and the full length brace on my left leg offer mute but undeniable testimony to that fact. Vocal evidence you hear; weak tongue muscles are likely to produce defective L and R sounds.

8 Childhood and early adolescence are the danger periods of a hemophiliac's life. As recently as November, 1950, *The Science Digest* reported that 85 per cent of all hemophiliacs die during that period. While the figure is exaggerated, it tends to indicate this salient point: if society can keep a hemophiliac alive until after adolescence, society has saved a member. During those years, society is given a responsibility it too often refuses to accept.

9 You might ask—but what can I do? What do you expect of me? The answer lies in the title of this oration: mingled blood. For all that boy needs is blood, blood, and more blood. Blood for transfusions, blood for fresh frozen plasma, blood for serum fractions. Not Red Cross Bank Blood, for stored blood loses its clot-producing factors. But fresh blood directly from you to him in a matter of hours. Your blood, dark and thick, rich with all the complex protein fractions that make for coagulation—mingled with the thin, weak, and deficient liquid that flows in his veins. Blood directly from you to the medical researcher for transformation into fresh frozen plasma or antihemophilic globulin. During those years, his very life is flowing in your veins. No synthetic substitute has been found—only fresh blood and its derivatives.

10 Because medical science had not advanced far enough, and fresh blood not given often enough, my memories of childhood and adolescence are memories of pain and heartbreak. I remember missing school for weeks and months at a stretch—of being very proud because I attended school once for four whole weeks without missing a single day. I remember the three long years when I couldn't even walk because repeated hemorrhages had twisted my ankles and knees to pretzel-like forms. I remember being pulled to school in a wagon while other boys rode their bikes, and being pushed to my table. I remember sitting in the dark empty classroom by myself during recess while the others went out in the sun to run and play. And I remember the first terrible day at the big high school when I came on crutches and built-up shoes carrying my books in a sack around my neck.

11 But what I remember most of all is the pain. Medical authorities agree that a hemophilic joint hemorrhage is one of the most excruciating pains known to mankind. To concentrate a large amount of blood into a small compact area causes a pressure that words can never hope to describe. And how well I remember the endless pounding, squeezing pain. When you seemingly drown in your own perspiration, when your teeth ache from incessant clenching, when your tongue floats in your mouth and bombs explode back of your eyeballs; when darkness and light fuse into one hue of gray; when day becomes night and night becomes day—time stands still—and all that matters is that ugly pain. The scars of pain are not easily erased.

12 Once a hemophiliac successfully passes through the dangerous period, his need for blood steadily decreases and his health improves. The nightmare of youth is gradually hidden behind a protective curtain of objectivity that is seldom raised. In contrast to my childhood days, I can look back on more than three years of college with joy and a sense of achievement. I've had some good breaks. I've been in debate and forensics for four years and had a variety of satisfying experiences. I've been lucky in politics. My constituents, the student body at our college, elected me President of Student Government. Like so many other American youths, I've worked my way through college as a clerk in a hardware store. On warm weekends, while not a Ben Hogan at golf, I have shot an 82. And back home, a girl wears my wedding band.

13 For today, except for periodic transfusions, my life is as normal as anyone else's, and my aims and ambitions are the same as anyone else's. But now, a different type of social relationship needs to be found. Because a hemophiliac is so totally dependent on society during his early years and because his very existence is sometimes then precarious, society now tends to lag in recognizing the change. It sometimes fails to realize that this hemophiliac's life is no longer in serious question and that now his right to aspire to any new height should not be frowned on by a society still vividly remembering the past. Now, he seeks neither pity nor privilege. He wishes to be regarded not as a hemophiliac but rather a human being to be evaluated like any human being.

14 I cannot change that part of my life which is past. I cannot change my hemophilia. Therefore, I must ask you to help those hemophiliacs that need help. For I remember too well my older brother Herbert, so shattered in adolescence by hemophilia, that his tombstone reads like a blessing: "May 10, 1927—April 6, 1950, Thy Will be Done." And I ask you to help hemophiliacs because one day my grandson may need your blood. But I also must ask you to recognize a hemophiliac for what he is today; to realize that past is prologue, that weakness sometimes begets strength; that man sometimes conquers. And so I pray:

15 "God give me the courage to accept the things that I cannot change; the power to change the things which I can; and the wisdom always to know the difference between the two."

CULTURE AND COMMUNICATION

Robert T. Oliver

Robert T. Oliver is Chairman of the Speech Department at Pennsylvania State University. During the Second World War he held various government posts and later served as a consultant to the

Republic of Korea. On the basis of his experiences in Korea, he published several books, including one on Syngman Rhee. His stay there also sparked a concern over the problem of intercultural communication; and, in 1962, he published a book titled Culture and Communication. *He delivered an address bearing the same title at the University of Denver on August 15, 1963.*

The introductory essay in this chapter states that a speaker wishing to create concern for a problem must first explore its nature. By using a vivid illustration of the problem in his introduction, Oliver sheds some light on his subject of culture and communication even before he gets to the body of his speech. Then, in the body, he proceeds to explore the nature of the problem. Why is the use of an illustration in the introduction especially desirable in speeches designed to create a concern for problems? How clear does Oliver make the nature of the problem he is discussing? The second thing a speaker must do is to get people genuinely concerned about a problem. This step means making the problem important to his audience—making them feel that unless they show an interest, they themselves may be threatened or their own values jeopardized. What elements create concern in this particular speech? Does Oliver make the problem seem vital to the needs and values of a university audience?

Of special importance in this speech is Dr. Oliver's credibility as a source of information on intercultural communication problems. What steps does he take during the speech to enhance this credibility and how effective are his efforts?

This speech is reprinted by permission from Vital Speeches of the Day *(September 15, 1963), pp. 721–724.*

1 As a professor of Speech I feel just a bit abashed to appear here before you with a manuscript in hand. But I do it for two reasons: first, because I was asked to do so, which surely is reason enough; and second, because, as the nature of the situation suggests, I have made a special effort to set forth some ideas in more definitive form than is likely to be accomplished extemporaneously.

2 Now, even if I do have a manuscript to read from, I want to assure you that I have written it myself. I know about ghost-writers, as you do. I know about them with special cogency, because I am one myself—and therein lies a point pertinent to the problem we are considering today.

3 It happens that some time ago I engaged over a span of

months in a running discourse—you might even call it an argument—with a professor who was on our campus as a visitor from his native land of India. The subject of our discussion was the nature of certain qualities of the Oriental value system with which our own democratic heritage could most readily interlock. For months he kept insisting to me that I had the ideas almost but never quite right. Then I had occasion to ghost-write a speech for a distinguished Oriental statesman on this very theme; and in a short time it appeared in print. A day or so afterwards the Indian Professor burst in to see me with the published speech in hand and said, "I want you to read this. Here is a statement by one of my fellow Orientals that says exactly what I have been trying to tell you and says it so clearly I don't think you can miss the point." Of course I never did tell him who the author was.

4 I tell this incident with a mingling of pride and frustration. It was pleasant, of course, to win my argument with the gentleman from India—even though I was trapped by circumstances and could not tell him I had won. But it was frustrating to be reminded so vividly and dramatically that no matter how hard I tried I could not communicate my ideas to him—at least not until they seemed to come not from me but from one of his own fellows.

5 The point, I am afraid, is all too clear. When we peoples of the world try to address one another across cultural gaps, we encounter two serious kinds of difficulties. The first is that we may not and probably usually do not understand one another's point of view. And the second is that even when we do, we speak to one another essentially as strangers, as foreigners, as spokesmen for and from differing and even competing ways of life.

6 This is my introduction to the topic I have chosen to discuss with you today. In a sense, it is an epitome of the whole speech. For, in essence, it contains the message I have in mind. What follows is chiefly elaboration, or interpretation or an effort to justify or to prove, together with an implied plea that we all work harder and more cooperatively than we have in the past to try to solve the problem I am trying to define.

7 Now, in these introductory comments, I have tried to accomplish two purposes: to indicate, first, that I shall have nothing either very new or very startling to say; and second, that there are some rather commonplace facts available to all of us that ought to be considered somewhat differently than they commonly are—and that if this is done we may become significantly more successful in our attempts at international and intercultural communication. It is, as you know, one of the strange characteristics of our minds that we find the obvious almost as elusive as the abstruse—so that, as it has been said, if water were unknown, fish would be the last creatures to discover it.

8 People are smarter than fish; but I think there are some facts about our world situation that are far too completely obvious to seem to most of us to be worthy of special attention.

9 What I chiefly have in mind is the truism that we now have become citizens of the world. This surely is one of the obvious facts.

10 This is a time in history in which it is difficult to be provincial. Technology has done wonders in compressing distance, so that our large world has become a small one. There are no strange places anymore. All roads lead to wherever one happens to live, whether it be in Teutopolis, Illinois, or in Tanganyika. Not only do we hear and read about the whole world, but we also go out into it.

11 Travel is supposed to be broadening; but in my observation, many times, for many people, it is actually narrowing. The farther they get away from Dubuque, the better Dubuque looks to them. When they are confronted with a delicious platter of steamed octopus, they long for a hamburger with catsup. We may go out into the world, but we never become a part of it as long as we take our own value systems, our own habits, our own expectations with us. I have known Americans who have lived for twenty years in the Orient without ever leaving home. On the other hand, there are receptive minds that know how to establish friendly contact with foreign cultures on the first meeting with them.

12 The point I want to make can be put into one single sentence, namely: We can communicate with people in another culture only in terms that make sense to them. Prime Minister Nehru, on his visit to America in 1950, made the same point a bit more explicitly, and cogently enough to merit quotation. "If we seek to understand a people," he said, "we have to put ourselves, as far as we can, in that particular historical and cultural background. . . . One has to recognize that . . . countries and peoples differ in their approach and their ways, in their approach to life and their ways of living and thinking. In order to understand them we have to understand their way of life and approach. If we wish to convince them, we have to use their language as far as we can, not language in the narrow sense of the word, but the language of the mind."

13 Now, the cultural anthropologists have gone a long way toward defining the special characteristics of differing societies. And the historians, and the political scientists, and the economists, and the

sociologists also have gone a long way toward identifying the problems that must be solved to eliminate the clashes of interest between competing groups. We in the Speech profession have not as yet made comparable contributions toward developing rhetorical methods suitable to bridge the gaps between divergent culture groups that are now in contact but not yet in communication.

14 If we have lagged behind in confronting our own professional challenge, this fact should occasion no surprise. The divergencies in world cultures have always existed and have long been readily available for our professional colleagues to examine. But the critical need for cross-cultural understanding has come hurtling upon the world with both a speed and an urgency that were wholly unexpected. The world did not really become one community even in the thirties, with its introduction of trans-global radio, nor in the forties, with a genuinely world-wide war in progress. It is only in the past ten years or so that planes, and missiles, and space satellites and now even trans-oceanic television have made universal communication a necessity, rather than a luxury. It is only in very recent years that the peoples of every portion of the globe have come into direct confrontation—sometimes in open enmity, sometimes with a wistful effort to be friendly.

15 What we must not ignore is the desperate urgency of the need for undertaking a new approach to the problem of people-to-people communication. Not only in our Cold War struggle with communism, but also in our relations with such old and close friends as France and Canada, it is evident that the rhetoric of international communication has proved inadequate to the demands made upon it. No one, I think, will deny that the survival of our civilization, if not of the human race itself, may depend upon the speedy development of effective means of bridging culture-gaps.

16 It is a task of such importance that governmental agencies and private research foundations should be initiating, encouraging, and supporting widespread inquiries and programs directed toward its solution. Yet nowhere in the world has there yet commenced a systematic and determined effort to devise means by which peoples of divergent value systems can come into close and cordial communication. Sir Winston Churchill has said that "Jaw, jaw, is better than war, war." Yet while we strive mightily to avoid falling behind in atomic weaponry, we don't as yet study the means of engaging in an effective global dialogue.

17 As you may well guess at this point, what I am trying to do is ask questions rather than to answer them. The answering will take the work of a great many people, armed with tremendous resources. What is of most urgency now is that we should direct our attention to the right question. And in my judgment this question may be stated as follows: *Should we abandon our traditional concept of a unitary or generic rhetoric and develop the ability to deal with a complex series of divergent rhetorics?*

18 Perhaps the question sounds a bit anticlimactic! First we confront the possible apocalyptic destruction of the world—through an atomic war; then I ask you to seek salvation through an academic inquiry into the nature of rhetorical theory. Let me try rephrasing the solution we should seek: the peoples of the world need to start talking to one another in ways that make sense to the listeners. You could say that what we need is better audience analysis—but it's more than that. What we need is to learn how to hook into one another's modes of thinking. What we need is to learn how to bridge from one culture to another.

19 But this is precisely, it may be argued, what rhetoric always has intended to do. Rhetoric, in fact, has been defined as the art of using language in such a way as to produce a desired impression upon the hearer or reader. It is, then, a generic term, of universal application. Whatever the communicative barriers may be, we utilize our rhetorical tools in an effort to penetrate them. But this is not the case. We have failed to confront the essential problem.

20 Let me back away for the moment from rhetoric to look at its companion science, logic. For a great many centuries logic was also considered to be an indivisible generic term. As late as the middle of the nineteenth century, it was quite proper for the Deacon in Oliver Wendell Holmes's poem, "The Wonderful One Hoss Shay," to exclaim, "Logic is logic, that's all I say." Alcuin, Spinoza, Hobbes, Locke, Hume, and Mill could introduce amendments or refinements to Aristotle's logic; but after all, it was a cardinal characteristic of logic as a system that it was unescapable—indivisible—inevitable. The laws of connection or of relationship or of definition that it described were in fact, it was assumed, prescribed by internal necessity. To speak of conflicting systems of logic was an absurdity.

21 But, as we know, the situation today is vastly different. In addition to Aristotelianism and Korzybskian or Bogoslovskyan Anti-Aristotelianism, we have now a dozen or more divergent systems, including the Classical Symbolic, the Intuitionist, the Combinatory, the Modal, etc. Each of these logics operates within its own conceptual universe. To a considerable degree they do not so much as touch upon one another. They offer to the logician a wide range of choice of analytical and synthesizing tools for dealing with quite different types of problems.

22 This is what is happening today in the field of logic, with astonishingly productive results. Yet listen to how logic *per se*, logic as a generic term, has been and often still is defined: "Logic works by obedience to inevitable connections between objectively existent facts. Its principal test is internal coherence." From this generic conception of logic, however, it was easy to proceed to a liberating realization that any system of logic is justified if it produces valid conclusions by a consistent methodology.

23 To remain with logic for a few moments longer, let us examine an article by C. Wright Mills, entitled "Language, Logic, and Culture," which he published in 1939 in *The American Sociological Review*, and which has just been reprinted in a collection of his essays, under the title *Power, Politics, and People*. "Problems set by one logic are, with a change in interests, outgrown, not solved," Professor Mills wrote. "The rules of the game change with a shift in interests, and we must accept the dominant rules if we would make an impress upon the profile of thought. Our logical apparatus is formulated by the rebuffs and approvals received from the audiences of our thought." In the same essay he also says, "Arguments which in the discourse of one group or epoch are accepted as valid, in other times and conversations are not so received."

24 Even so rigid a logician as John Stuart Mill once wrote that if the rules of geometry had not proved to be useful, mankind would have pronounced them to be false. Now, I shall leave it to the logicians whether or not they accept this doctrine. To me it seems antithetical to the conception that logic deals with immutable relationships that are immune from the accidents of time or place. But whatever the logicians may do with it, it seems to me that we rhetoricians should welcome the statements by both Mills and Mill as a description not of logic but of rhetoric.

25 Rhetoricians are not concerned with immutable relationships but with probabilities. Our problems are not objective but subjective. Of rhetoric it surely may be said that "the rules of the game change with a shift in interests" and that "we must accept the dominant rules if we would make an impress upon the profile of thought."

26 This may seem harmless enough and simple enough. Remember, I warned you at the outset that my purpose was to emphasize the obvious. But if we simply accept what we are saying here, a tremendous difference would be introduced into the scholarship of our field. And if our professional colleagues would go along with us, it may be that collectively we could solve some of the problems of impenetrable distance that prevent the flow of understanding from one culture to another. For what this "obvious" interpretation leads to is an abandonment of the term *rhetoric,* and a replacement of it with the plural, *rhetorics.* What we would then need to deal with is not rhetoric *per se,* but a Confucian rhetoric, a Taoist rhetoric, a Buddhist rhetoric, a Communist rhetoric, a Muslim rhetoric, indeed even a Swahili rhetoric, and a Congolese rhetoric.

27 At this point it may appear that I am dealing less with the obvious than with chaos. To insist upon a different rhetoric for every different cultural entity may appear the same thing as having no rhetoric at all. I would ask us to remind ourselves, however, that our brethren in Speech Therapy made comparatively little advance upon the problem of stuttering until they recognized that it is not one problem after all, but a cluster of problems—that instead of stuttering, they are confronted with stutterings. Then, upon this revolutionary change of approach, they began to develop differential diagnoses, which, in turn, led to individuation of proposed remedies.

28 The rhetoric we think of as generic was in fact devised for a specific kind of society, with its own view of the nature of human nature. It was designed for the use of free men who have the right to cast free ballots. It was developed for individuals who were considered to be essentially rational—beset by emotionalism, of course, but finally "available" to the prescriptive conclusions of fact and logic. Its field of concern was with probabilities, or with relativistic values—with propositions concerning which a choice had to be made by weighing considerations of greater or lesser, better or worse. The decision finally, was intended to accord with the "greatest good for the greatest number" by the mechanism of a majority vote.

29 It is no accident that this rhetoric was invented by Corax in Syracuse when Syracuse adopted a democratic form of government, nor that it was elaborated and given its final structure by Aristotle for use by the self-governing minority in Athens. For the relatively closed world of Europe and America, this rhetoric has, by and large, met the pragmatic test: it has worked, at least well enough to escape serious question.

30 However, we have all of us been propelled out into a world nowadays where no single one of the presumptions upon which this rhetoric works is universally true.

31 Freedom, for example, is a matter of degree, varying widely from one country to another. Some cultures flatly reject the notion that man is rational, lending their prestige, rather, to appeals and responses based upon intuitive insight. Relativism concerning ultimate values is in some cultures regarded as a sinful philosophy, with authoritarianism the court of final appeal. Still other cultures reject the idea that a majority vote is superior—or, as in communist states, control the voting to assure virtual unanimity.

32 It is obvious, also, that in different cultures people think about different subject-matter. Industrialization, with its whole complex of problems and attitudes, means nothing to a Zulu. On the other hand, the very elaborate and all-embracing system of witchcraft of a Bushman dominates his thinking but scarcely so much as brushes against the edges of our minds. The Australian Aborigines, to cite another example, could not count beyond ten; hence their awareness of number was limited. Cultural anthropologists have multiplied such instances.

33 Beyond this, different peoples also think in different ways about the same or similar subject matter. For example, it is a matter of pride to an American boy to rise to a higher status than that of his parents. But for an Oriental it would be a cause of shame even to contemplate doing so. To us self-preservation is the first law of life. But to a Japanese who values the Shinto tradition, the state is of more consequence than the individual. Equality, individuality, and freedom of the will are valued in some cultures; whereas, subordination, conformity, and predestination are preferred in others.

34 As we all know, Benjamin Lee Whorf, following the cue of Edward Sapir, correlated some of these ideas with his study of language and formulated what has come to be known as the Sapir-Whorf Hypothesis—that language serves as a perceptual mold, shaping how people think and also influencing their choice of objects of attention or interest. And we know, too, that Harry Hoijer and his associates have directed some very telling criticism at what appears to have been Whorf's exaggeration of the dominant power of linguistic forms. Culture, these critics point out, influences language, as well as the reverse. However, both Whorf and his critics combine to direct our thinking toward the same point: namely, that language and culture together do either reflect or cause basic and significant group differences in modes of thinking.

35 We as rhetoricians can afford to be relatively indifferent to the question of whether the cultural characteristics or their linguistic expression come first. What we cannot be indifferent to is the very evident fact that every culture, by definition, constitutes a unique value system, with its own mode of thought. A Hindu cannot think as an American does; he cannot be similarly motivated; he cannot follow the same kind of mental processes. The two are unlikely to start from the same premises and even when they do they are unlikely to reach the same conclusions.

36 I don't see how anyone can doubt this interpretation. Indeed, it is less likely to be doubted than to be accepted with a shrug as being obviously true but relatively unimportant. To deny its truth would be to wipe out at one stroke the whole field of cultural anthropology and to deny to sociologists the validity of one of their key terms—culture.

37 But if it is true that every culture has its own typical mode of thinking, this fact must inevitably demand a renunciation of the concept of rhetoric, in favor of the idea of a cluster of rhetorics. It must, that is, if we think of rhetoric as a mode of thinking, comparable, let us say, to dialectic, and logic, and the so-called scientific method.

38 Within the scope of this lecture time does not permit me to develop the ideas I have so hastily sketched. For those who may wish to pursue them further, I can only suggest that they are spelled out in greater detail, with rather complete if far from exhaustive illustrations from the areas of rhetoric represented by Communism, Confucianism, Taoism, Shintoism, and the Hindu-Buddha idea system in my recent book, *Culture and Communication,* especially in Chapters VII through XII.

39 I shall conclude with a simple instance of changing the tone of an international dialogue by the use of an appropriate cultural rhetorical frame of reference.

40 I recall very well a scene of some years ago, just as daylight was breaking, on the island of Wake, in the mid-Pacific. The commercial passenger plane on which I was flying from Tokyo to San Francisco had put down to refuel, and we passengers were shepherded into the restaurant at the terminal building to have breakfast. All of us were sleepy, disheveled, and tired after a night-long flight. As a consequence, we did not feel particularly sociable. I took my seat at a small table along with two other American men, who appeared to be businessmen, and a middle-aged Japanese, who proved to be a college professor barely able to speak a few words of English.

41 None of us paid any attention to any of the others until I noticed that the Japanese was regarding his American companions with rather obvious distaste. Then I smiled at him, and handed him the salt cellar for his eggs, holding it toward him in my right hand, with the fingers of the left hand lightly touching the base of my right hand palm—a typical Japanese gesture of respect. For a moment he looked unbelievingly at the unexpected behavior of this strange foreigner. Then his face broke into a broad smile of sheer relief and I could almost hear him say to himself, "Perhaps they are not barbarians, after all." It was quite a lot to accomplish by so simple a device as knowing how to hold one's hands.

42 This, I think, is a good point at which to come to rest. The change in theory and in method for which I am asking is neither complex nor considerable. But if we should make the shift and learn how to operate upon the concept of multiple rhetorics, the change in effect might be as great as was the change in medicine when Pasteur said to his colleagues, "It is not vapour or dirt, gentlemen, that carries the disease, but germs."

A PLAGUE OF PEOPLE

Daniel R. Crary

Daniel R. Crary was a senior at the University of Kansas when he won first place with this speech in the school's annual Delta Sigma Rho Public Affairs Speaking Contest in April 1963.

Crary begins his address by graphically illustrating the population explosion. How does he use evidence to develop an awareness of this problem and to make the fact of the burgeoning population vivid for his audience? Do you think that any listener would be likely to dispute the existence of the increase? As you read the speech, note any characteristics of style that supplement Crary's evidence and help make his material especially vivid.

Also note that Crary's introduction not only states and illustrates the problem but also suggests that it holds a threat for the audience. The body of his speech then explores the nature of the problem and its implications for society. Do you think the introduction is effective in setting up the subject of the speech or do you find it confusing? How does Crary give scope to the significance of the problem in the body of the speech? What values does he indicate as threatened? Does he make these threats seem to be of a vital nature?

At the close of a speech designed to create concern for a problem, the listener should feel a sense of urgency. How does the speaker try to make his problem especially vital and urgent in his conclusion? Does he capitalize on the title of his speech to secure a feeling of urgency?

This speech is reprinted by permission of Mr. Crary.

1 In Los Angeles, California, during rush hour on a heavily traveled, fog-shrouded freeway twelve-lanes-wide, a woman's car blew a tire, careened to the side of the lane and stopped. But out of the fog came another car which could not stop in time, and it struck the first . . . and another and another until one of the worst automobile accidents in history had involved a string of 200 cars, over a mile long, and had resulted in one death and several injuries.

2 In February, the United Nations called together several thousands of the world's experts in science and technology to the greatest conference of its kind ever held. The purpose: the application of science and technology to the needs of the world's emerging and under-developed countries.

3 The powerful leader of millions of Red Chinese has declared repeatedly that he will arm his people with nuclear bombs and missiles.

4 Now, at first glance, each of the things I have mentioned seem unrelated, but in fact they all have something very much in common. They are all things which have a direct bearing on something which was predicted in the waning years of the 18th century by a rather obscure British scholar and theologian. This man was Thomas Malthus, who was one of the first to recognize that the issue of crowded population in some areas was to become a world-wide issue.

5 It was the Malthusian Theory which stated generally that population growth proceeds geometrically, while the available food supply increases arithmetically. This is like saying that both food and population increase, but with the population, the *increase itself* increases, to the extent that eventually the number of people in the world will outstrip the food supply. For a moment let's look at the incredible and almost unbelievable facts of that fulfillment of Malthus' fears.

6 It has been estimated that at the beginning of the Christian era the population of the world was something like 300 million. Today, 1,960 years later, the world population is estimated just at three billion, ten times greater than it was in New Testament days. But the best

conservative information, which is now available from United Nations demographers, says flatly that this increase in population, which has taken us nearly 2,000 years, is going to be *repeated,* not in 2,000 years, but in 40. The 1958 publication, *Future Growth of World Population* from the U.N. states that the population of the world by 2,000 A.D. will be seven billion. I suppose we've all heard population-explosion statistics, which are designed to scare us into subscribing to some socially beneficient endeavor or another, but the United Nations is not passing the hat or trying to scare anyone when it says this (and I quote): "With the present rate of increase, it can be calculated that in 600 years the number of human beings on earth will be such that there will be only one-square meter for each to live on." Now this puts into question one of the rather old and often-used jokes, which goes: "If all the people of the world were laid end-to-end around the equator, they'd be more comfortable." But if the United Nations facts are correct, in a few hundred years it may be decidedly more comfortable to stand, thank you. That is purely speculative, but the expectation that world population is going to double in the next 35 or 40 years is not just a speculative game played with almanac and slide-rule. Rather this incredible prospect is the logical implication of what we know to be the facts. And the results are already becoming clear.

7 The United States, of course, is beginning to wake up to the domestic implications of the population question. Here at home, we are building millions of dollars of superhighways, automobiles, homes, and new businesses to keep up with demand for them. Experts are predicting here at Kansas University that in 20 years the United States will have a dozen or more supercities, larger than anything we now know. One of these will be Kansas City, whose western limits will be somewhere between Lawrence and Topeka. With greater population in the United States has come great social and economic problems: racial strife in crowded and teeming cities, and unemployment almost everywhere. And the prospects for more spectacular fender-crunching sessions are very promising.

8 On the international scene the spectacular rise in population has some challenging, and sometimes rather frightening, aspects. For example, a deeper analysis of the facts of population shows that most of the increase in the next 40 years is going to occur not in Europe, which actually has one of the lowest rates of increase in the world, *and* not in the United States—either of which would be infinitely better able to sustain this increase than those nations where it is occurring. In fact, the vast majority of substantial population increases are to be found in

the less developed countries, many of which sustain annual population increases of over twice that of the world average. And this is important too, because many authorities believe that the important world decisions of the next decades are going to be influenced by, if not *made in*, these emerging areas. So, we give billions a year, international conferences are held, and organizations are established to give money and food, to apply science and technology, and to industrialize. How are we doing in this? We are facing tremendous odds. For example, the country of Brazil is developing economically but can barely keep up with the rise in population. In India, population increases *every year* by the total population of Canada! Egypt's Aswan Dam, which was to spur Egypt to greater economic heights, will soon be completed, but when it is, Egypt's economy will be behind what it was before the construction began, because the population has grown faster than the benefits of the project. According to statistics of the United Nations and the International Monetary Fund, these examples are typical of 70 to 80 per cent of all less developed countries. Instead of advancing economically, in terms of population growth and internal problems they are stagnating or regressing.

9 The number of people in the world is also having an effect in the communist nations. Western leaders who have been able to arm themselves into a position where they feel the U.S.S.R. is unlikely to risk nuclear war, are stumped by Mao Tse-Tung's statement that when Red China acquires nuclear power she *will* declare unlimited war with the West. And Mao admits that millions of Chinese would be killed in such a war, but he says that because of the huge increase in Chinese population elimination of even a majority of China's millions would be the best thing that ever happened to the People's Republic of China.

10 So to say that the world is getting smaller doesn't only have meaning in terms of transportation but also in terms of the food, territory, and opportunities available for every man. Medical science curbs disease, protects childbirth, and makes the old live longer. More and more people are born, and the masses who are the most deprived are doing the most to insure that their problems will multiply.

11 It is urgent that all nations realize that the problem exists and gather information about it. As elementary as this seems, the population explosion remains one of our most neglected social problems. Major religions need to examine their positions on the question of birth control; and this applies not only to the Roman Catholic Church, which disavows use of artifical methods of birth control but which, at the same time, has made some of the most significant pronouncements regarding family planning and responsibility; it also applies to other churches, which need to pursue the moral issues at hand in this problem. National governments are going to have to investigate the role of government in population control, inasmuch as the dimensions of the crisis has made it the property of society.

12 Whatever eventual course of action is taken, we must realize that some action must be taken without delay. Since I have been speaking, hundreds of people have died and several hundreds have been born. But during this ten minutes, the total world population has increased by a thousand people. These thousand people are going to need food and space in which to live, it's true. But they're going to need more—much more. They are going to need access to the world's resources of educational and economic opportunities and access to opportunities to make their own descendants' world a reasonably livable one. The question of whether they'll have that chance is a very important one to answer because by now the number has risen to nearly 1,100.

ON MOUSETRAPS

Sally Webb

A student at Southeast Missouri State College, Sally Webb delivered this speech as a representative for her state in the 1963 Interstate Oratorical Contest held at Northwestern University. Miss Webb's speech creates concern for a problem of values, that of thinking in terms of stereotypes. As you read the speech, you will observe that she establishes the seriousness of the problem by pointing out some of the harmful results it produces. She underscores these dangers by also showing that careless stereotyping is often at the root of other problems. In what ways does the problem involve violation of certain social values or ideals? Does this kind of stereotyping seem thoroughly repugnant by the end of the speech?

"On Mousetraps" is a one-point speech *in which Miss Webb brings many factual and hypothetical illustrations to bear on the same problem and thus makes its various dimensions vivid to her audience. The success of this talk depends upon how well these illustrations make listeners aware of the existence, scope, and repugnancy of her one*

point, stereotyping. Analyze carefully the relative merits of each of the illustrations used in fulfilling this objective. Do they all contribute a slightly different view to the problem or do some of them seem redundant?

This speech is reprinted by permission from Winning Orations, 1963 (*Evanston, Ill.: The Interstate Oratorical Association, 1963*), *pp. 31–33.*

1 In the local newspaper of my community recently, there was a story about a man named Virgil Spears. He lived in a small town about 40 miles from my home. He had served five years in the Missouri State Penitentiary for passing bogus checks. When he returned to his family, Mr. Spears couldn't find a job. Everyone knew he was an ex-con and everyone knew that ex-cons aren't to be trusted. Finally in what was described as calm desperation, he walked into a local barbershop where he was well known, pulled a gun, and took all the money the barber had. Up to this point it had been a fairly routine robbery, but then something unusual happened. Mr. Spears didn't try to get away. He got into his car, drove slowly out of town, and waited for the highway patrol. When they caught him, he made only one request. He turned to the arresting patrolman and said: "Would you please ask that the court put my family on welfare just as soon as possible?"

2 To the people of Clarkston, Missouri, Virgil Spears wasn't to be trusted because he was an ex-con. And their thinking about Virgil Spears was similar to the thinking of the late Senator Theodore Bilbo of Mississippi about Ralph Bunche, Under Secretary of the United Nations. When Dr. Bunche and Senator Bilbo were introduced several years ago, the Senator refused to shake hands with Dr. Bunche. Later, a friend asked the Senator, "Why didn't you shake his hand?" Senator Bilbo replied, "I don't care if he has a Ph.D. A 'coon' is a 'coon'."

3 Virgil Spears is back in jail. His fellow townspeople have put him there. Theodore Bilbo died still denying himself the possibility of enriching his life through contacts with the winner of the 1950 Nobel Peace Prize. These men and millions of others suffer the consequences of stupidity, not illiterate stupidity but the kind of ignorance the noted psychologist Dr. Gordon Allport has described as "the commonest trick of the human mind." We don't look at what people do, we think in terms of what people are. After we've decided what they are, too frequently we stop paying attention to what they do. For many people, once they learn that Virgil Spears is an ex-con, he never appears the

same again. And this is understandable because we've been trained to think that way. As children, we see details; but when we go to school we're taught, perhaps too well, to classify, to order, to categorize. And our perception of details and differences decrease. Much of your education and my education has been like this. It's a beautiful system. Once you learn what traits canines, felines, and bovines have, you know how you should react to the cats, dogs, and cows you meet on the street. That's the system. It provides some order. It also provides misunderstanding, misery, and lots of trouble.

4 The late Irving Lee of Northwestern University told a story about a Jewish merchant named Goldstein, who moved into a small community. One night Mr. Goldstein heard a knock at his door and found one of his neighbors there. The man was obviously embarrassed. He didn't quite know how to start what he had to say. Finally, he said, "Mr. Goldstein, I don't know how to tell you this, but I've been selected by a neighborhood committee to ask you to move." Mr. Goldstein asked, "But why? Have I cheated someone or offended anyone?" The caller replied, "You don't understand, Mr. Goldstein. You haven't cheated someone or offended anyone. We don't have anything against you. You just don't understand." Mr. Goldstein hesitated, looked calmly at his visitor, and finally said, "I think I do understand. What you're saying is when you look at me, you don't see me." And he was right.

5 All of us know in a vague sort of way that the world isn't made up of things with characteristics. The world is composed of people and objects, which are all to some extent different from one another. The nub of our education has to be to teach us to see those differences and evaluate their significance, whether those differences are great or small. And in this regard, some people, even some with several college degrees, are woefully uneducated.

6 I recently read a story of a personnel manager, a college graduate, who wouldn't employ a blind man. The man wanted to work as a typist in a department-store order room, where employees typed orders dictated over the telephone. The man kept saying, "Just give me a chance. I know I can do it." The executive's reply was, "But you're blind." Because of this classification, he kept overlooking the fact that the man was also an expert typist, a conscientious worker, and a careful listener. A company and a handicapped man both lost because that personnel manager took the easy way. It's easier to think in terms of gross classifications than in terms of subtle differences.

7 A graduate of my school, Mr. Jerry McNeely, has written a play entitled *The Staring Match*, which won the Writers' Guild Award for the Best Television Drama of the 1957–1958 Season. In the play Mr. McNeely deals with the same idea I've been discussing with you. You may remember this play. Its setting is a small community. The water supply of the town is quickly drying up and people know that in order to survive they must find a new source of water. Time is precious. They're unable to decide where their digging should be concentrated, when two strangers appear in town. One stranger is dressed completely in white and is called Mr. White. The other man is dressed completely in black. His name is Mr. Black. Each claims to know where the new well should be dug, but they disagree about the spot. Some of the people follow Mr. White, arguing that he "must be an angel of the Lord" and insisting that the man in black "must be an emissary of Satan." But no one knows for certain. Finally, they decide to use an old folk custom to decide. They'll have a staring match. In the staring match the two men must stand inside a circle of townsfolk, gazing at one another until one drops from exhaustion. The winner, of course, will be sustained by the power of goodness, and therefore must be the one who knows where the water will be found. In the play Mr. White and Mr. Black stood in the circle and stared at each other. Neither one broke the gaze, and finally the spectators began to tire. Suddenly, a little girl on the edge of the crowd fainted. One of the adversaries saw her out of the corner of his eye. He broke the gaze and ran to the child to pick her up. The man was Mr. Black. The play ends here, but its questions remain. Is the angel of the Lord the man who lost the staring match out of compassion for another human being, or is the angel the man who won the staring match? According to the classification system of the townsfolk, Mr. White is the angel. But, I'm not so sure. The answer shouldn't come from classifications. The answer ought to come from observations and lots of them, for observations are the very essence of wisdom.

8 Those people who classify but don't observe are gradually decreasing in number, but we face daily reminders of their presence. They range from the tragedy of Virgil Spears to the travesty of Theodore Bilbo to the bizarre segregation of animal cemeteries in Washington, D.C., in which dogs belonging to colored families aren't permitted to be buried beside dogs belonging to white families. As long as we govern our actions by classification systems without tempering those classifications with careful and continuous observations, we'll continue to have those same problems. Men like Virgil Spears won't be able to support their families. Goldsteins will be asked to move. One recent writer has put it succinctly: He said, "To a mouse, cheese is cheese and

that's why mousetraps are effective." You and I know, however, that there is cheese, and there is cheese, and there is cheese. We also know and should busy ourselves teaching others that there are people, and there are people, and there are people.

WHO IS TAMPERING WITH THE SOUL OF AMERICA?

Jenkin Lloyd Jones

Jenkin Lloyd Jones, editor of the Tulsa Tribune *since 1941 and recipient of the William Allen White Award from the American Society of Newspaper Editors in 1957, first delivered this speech before the Inland Daily Press Association in Chicago, on October 16, 1961. He gave substantially the same address to the American Society of Newspaper Editors at New Orleans on April 18, 1962.*

In direct constrast to "On Mousetraps" by Sally Webb, this speech covers many points. In fact, Jones makes a rather complete examination of the "moral failures" of contemporary American society. Does the broad scope of his speech topic present any special problems?

As you read the introduction of this speech, observe the special role historical example and the lamentations of Jeremiah play in developing a rationale and justification for the type of speech Jones is about to give. Does the introduction set a proper tone for the speech?

To demonstrate that contemporary America suffers from a moral failure, Jones uses value judgments. Keep this fact in mind as you read the speech and search for answers to these questions: Are the value standards Jones employs primarily his personal ones or are they part of the established moral fabric of American society? How adequately does he prove his charges about American morals? Does he make any unwarranted generalizations? How well, for example, does he prove his assertion that there is a causal relationship between progressive education and its results, such as juvenile delinquincy and low educational achievement? What threat appeals does Jones use to create concern for the problem of American morals?

In paragraph 49, in which Jones formulates a list of suggestions, his apparent intent is to present a solution for the problem he has outlined. Do you think these suggestions are clear-cut and well-defined? Do you feel that he presents a sufficiently comprehensive plan or course of action to warrant classifying this speech as one that advocates a policy?

This speech is reprinted by permission from Vital Speeches of the Day *(January 1, 1962), pp. 180–183.*

1 This afternoon I am about to inflict upon you a jeremiad. Long before the prophet, Jeremiah, uttered his lamentations about the evil behavior of the Children of Israel the world had seen many calamity-howlers. We have cunieform tablets describing the moral decay of Babylon and Chaldea. We have hieroglyphic inscriptions predicting that Osiris and Ra will smite the Egyptians for their wickedness. And so when I rise today and make some comments about the moral climate of America, and about our responsibilities therefor as temporary custodians of America's press, I speak in a very old tradition.

2 The calamity howler! It is customary to dismiss such fogeyism as I am about to display with a tolerant laugh. For while it was freely predicted all through the ages that the world was going to Hell, it hasn't gone to Hell yet. Who can deny that in practically all the crafts and certainly all of the sciences we are farther advanced than we ever have been? Why not be cheerfully optimistic?

3 I think I can tell you why. Human progress has never been steady. It has washed back and forth like waves upon a beach. Happily, there has also been an incoming tide, so the waves have washed higher and higher as each great civilization came on.

4 But the pathway of history is littered with the bones of dead states and fallen empires. And they were not, in most cases, promptly replaced by something better. Nearly a thousand years elapsed between the fall of Western Rome and the rise of the Renaissance, and in between we had the Dark Ages in which nearly all of man's institutions were inferior to those which had gone before. I don't want my children's children to go through a couple of centuries of dialectic materialism before the sun comes up again.

5 So the Jeremiahs haven't been so wrong, after all. It is sad to watch the beginnings of decay. It is sad to see an Age of Pericles replaced by the drunken riots of Alcibiades. There was, indeed, just cause for gloom when into the palaces of the Caesars went Nero and

Caligula, and when the once-noble Praetorian Guard became a gang of assassins willing to sell the throne to the top bidder.

6 Alaric's Goths finally poured over the walls of Rome. But it was not that the walls were low. It was that Rome, itself, was low. The sensual life of Pompeii, the orgies on Lake Trasimene, the gradually weakened fibre of a once self-disciplined people that reduced them at last to seeking safety in mercenaries and the payment of tribute—all these brought Rome down. She went down too early. She had much to teach the world.

7 And so, ladies and gentlemen, I look upon our own country and much that I see disturbs me. But we are a great people. We have a noble tradition. We have much to teach the world, and if America should go down soon it would be too early.

8 One thing is certain. We shall be given no centuries for a leisurely and comfortable decay. We have an enemy now—remorseless, crude, brutal and cocky. However much the leaders of the Communist conspiracy may lie to their subjects about our motives, about our conditions of prosperity, about our policies and aims, one thing they believe themselves implicitly—and that is that we are in an advanced state of moral decline.

9 When Nikita Khrushchev visited Hollywood he was shown only one movie set, that of a wild dance scene in Can-Can. He said it represented decadence and I am sure he really thought so. It is a dogma of current Communist faith that America is Sodom and Gomorrah, ripening for the kill.

10 Do you know what scares me about the Communists? It is not their political system, which is primitive and savage. It is not their economic system which works so badly that progress in a few directions is purchased at the price of progress in all the rest. It is their puritanism. It is their dedication and self-sacrifice.

11 It does no good to comfort ourselves with the reflection that these are products of endless brainwashings, of incessant propaganda, of deprivation by censorship and jamming of counter-information and contrary arguments. The dedication is there. The confidence that they are morally superior is there.

12 The naive questions of your Intourist guide reveal only too quickly that she thinks she is talking to a self-indulgent fop from the court of some latter-day Louis XIV. In the school yard the children rush up to show you, not their yo-yos, but their scholarship medals. And when you offer them new Lincoln pennies as souvenirs they rip off their little Young Pioneer buttons and hand them to you, proud that they are not taking gifts, but are making a fair exchange.

13 The Russian stage is as austere as the Victorian stage. Russian literature may be corny but it is clean, and it glorifies the Russian people and exudes optimism and promise. Russian art is stiffly representational, but the paintings and the sculpture strive to depict beauty and heroism—Russian beauty, of course, and Russian heroism.

14 And what of us?

15 Well, ladies and gentlemen, let's take them one at a time.

16 We are now at the end of the third decade of the national insanity known as "progressive education." This was the education where everybody passes, where the report cards were non-committal lest the failure be faced with the fact of his failure, where all moved at a snail pace like a transatlantic convoy so that the slowest need not be left behind, and all proceeded toward adulthood in the lockstep of "togetherness." Thus the competition that breeds excellence was to be sacrificed for the benefit of something called "life adjustment."

17 With what results? We have watched juvenile delinquency climb steadily. We have produced tens of thousands of high school graduates who move their lips as they read and cannot write a coherent paragraph. While our Russian contemporaries, who were supposed to be dedicated to the mass man, have been busy constructing an elite we have been engaged in the wholesale production of mediocrity. What a switch!

18 When was the last time you, as editors and publishers, examined the curricula of your local schools? How did your schools rank on the standardized Iowa tests? When have you looked at your schools' report cards and the philosophy behind their grading system? Have you asked to examine any senior English themes? Have you offered any recognition to your schools' best scholars to compare to the recognition you accord your schools' best football players?

19 For the funny thing about "progressive educators" is that theory vanishes when the referee's whistle blows for the kick-off. In the classroom they pretend to grade subjectively; against the student's supposed capacity, lest he be humiliated by natural inadequacy. But on the football field they never put in a one-legged halfback on the theory that, considering his disability, he's a great halfback. They put in the best halfback they've got, period. The ungifted sit on the bench or back in the stands even though they, too, might thirst for glory. If our schools were as anxious to turn out brains as they are to turn out winning football teams this strange contradiction wouldn't exist.

20 Having neglected disciplines in education it was quite logical that we should reject disciplines in art. The great painters and sculptors of the past studied anatomy so diligently that they often indulged in their own bodysnatching. And today, after many centuries, we stare at the ceiling of the Sistine Chapel or at the walls of the Reichsmusee and marvel at their works.

21 But this self-discipline is of little concern to the modern non-objective painter. All he needs is pigment and press agent. He can throw colors at a canvas and the art world will discover him. He can stick bits of glass, old rags and quids of used chewing tobacco on a board and he is a social critic. He can drive a car back and forth in pools of paint and *Life* magazine will write him up.

22 Talent is for squares. What you need is vast effrontery. If you undertake to paint a cow it must look something like a cow. That takes at least a sign-painter's ability. But you can claim to paint a picture of your psyche and no matter what the result who is to say what your psyche looks like? So our museums are filled with daubs being stared at by confused citizens who haven't the guts to admit they are confused.

23 But the Age-of-Fakery in art is a mild cross that American civilization bears. Much more serious is our collapse of moral standards and the blunting of our capacity for righteous indignation.

24 Our Puritan ancestors were preoccupied with sin. They were too preoccupied with it. They were hag-ridden and guilt-ridden and theirs was a repressed and neurotic society. But they had horsepower. They wrested livings from rocky land, built our earliest colleges, started our literature, caused our industrial revolution, and found time in between to fight the Indians, the French and the British, to bawl for abolition, women suffrage and prison reform, and to experiment with graham crackers and bloomers. They were a tremendous people.

25 And for all their exaggerated attention to sin, their philosophy rested on a great granite rock. Man was the master of his soul. You didn't have to be bad. You could and should be better. And if you wanted to escape the eternal fires you'd damned well better be.

26 In recent years all this has changed in America. We have decided that sin is largely imaginary. We have become enamoured with "behavioristic psychology." This holds that a man is a product of his heredity and his environment, and his behavior to a large degree is foreordained by both. He is either a product of a happy combination of genes and chromosomes or an unhappy combination. He moves in an environment that will tend to make him good or that will tend to make him evil. He is just a chip tossed helplessly by forces beyond his control and, therefore, not responsible.

27 Well, the theory that misbehavior can be cured by pulling down tenements and erecting in their places elaborate public housing is not holding water. The crime rates continue to rise along with our outlays for social services. We speak of underprivilege. Yet the young men who swagger up and down the streets, boldly flaunting their gang symbols on their black jackets, are far more blessed in creature comforts, opportunities for advancement, and freedom from drudgery than 90 per cent of the children of the world. We have sown the dragon's teeth of pseudo-scientific sentimentality, and out of the ground has sprung the legion bearing switch-blade knives and bicycle chains.

28 Clearly something is missing. Could it be what the rest of the world's children have been given—the doctrine of individual responsibility?

29 Relief is gradually becoming an honorable career in America. It is a pretty fair life, if you have neither conscience nor pride. The politicians will weep over you. The state will give a mother a bonus for her illegitimate children, and if she neglects them sufficiently she can save enough out of her ADC payments to keep herself and her boy friend in wine and gin. Nothing is your fault. And when the city fathers of a harassed community like Newburgh suggest that able bodied welfare clients might sweep the streets the "liberal" editorialists arise as one man and denounce them for their medieval cruelty.

30 I don't know how long Americans can stand this erosion of principle. But I believe that some of my starry-eyed friends are kidding themselves when they pretend that every planeload of Puerto Ricans that puts down at Idlewild is equivalent in potential to every shipload of Pilgrims that put into old Plymouth. Nations are built by people capable of great energy and self-discipline. I never heard of one put together by cha-cha-cha.

31 The welfare state that taxes away the rewards for responsible behavior so that it can remove the age-old penalties for irresponsible behavior is building on a foundation of jelly. It is time we stopped this elaborate pretense that there is no difference between the genuinely unfortunate and the mobs of reliefers who start throwing bottles every time the cops try to make a legitimate arrest.

32 Finally, there is the status of our entertainment and our literature.

33 Can anyone deny that movies are dirtier than ever? But they don't call it dirt. They call it "realism." Why do we let them fool us? Why do we nod owlishly when they tell us that filth is merely a daring art form, that licentiousness is really social comment? Isn't it time we recognized Hollywood's quest for the fast buck for what it is? Isn't it plain that the financially-harassed movie industry is putting gobs of sex in the darkened drive-ins in an effort to lure curious teen-agers away from their TV sets? Last week the screen industry solemnly announced that henceforth perversion and homosexuality would no longer be barred from the screen provided the subjects were handled with "delicacy and taste." Good Lord!

34 And we of the press are a party to the crime. Last year the movie ads in our newspaper got so salacious and suggestive that the advertising manager and I decided to throw out the worst and set up some standards. We thought that due to our ukase there might be some interruption in advertising some shows. But no. Within a couple of hours the exhibitors were down with much milder ads. How was this miracle accomplished?

35 Well, it seems that the exhibitors are supplied with several different ads for each movie. If the publishers are dumb enough to accept the most suggestive ones those are what they get. But if publishers squawk the cleaner ads are sent down. Isn't it time we all squawked?

36 I think it's time we quit giving page 1 play to the extramarital junkets of crooners. I think it is time we stopped treating as glamorous and exciting the brazen shack-ups of screen tramps. I think it is time we asked our Broadway and Hollywood columnists if they can't find something decent and inspiring going on along their beats.

37 And the stage: They raided Minsky's so Minsky's has spread all over town. Bawdiness has put on a dinner jacket, and seats in the orchestra that used to go for six-bits at the Old Howard and Nichols' Gayety are now scaled at $8.80. Oh, yes. And we have lots of "realism." Incestuous Americans. Perverted Americans. Degenerate Americans. Murderous Americans.

38 How many of these "realistic" Americans do you know?

39 Two months ago an American touring company, sponsored by the State Department and paid for by our tax dollars, presented one of Tennessee Williams' more depraved offerings to an audience in Rio de Janeiro. The audience hooted in disgust and walked out. And where did it walk to? Right across the street where a Russian ballet company was putting on a beautiful performance for the glory of Russia! How dumb can we get?

40 We are drowning our youngsters in violence, cynicism and sadism piped into the living room and even the nursery. The grandchildren of the kids who used to weep because The Little Match Girl froze to death now feel cheated if she isn't slugged, raped and thrown into a Bessemer converter.

41 And there's our literature. The old eye-poppers of the past, which tourists used to smuggle back from Paris under their dirty shirts, are now tame stuff. Compared to some of our modern slush, "Ulysses" reads like the minutes of the Epworth League. "Lady Chatterley's Lover" has been draped with the mantle of art, and it is now on sale in the corner drugstore to your high-school-age son or daughter for 50c. Henry Miller's "Tropic of Cancer," which resembles a collection of inscriptions taken from privy walls, is about to join Lady Chatterley. The quick-buck boys have apparently convinced our bumfuzzled judges that there is no difference between a peep show and a moral lecture.

42 And, of course, we have our latter-day historical novels in which the romance of man's upward movement from savagery is lost in a confused welter of bundlings and tumblings. The foreign reader of one of these epics on the development of the American West must marvel that our forefathers found time to quell the Comanches, plow up Kansas and build the transcontinental railroad while spending practically all their time in the hay.

43 Don Maxwell of *The Chicago Tribune* has recently asked his book department to quit advertising scatological literature by including it in the list of best sellers. The critics and the book publishers have denounced him for tampering with the facts. I would like to raise a somewhat larger question: Who is tampering with the soul of America?

44 For nations do have souls. They have collective personalities. People who think well of themselves collectively exhibit elan and enthusiasm and morale. When nations cease believing in themselves, when they regard their institutions with cynicism and their traditions with flippancy they will not long remain great nations. When they seek learning without effort and wages without work they are beginning to stagger. Where they become hedonistic and pleasure-oriented, when their Boy Scouts on their 14-mile hikes start to hitch, there's trouble ahead. Where payola becomes a way of life, expense account cheating common, and union goonery a fiercely defended "right" that nation is in danger. And where police departments attempt to control burglary by the novel method of making it a department monopoly then the chasm yawns.

45 Ladies and gentlemen: do not let me overdraw the picture. This is still a great, powerful, vibrant, able, optimistic nation. Americans—our readers—do believe in themselves and their country.

46 But there is rot and there is blight and there is cutting out and filling to be done if we, as the leader of free men, are to survive the hammer blows which quite plainly are in store for us all.

47 We have reached the stomach-turning point. We have reached the point where we should re-examine the debilitating philosophy of permissiveness. Let this not be confused with the philosophy of liberty. The school system that permits our children to develop a quarter of their natural talents is not a champion of our liberties. The healthy man who chooses to loaf on unemployment compensation is not a defender of human freedom. The playwright who would degrade us, the author who would profit from pandering to the worst that's in us, are no friends of ours.

48 It is time we hit the sawdust trail. It is time we revived the idea that there is such a thing as sin—just plain old willful sin. It is time we brought self-discipline back into style. And who has a greater responsibility at this hour than we, the gentlemen of the press?

49 So I suggest: Let's look to our educational institutions at the local level, and if Johnny can't read by the time he's ready to get married let's find out why.

50 Let's look at the distribution of public largesse and if, far from alleviating human misery, it is producing the sloth and irresponsibility that intensifies it, let's get it fixed.

51 Let's quit being bulldozed and bedazzled by self-appointed longhairs. Let's have the guts to say that a book is dirt if that's what we think of it, or that a painting may well be a daub if you can't figure out which way to hang it. And if some beatnik welds together a collection of rusty cogwheels and old corset stays and claims it's a greater sculpture than Michelangelo's "David" let's have the courage to say that it looks like junk and probably is.

52 Let's blow the whistle on plays that would bring blushes to an American Legion stag party. Let's not be awed by movie characters with barnyard morals even if some of them have been photographed climbing aboard the Presidential yacht. Let us pay more attention in our news columns to the decent people everywhere who are trying to do something for the good of others.

53 In short, gentlemen, let's cover up the cesspool and start planting some flowers.

54 Well, that's the jeremiad. I never thought I'd deliver one of these. I never dreamed I'd go around sounding like an advance man for the Watch-and-Ward Society. I used to consider myself quite a liberal young man. I still think that on some people bikinis look fine.

55 But I am fed up to here with the educationists and pseudo-social scientists who have under-rated our potential as a people. I am fed up to here with the medicine men who try to pass off pretense for art and prurience for literature. I am tired of seeing America debased and low-rated in the eyes of foreigners. And I am genuinely disturbed that to idealistic youth in many countries the fraud of Communism appears synonymous with morality, while we, the chief repository of real freedom, are regarded as being in the last stages of decay.

56 We can learn a lesson from history. Twice before our British cousins appeared heading into a collapse of principle, and twice they drew themselves back. The British court reached an advanced stage of corruption under the Stuarts. But the people rebelled. And in the wild days of George IV and William IV it looked as though Britain were rotting out again. But the people banged through the reform laws, and under Victoria went on to the peak of their power.

57 In this hour of fear, confusion and self-doubt let this be the story of America. Unless I misread the signs a great number of our people are ready. Let there be a fresh breeze, a breeze of new honesty, new idealism, new integrity.

58 And there, gentlemen, is where you come in. You have typewriters, presses and a huge audience.

59 How about raising hell?

Chapter Eight

SPEECHES THAT AFFIRM PROPOSITIONS OF POLICY

Whenever men have been free to choose their personal or corporate destinies, speakers have risen to advocate courses of action. Aristotle observed this phenomenon in ancient Greece. So too may we in modern America. When the President of the United States stands before a television camera to encourage popular approval of a Supreme Court ruling, he is proposing a course of action. When an assemblyman stands at the rostrum of a state legislative body to recommend adoption of a new taxation program, he is advocating a proposition of policy. When a social reformer urges the abolition of capital punishment or a union official, the rejection of a contract or a theologian, an end to doctrinal conflict or a politician, a vote in his behalf, they are all engaged in the affirmation of policies of individual or collective action. That this form of advocacy is of central importance in a free society has long been recognized. Aristotle, having observed speakers as they exhorted and dissuaded legislative and popular assemblies on future action, treated the essential constraints of this speech form under the heading of *deliberative* rhetoric. Although societies have grown increasingly complex, the speaker of today who would give counsel on matters of personal or collective behavior is governed by the same kind of constraints Aristotle noted in his time.

CONSTRAINTS IMPOSED BY SPEECH PURPOSE

Although speakers try to win acceptance of propositions of fact and value and create concern for problems on the basis that they are *true, good,* or *significant,* they affirm propositions of policy because they believe they are *necessary* and/or *desirable.* However, an advocate affirming a proposition of policy may affirm related propositions of fact and value in order to establish a need for action. For example, a speaker who is trying to demonstrate that it is expedient and practical for "the federal government to subsidize the higher education of superior students" may first affirm these propositions of fact and value: "that many qualified high school graduates are unable to attend college for financial reasons"; "that the development of the nation's intellectual resources is socially desirable"; or "that the loss of intellectual resources constitutes a significant economic problem in America."

Though stereotyped formulas must be qualified when applied to popular discourse, they do provide a starting point for the analysis of propositions of policy. In 1922, Shaw,[1] presenting a specimen analysis of Edmund Burke's speech, "On Conciliation with the American Colonies," applied the four commonly identified issues of propositions of policy: (1) Is some change from the present policy of taxation necessary to restore peace in America? (2) Would Burke's policy of conciliation restore peace in America? (3) Would Burke's policy of conciliation introduce new and worse evils? (4) Would any other policy be more satisfactory than Burke's policy of conciliation? Although these stock issues— (1) Is there a need for a change from the status quo? (2) Is the proposed course of action capable of meeting this need? (3) Do the advantages of the proposed policy outweigh its disadvantages? and (4) Is it the best solution to the problem?—ask the questions each advocate must basically answer in preparing for popular discourse, he may in practice considerably abbreviate the process.

Although the advocate may sometimes find it expedient to explore each of these points publicly, he may at other times find it unnecessary to consider all of them. He may neglect to elaborate on a problem because he is confident that his audience shares his concern for it. He may avoid a detailed statement of policy because he believes it sufficient to show that a general course of action is in some ways superior to the philosophy currently pursued. He may avoid mention of the negative effects of a proposed policy because he feels that such an analysis runs counter to his best interests as an advocate. He may pose a theoretical ideal and demonstrate the superiority of his course of action in the light of that ideal. But whatever the demands of his audience, setting, or subject, the speaker who seeks to affirm a proposition of policy must demonstrate that the course of action he proposes is *necessary* and/or *desirable* (or that a course of action he hopes to

[1] W. C. Shaw, *The Art of Debate* (Boston: Allyn and Bacon, 1922), pp. 201–202.

deprecate is *unnecessary* and/or *undesirable*), and that the consequences of his proposal will be beneficial to his audience.

CONSTRAINTS IMPOSED BY THE PARTICULAR AUDIENCE

Whenever a speaker seeks to affirm a proposition of policy, he must be aware of the *interest* his subject holds for his audience. A senator who speaks, in turn, to an assembly of high school students and a convention of the American Medical Association on socialized medicine will experience quite different interpretations of this constraint. In the first instance, the members of his audience will be less interested in the measure because at their age they normally will not be affected much by the consequences of the legislation nor be directly able to influence its passage. In the second instance, his audience is both immediately involved with the consequences of the legislation and in a position to influence its passage through a corporate lobby. While in the first situation the speaker may choose to demonstrate that proper medical care is of concern to all Americans regardless of age, in the second, he may choose to expend his efforts elsewhere.

The second order of constraints imposed on the advocate's behavior concerns the *meaning* the proposed course of action holds for his audience. In addressing high school students on socialized medicine, our hypothetical United States senator may choose to explore in depth the economic and medical problems of the nation, to interpret carefully the essential features of the proposed legislation, and to examine in detail its advantages and its superiority over alternate courses of action. This approach is based on his assumption that many members of his audience are unaware of the facts intrinsic to his proposed course of action and the problem that gave it birth. In addressing the American Medical Association, he would probably decide to treat only those aspects of the legislation in need of clarification so that he could consider, in detail, the consequences of the proposed legislation for the medical profession and for the American public at large.

A third constraint influencing a speaker's behavior concerns the *credibility* he holds for his audience as an authority on future policy. The speaker who wishes to advise his audience on personal or corporate behavior must recognize that he is closely and personally identified with his subject. His credibility both influences and is influenced by the course of action he proposes. Thus a speaker who wishes to win a favorable response to his proposed course of action must demonstrate to his audience that he fully understands his subject, that he is being honest in both the content and presentation of his message, and that the counsel he offers has their own best interests in mind. Although his previous reputation usually will influence his credibility, his ethos is greatly determined by the choices he makes in the immediate speaking situation. He may demonstrate wealth of knowledge and mental dexterity through use of evidence, reasoning, and refutation. He may convey assurance, enthusiasm, interest, and conviction through vocal, physical, and linguistic dynamism. He may demonstrate good will toward his audience through the judicious handling of questions and reactions, consideration of their immediate problems, and reference to his associations with persons, places, institutions, and ideas that they value.

The final order of constraints an audience imposes on a speaker's behavior concerns the *validity* they assign to his message. Since most listeners expect an advocate to demonstrate that the course of action he is proposing is reasonable, he must select those rhetorical strategies that help them to believe in the policy he is advancing. Although there are no absolute rules a speaker must follow, a few strategies have proven to be especially useful. The speaker may show that the course of action he is proposing has worked effectively elsewhere, or that experts have widely supported it, or that it will remove the causes of certain personal or social problems, or that it will minimize the symptoms of a specific disorder. And since men characteristically resist new courses of action in favor of policies they revere, the speaker will often find it to his advantage to recognize and refute positions that run counter to his own. His task, then, involves more than providing adequate reasons for the adoption of his own propositions; it concerns itself also with refuting opposing programs.

But men also judge the validity of policies on the basis of self-interest or personal values. An audience of businessmen may judge a program by the effect it will have on corporate profits. An audience of clergymen may judge a policy by its consistency with spiritual values. An audience of working men may judge a policy by its effect on their pay envelopes. An audience of Negroes may judge a proposal by the contribution it will make to the cause of social equality. So no matter who composes his audience, the speaker advancing propositions of policy must recognize the influence that personal values and self-interest exert on its members' judgments in selecting a course of action.

CONCLUSION

In a free society men often assemble to consider courses of future action. At such times the speaker serves as an adviser on personal or corporate conduct. In this capacity he must consider, among other things, the consequences of the course of action he is advising, so that his audience can determine whether the results are either *necessary* or *desirable.* Since an audience's acceptance of a policy presupposes a willingness to listen and an ability to understand, the speaker must also give *interest* and *meaning* to his message. A third constraint concerns an audience's willingness to assign *credibility* to the speaker as an authority on policy. This constraint is especially important in this speech form since audiences are unlikely to accept a course of action if they consider the speaker foolish, dishonest, or opposed to their own best interests. The final constraint imposed on the speaker concerns the standards an audience uses for judging the *validity* of a proposed course of action. In complying with this constraint the speaker must choose those rhetorical strategies that enable his audience to justify adoption of his policy on the grounds of logic and self-interest.

In the following speeches, the student may consider the choices other speakers have made in affirming propositions of policy. The constraints set forth in this chapter should be used as evaluative criteria. "Anti-Westernism: Cause and Cure" by Vera Micheles Dean is a clear example of a problem-solution approach to a question of policy. The next speech, "A Matter of Necessity" by Anthony F. Arpaia, is a problem-solution speech that examines and then eliminates alternate courses of action; as such, it illustrates the "this-or-nothing" approach to a question of policy. "Trial Outside the Courtroom" by Bert C. Goss exemplifies the use of expert testimony to illuminate a problem and to support the policy advocated. "Man's Other Society" by Richard M. Duesterbeck advocates a three-pronged program for prison reform. The policy Daniel P. Loomis recommends in "Why Not Let Competition Go to Work in Transportation?" consists of removing restrictive government regulations. John F. Kennedy shows the interrelationship between "The Intellectual and the Politician" and points out the advantages of a policy of increased cooperation. Finally, Adlai E. Stevenson uses propositions of value as the basis for the policy he advocates in "Let Us Work While It Is Yet Day."

For Further Reading

Baird, A. Craig, *Argumentation, Discussion, and Debate,* McGraw-Hill, 1950, pp. 41–49, 65–68. Examines in detail Dewey's pattern of reflective thinking; discusses questions to be considered when advocating a policy.

Ewbank, Henry L., and J. Jeffery Auer, *Discussion and Debate,* 2nd ed., Appleton-Century-Crofts, 1951, pp. 53–56, 180–192. Discusses Dewey's pattern of reflective thought; presents procedures for examining suggested solutions to problems and for choosing the best solution.

Gilman, Wilbur, Bower Aly, and Hollis White, *Fundamentals of Speaking,* 2nd ed., The Macmillan Co., 1964, pp. 348–367. Focuses on procedures for and types of speeches that advocate policies and programs.

Graves, Harold F., and Bernard S. Oldsey, *From Fact to Judgment,* The Macmillan Co., 2nd ed., 1963. Chapter 6 analyzes questions of policy.

Leys, Wayne A. R., *Ethics for Policy Decisions,* Prentice-Hall, 1952. Chapters 1, 12, and 22. Pages 189–192 list the critical questions relevant to policy decisions developed in ten major systems of ethics.

Minnick, Wayne, *The Art of Persuasion,* Houghton Mifflin Co., 1957, pp. 198–216, 262–268. Discusses winning audience belief and action through appeals to their wants and values.

Monroe, Alan H., *Principles and Types of Speech,* 5th ed., Scott, Foresman and Co., 1962, pp. 280–301, 414–416, 423–432. Explains the nature and uses of the five-step "motivated sequence" pattern of organization; this pattern is especially useful in speeches advocating policies.

Walter, Otis, and Robert L. Scott, *Thinking and Speaking,* The Macmillan Co., 1962, pp. 148–157. Presents suggestions for thinking and speaking about solutions to problems.

ANTI-WESTERNISM CAUSE AND CURE

Vera Micheles Dean

Vera Micheles Dean, born in Petrograd, Russia, and naturalized as an American citizen in 1928, has been Professor of International Development in New York University Graduate School of Public

Administration since 1962. She is the author of several books on Europe, Asia, and American foreign relations, including The Nature of the Non-Western World, *published in 1957. Mrs. Dean delivered this address at the conference of the National Association of Women Deans and Counselors in Cleveland, Ohio, on March 21, 1959.*

The organizational pattern the speaker uses in the course of action she advocates is a clear problem-solution one. She identifies the problem, searches out its causes, briefly demonstrates the weaknesses of several alternative approaches, and then provides a remedy for the ills. This method is a common and useful approach to a proposition of policy. It will be useful to evaluate this speech by applying the stock questions listed for policy speeches in the introductory essay to this chapter. However, since Mrs. Dean presents causes of the problem, two additional questions are useful. Are the causes she gives the real ones? Does her solution eliminate or alleviate each *of the causes? Note that when a speaker sets forth causes of a problem he is specifically outlining those factors with which a plan of action must deal.*

This speech is reprinted by permission from Representative American Speeches: 1959–1960, *ed. Lester Thonssen (New York: H. W. Wilson Co., 1960), pp. 116–122; and by permission of Vera Micheles Dean.*

1 In Cuba, one of our Latin American neighbors, Fidel Castro denounces the United States. In Iraq, until 1958 an active member of the Baghdad pact, crowds jeer at an American diplomat, and a Communist-dominated regime comes to power. The mayor of Manila, speaking on Edward R. Murrow's *Small World* TV program, tells us why we are losing friends in Asia in terms so bitter as to befit a foe rather than a friend of the United States.

2 As these and other incidents are reported from around the globe, Americans ask themselves: Why are these non-Western peoples against the West—and particularly why are they against the United States? What is anti-Westernism? And how can it be cured?

3 So deeply is the West imbued with the sense of benefits it has conferred on the non-Western areas in the past, and is ready to confer in the future, that we find it difficult to believe anti-Westernism can exist and flourish without the help of communism. Yet, this is the harsh reality we must face in Asia, the Middle East, and Africa if we are not to fall prey to perilous illusions.

4 The Russians did not need to lift a finger, fire a gun, or spend a single ruble to foment anti-Westernism in Egypt or Saudi Arabia, in Indonesia or Jordan. It's in the air. It is deeply imbedded in the consciousness of peoples who have lived under the rule of Britain, France, or the Netherlands, not of Russia. True, the Russians capitalize with marked success on a sentiment against the West which corresponds to their own, but they did not in the first place create it. This sentiment can exist and has existed apart from communism—just as some plants need no soil or fertilizer to remain alive. In fact, anti-Westernism was a sturdy plant in Russia itself during the nineteenth century under the czars, long before the Bolsheviks came on the scene.

5 But, if these manifestations in Russia were not initially a product of communism, were they an exclusive product of Russia's historical development? Is the anti-Westernism we see today in other areas of the world just a carbon copy of that practiced in Russia? Would it vanish if the West could discover some magic formula for eliminating Russia or sealing it off from the rest of the world?

6 The answer, disappointing as it is for the West, must be in the negative. From New Delhi to Cairo, from Jakarta to Karachi and Nairobi, men and women who have never read Marx, Lenin, or Stalin, and who often abhor what they know of Russia, are in the grip of the same emotions and ideas which fan the as yet unfinished controversy between Westernizers and Slavophiles in Russia. Their anti-Westernism, like that of the Russians, is an explosive mixture of contradictory reactions inspired by rising nationalism.

7 Non-Westerners admire our material achievements—the fruits of modern science and technology. They long to have their own peoples benefit by these fruits, to which they feel entitled by reason of living in the twentieth century; this is the essence of what has been well called the revolution of rising expectations. But they realize, with a poignancy which no Westerner, however sympathetic, can possibly understand—because like intense fear or joy it cannot be expressed in rational terms but must be experienced to be known—that their own countries are poor and retarded, ridden with disease and ignorance. The contrast between what they see around them, in Egypt or Indonesia, and what they painfully wish to achieve is so staggering as to fill them with a sense of hopelessness and frustration. Instead of trying to escape from this state of mind by tackling the nearest practical job, no matter how modest it may be, they are likely to vent their feelings of disappointment against the West, making it the scapegoat for all the ills from which they and their countrymen suffer.

8 The situation becomes all the more painful—for non-Western peoples and for the West—where the rulers, today or in the recent past, are or have been Westerners who may well have concentrated on their own interests such as the building of strategic facilities or the development of resources needed by Western industry, rather than on improvement of the economic, social, and political conditions in the areas under their control. Then the anti-Westernism which is found even in independent nations such as Japan becomes dangerously aggravated by anticolonialism and, since the foreign rulers are representatives of white nations, also by racialism. To all these feelings must be added the fear of some, who want to maintain ancient political and religious customs, that the impact of the West will destroy the fabric of the nation's traditional life. They want to oust all Westerners before this horrifying prospect has come to pass.

9 We, however, are particularly puzzled by the tendency of the non-Western nations to denounce Western colonialism yet say little or nothing about the colonialism of the USSR. Here again Russia's past experience is much closer to that which Asia, the Middle East, and Africa are now undergoing than is the experience of the Western nations. Russia itself was a relatively backward nation as late as the 1920's. It, too, both wanted to learn from the West yet feared its impact on institutions and on national security.

10 This does not mean, and should not be interpreted to mean, that the Asian and African countries accept Russia without criticisms or qualms. They are aware of the dangers of eventual pressure from Moscow. They are not enthusiastic about Russian dictatorship—although, being often accustomed to authoritarianism at home, they are less repelled by it abroad than the nations of the Atlantic community, where democracy is—more or less—an old story. Russia was not invited to the Afro-Asian conference at Bandung in 1955, presumably because it is a Eurasian, not an Asian or African, country. But Russia's experience in modernizing its economy and in making the difficult transition from ancient times to the nuclear age within a third of a century is of intense interest to all non-Western areas, which feel that they have more to learn, in a practical way, from a country far closer to their current problems and experiences than from such advanced nations as the U.S.A. and Britain. This sense of affinity with Russia—economic and social if not always political—on the part of non-Western peoples of diverse religious faiths, political traditions, and international aspirations constitutes our most difficult hurdle in our efforts to find a cure for anti-Westernism.

11 This cure cannot be found by denouncing communism, by demanding that the non-Western nations abandon all contacts with Russia and Communist China, or by threatening to cut off aid unless they agree to join our side. Such moves would merely reinforce their hostility to and suspicion of the West and cause them to strengthen rather than weaken their still tenuous bonds with Moscow.

12 As in the case of some other troubles, the most promising remedy is the hair of the dog. The cure for anti-Westernism is Westernization, but it cannot be forced on peoples by military pressure or financial handouts. Nasser in Egypt or Nehru in India, like the Japanese after 1867 or the Russians after 1917, must be free to take the initiative in accepting or rejecting what the West has to offer. They must be free to pick and choose those features of our development they think best adapted to their own particular needs.

13 The essence of anti-Westernism, in Czarist Russia as in the USSR and other areas, is resistance to the assumption, which the West makes as a matter of course, that our civilization is superior to the civilizations of other regions and represents a norm which should be the ideal goal of Asians, Arabs, and Africans. When Glubb Pasha, upon reaching London after his expulsion from Jordan, was asked what it was the West had done wrong, he said that, while the West had committed mistakes, it had also done much good but that its main error is its "superciliousness" toward the non-West. If the West is to succeed, it must learn to restrain its natural feeling of pride in its own achievements—a feeling which, when transposed to non-Western lands, looks and sounds like arrogance—and display modesty in offering to improve the conditions of Egyptians or Indians.

14 We must, moreover, constantly bear in mind that, as a matter of historical fact, many of these today economically underdeveloped countries had achieved a high type of civilization and culture when our own ancestors were still relative savages. It is no wonder, then, that they think they have something to preserve.

15 Nor is it enough for us to point out that the Communist powers now practice the imperialism which the Western nations are in process of relinquishing. For Asia, Africa and the Middle East, colonialism and imperialism have been associated with the West, and symbolized by the unequal treatment accorded by whites to non-whites. What Russia does in Eastern Europe, repugnant as it may be to all non-Communists, is regarded as a conflict between white peoples. The situation changes, however, when non-whites try to subjugate and repress non-whites, as shown by the sharp reaction in Asia against Communist China's actions in Tibet.

16 What, then, can the United States do to counter Soviet influence? First, we must renew our efforts to facilitate orderly self-determination for those peoples who are still under colonial rule. This does not mean that all will benefit by achieving independence overnight but that we should show genuine concern for their desire to rule themselves in at least a limited form—perhaps, for a stated period of time, under the supervision of the United Nations.

17 Second, when we advocate independence, we must accept the fact that independence includes the right for a free nation to choose its own course in world affairs. We must stop criticizing those of the non-Western nations which, like India or Burma, choose neutralism in preference to membership in one or other of the military blocs that have emerged out of the cold war.

18 Third, we must look at foreign aid not merely as a weapon in the cold war. We must understand that it is in our national interest to give aid to the underdeveloped countries, even if communism did not exist, in order to improve economic and social conditions in the world community of which we are a part. Once we realize that the goal of foreign aid is not just to defeat communism but to advance the development of non-Western areas, then we should think of long-term aid of a more substantial character than we have undertaken in the past. Economists calculate that we could and should allocate $3 billion a year during two or three decades for economic, as distinguished from military, aid. This figure may seem large, but it is less than 1 per cent of our national income.

19 Fourth, we must realize that foreign aid cannot be considered apart from foreign trade. The non-Western nations have no desire to become permanent pensioners. They do not just want to receive handouts; they want to stand on their own feet and gain self-respect. But they can do this only if they can repay the long-term loans we may make to them. And this they can do only if they can sell their products in Western markets. This means that we and our allies must rethink the character of world trade.

20 And, finally, we must learn that relations with the non-Western nations, if they are to be successful, have to be a two-way street. We have much to offer in terms of democratic procedures and technological skills, but we can greatly enrich ourselves by sharing their contributions to the world's cultural heritage through religion, philosophy, art, literature, and music.

21 This five-point program may sound like a tall order. But no one who has faith in the American way of life can believe that we are unable to meet Russia's challenge for peacetime competition in the non-Western World. As the *New Yorker* said about the world domination dreams of the Nazis when Germany conquered France in 1941: "We, too, can dream dreams and see visions."

A MATTER OF NECESSITY

Anthony F. Arpaia

Anthony F. Arpaia is vice president of International Services of the Railway Express Agency. He delivered this speech on April 2, 1964, at the Sixth Annual Transportation Conferences of Texas A. & M. University.

This speech by Arpaia utilizes the "this-or-nothing," or residual reasoning, pattern of speech organization: the speaker evaluates leading alternative solutions for a problem, shows why each in turn is ineffectual, and finally presents his policy as the only sound choice. This approach raises the important question: when should an advocate for a cause deal with alternative proposals? A suitable answer seems to be that he should discuss other solutions if his listeners are so familiar with them that they will make comparisons, no matter what he does. In your study of this speech, analyze Arpaia's motive for eliminating alternate proposals. How does he attempt to eliminate them? How well does he succeed?

It is doubly important for a speaker using a "this-or-nothing" approach to demonstrate that his solution is both workable and desirable. Is the information Arpaia provides sufficiently detailed for us to evaluate the desirability of his proposed policy? Is the information adequate for judging his policy's efficiency and economy in operation, as well as its potential for solving the problem? Do you think it was important for him to refute the major arguments that his opponents might raise against the workability and desirability of his plan? When is it important for a speaker to recognize major objections to his plan and refute them?

Arpaia uses many factual examples. Try to determine what functions they serve in the speech. What tests should you apply when they are used as evidence? Do the historical examples function primarily as informative background on the nature of the problem Arpaia is delineating or as precedents for the proposed policy?

This speech is reprinted by permission from Vital Speeches of the Day (*May 15, 1964*), *pp. 477–480.*

1 Last August a new page was written in labor-management history. For the first time, by an overwhelming vote in both houses, Congress passed a resolution setting up compulsory arbitration of the rail labor work rules dispute. The occasion was the imminence of a nation-wide rail strike. This, after the collective bargaining process, mediation, fact-finding by two Emergency Boards, recommendations by a Presidentially appointed Commission, and every other approach during four years of effort had failed to produce a settlement.

2 There was strong public support for this action by the Congress. Resentment against the failure of those involved to accommodate their claims to the public interest left no alternative. A nation-wide rail tie-up would have done catastrophic damage to our entire economy, to our nation's defense posture and to the daily living of its people.

3 I shall point out later that the Government has been forced to intervene under other circumstances when the movement of goods and people was interrupted. However, never before has such intervention taken the form of directly setting up the machinery to adjudicate the actual issues in dispute, binding on both management and labor. Although this action was intended to resolve a specific problem and might be considered as a stop-gap measure, it does mark a milestone in the evolution of labor-management relations.

4 Labor has come a long way since 1935, when the Wagner Act brought millions of workers into unions and buttressed collective bargaining with Government guarantees. Its purpose was to balance the power of individual, unorganized employees against that of employers. Conditions have changed. With the growth of power and the maturity of unions, a new responsibility has arisen for both labor and management to negotiate with greater consideration for the public and broad national interest. The use of strikes and lockouts in a key industry, such as transportation, as the ultimate test of strength is even less acceptable or tolerable. As Senator Magnuson pointed out, the public interest in this last dispute was far superior to the interests of either side. So complex has our industrial machine become that irreparable hardship and damage are caused when its transport is tied up.

5 Unions serve a useful purpose and should continue to serve a useful purpose. They have contributed to an increased standard of living for employees and improved the conditions and terms of employment. Earlier in this century, demands for pensions, social security, unemployment insurance, vacations and paid sick leave were regarded as revolutionary, as radical. Today, these objectives have been gained not only through the collective bargaining of unions, but because of the changed philosophy of both business and Government and Government's attitude toward the welfare and health of its population. As a result, the intervening years have brought about a change not only in aims of union organizations but also in the social, political and economic attitude of their members. Workers, organized and unorganized, suffer the same hardship and loss and have the same stake in the nation's well-being as those directly involved in a strike.

6 Irresponsibility, even in a free society, has its limitations. As David J. McDonald of the United Steelworkers said in a recent speech, "We must perform our roles as Americans concerned first with the common good." A better way than tests of raw economic force must be found to resolve labor-management issues when collective bargaining fails.

7 What is to happen when collective bargaining fails in such instances? Ad hoc legislation forcing compulsory arbitration, or specific legislation dealing directly with the issue in dispute, is not satisfactory. Everyone is adversely affected. This not only includes the ultimate consumer, but the employees of other industries and businesses which are not concerned in the dispute, which are closed down entirely or restricted to limited operations because goods and people cannot move.

8 It becomes more clear that a different approach is necessary and desirable if extensive economic dislocation and danger to the national welfare are to be avoided. Various suggestions have been made and certain alternatives are available. Before we can evaluate the alternatives and determine what type of machinery should be used to protect the public interest and yet preserve the integrity and interests of both labor and management, I think we should first review briefly the history of emergency strikes and labor disputes and, second, consider each possible alternative.

9 It is not remarkable that the first national emergency involving labor occurred on the railroads. It came in 1877 as a result of a railway "strike." I use the word strike in quotes because this was not a strike in the conventional sense. It was not "called" by a union. In response to the railroads' proposal to cut wages, widespread rioting broke out. Federal troops were called in and the rioting was quelled. The use of troops was not directed at breaking the strike itself but was justified by the violence which resulted from the strike. Nevertheless, the strike was broken by direct action and contributed nothing to improved relations between management and labor.

10 The next railway strike was the Pullman strike in 1894. The American Railway Union, an industry-wide union, now represented the rail employees. The union requested bargaining privileges and when its proposals were rejected it called upon the employees to handle no more Pullman cars. The railroads retaliated by firing employees who refused to handle the cars. This, in turn, led to train crews quitting. And, when the railroads sought to use replacements, violence occurred. Federal troops were again called out and the strike was broken.

11 Although, again, there was direct action against the strike, an interesting development came about during this episode. Legal steps also were taken to halt the strike. The Attorney General of the United States sought an injunction, not only against violence but against any effort by union leaders to persuade employees not to work. The lower Federal Court granted the injunction, holding that concerted action to induce a strike constituted a combination in restraint of interstate commerce, barred by the Sherman Act.

12 Eugene Debs, head of the American Railway Union, was jailed for violating the injunction. It is noteworthy that although the Supreme Court denied a writ of habeas corpus to Debs, it did not rely on the Sherman Act, as did the lower court. It held, instead, that the Federal Commerce Power and its exercise in other statutes dealing with interstate commerce gave the Federal courts inherent power to protect such commerce from obstruction.

13 While this injunction was effective in halting the strike, it generated a persistent campaign by labor against "government by injunction." This campaign, years later, led to the passage of the Norris-LaGuardia Act in 1932. The Act restricted the power of the Federal courts to issue injunctions in labor disputes. It also barred antitrust suits based upon trade union conduct and thus effectively overruled the interpretation of the Sherman Act by the lower Federal Court in the Debs case.

14 By 1916 railway labor was thoroughly organized. A third nation-wide labor dispute arose in that year. The demand was for an 8-hour day without reduction in wages. Since it was rejected by the railroads, there was a complete impasse and a strike was imminent. Congress realized that in order to prevent irreparable damage to the public and the national economy (we were then on the threshold of World War I) effective action was necessary. It resolved the problem by passing the Adamson Act, which made the 8-hour day mandatory. In order to soften the impact of its intervention, a provision was included setting up a temporary period of two years during which its operation was to be observed by a commission.

15 Thus, for the very first time, Government action was directed not to preventing a strike as such, but instead dealt with the basic substantive issue which was in dispute between labor and management. In other words, the principle applied was to legislate on the basic merits of the dispute between the parties rather than take direct action against the strikers.

16 And the second feature of the Adamson Act—the temporary mandatory period for which the relief was imposed—was also a novel technique. The Adamson Act was upheld by the Supreme Court as a legitimate exercise of Federal Commerce Power by Congress.

17 Public concern over the harm caused by transport paralysis led to the enactment of the Railway Labor Act in 1926. Its purpose was to provide a permanent basis for resolving labor disputes affecting railroads. As amended in 1934, it provided machinery for settling grievances under existing collective bargaining agreements and also some procedures for seeking to resolve major disputes relating to new agreements. The Act did not ban strikes. Therefore, after all the required procedures are exhausted, the rail unions can still call a strike.

18 The first railway strike following the Railway Labor Act came in 1946. The procedures required by the Act had been exhausted. President Truman sought to deal with this emergency by proposing legislation which, in addition to permitting the President to ban an emergency strike by proclamation, would permit him to draft strikers into the Army if they still persisted in refusing to work. Although this bill was adopted by the House, it was blocked in the Senate, chiefly through the efforts of Senator Robert A. Taft. In this instance the mere threat of legislation was sufficient to force the parties into a settlement.

19 We have had other national emergency disputes; one in coal in 1946 and two in steel in 1952 and 1959, in which the Government intervened. The postwar coal strike of '46 was terminated by the use of the World War II Seizure Statute. The Government also successfully contended that the union was responsible for this strike and imposed a fine. The fine and the injunction were upheld by the Supreme Court. The Norris-LaGuardia Act was held inapplicable in view of the fact that the Government had seized the property.

20 The steel strike in 1952 was postponed by Presidential seizure. However, in this instance the Supreme Court held that the President's constitutional authority did not permit seizure since the War Powers Act had expired. After the seizure was voided the strike resumed, but it was finally settled by voluntary agreement, after it was made plain to both parties that the continuation of such a strike was intolerable and against the public interest because of its impact on the defense effort.

21 There was another steel strike in 1959. It lasted quite a while before it was halted by the 80-day injunction under the national emergency provisions of the Taft-Hartley Act. This Act, as you know, permits such temporary injunction on motion of the Attorney General, after a Presidential fact-finding board has made a finding that national health or safety is in danger. This injunction was challenged by the union but was upheld by the Supreme Court on the ground that the shortage of steel affected defense production and, therefore, national safety.

22 Up to this point, it is obvious that strikes or injunctions in themselves do not resolve underlying substantive issues between the parties. Attack upon the power to strike alone as the evil, not resolving the issues in dispute, proves nothing. All that is left is bitterness and waste in its wake. To date, each dispute has been treated in a case-by-case fashion, the progress of which could not be predicted or predicated in advance. Both the Railway Labor Act and the Taft-Hartley Act imply the use of this same ad hoc approach. After the procedures of mediation and reference to an emergency board have failed, the President may decide to refer the dispute to Congress. Without predictable definitive action, the uncertainty, the delay in setting up the arbitration machinery, the continual pressure on Congress and the tremendous dislocation in employment and of the economy because of recurring imminent strike deadlines, cause unnecessary damage to the general public which is hard to measure and which is irreparable.

23 In the work rules dispute, I think everybody will agree that the uncertainty, the long delays, the economic waste, the inability of industry and business to plan, the threat of a strike hanging over their heads, the preparation of alternative plans, makeshift plans, all did extensive damage. Continuity and dependability of transportation service is indispensable to keep our economy on an even keel.

24 What then should be the solution? I think it is in the interest of both labor and management, all employees, and the general public, that the complex economic issues of today be resolved in an atmosphere of calm and without hostility and without the emotional and subjective considerations which inhibit frank discussions and new ideas. Labor has the capability and resources to represent itself at the bargaining table, or in any other forum, with confidence. There is no inequality today between the strength of labor and that of management. As a matter of fact, the claim is made that labor has and can exercise far greater power than management.

25 If we are agreed that damaging strikes must be avoided, as they have been in the past, we will have to face up to the reality that rapid and far-reaching economic changes have created difficult issues. Since they cannot be settled by strife without jeopardizing the larger interest of the public, some solution must be found which is fair to labor and management. Let us now consider every possible alternative.

26 One alternative is outright permanent ban against strikes of any kind in transportation. This is the approach which was followed in 1877 and 1894, which caused violence, loss of life and disorder, and which was wisely blocked by Senator Taft when it was again revived as a solution in 1946.

27 The real objection, and we have to be fair about this, to any suggestion of this kind is that only one side is coerced. It ignores the existence of a real dispute involving two parties, each of whom may have just claims which remain unresolved under such a proposal. Furthermore, such an approach does violence to political reality.

28 Another alternative suggested is administrative wage determination by the Government itself. This is abhorrent to our system of private enterprise and can't be taken seriously. You can't fix wages unless you fix prices and, in the absence of extreme emergency, nobody wants Government intervention in wage and price control. It violates fundamental economic law, distorts the economy, wastes and misapplies resources, and results in a tremendous government bureaucracy, which is inefficient, imperfect and intolerable.

29 A third alternative is seizure by the Government. This is objectionable from every angle. It is the first step toward Government ownership. It is Government intervention of the worst kind. Furthermore, the owners of the facilities are entitled to compensation from the Government during the period of seizure, which creates many problems. Such action would be justified only in periods of war, or other dire national emergency, and then only as an intermediate measure.

30 Much serious consideration has been given to the application of antitrust laws, or other anti-monopoly provisions, to unions in key industries. The purpose is to take away the power of unions to paralyze the economy of the country on an industry-wide basis. The theory is that unions shouldn't be permitted to wield this power to public disadvantage.

31 Frankly, I have strong reservations about this as a cure. First, let me say that the argument is made that because the Sherman Act has been interpreted to ban price-fixing agreements among producers, therefore, in fairness the unions should be curbed against taking similar industry-wide action. That situation is radically different from that in which labor is involved. Price-fixing is not an irrevocable thing; it can be changed at any time. Secondly, price-fixing is unilateral; taken by sellers alone. In such instances, since the consumers themselves are not organized and, therefore, cannot consult or combine in order to take a position to protect themselves, only the Government can do so.

32 Furthermore, I think the application of the anti-monopoly provisions to labor unions would be ineffectual. How much difference would it make to a labor union to strike the whole industry at one time when it has the power to strike against a single enterprise or a single area? The pressure in such a situation is intolerable. The struck enterprise will yield when it is in danger of losing its market to those who continue in operation. I think the union leaders appreciate the whipsaw effect of localizing strike action. Hoffa said he would use "selective" strikes to obtain his objective of national contract terms.

33 Theoretically, employers could combine to meet such tactics by joint lockout. But the application of antitrust laws in labor matters would probably also prohibit employers from doing this. For instance, as of now the CAB has held that in the airline industry employers may pool strike losses in order to counteract the whipsaw effect of such strikes. Therefore, the application of anti-monopoly laws to unions might stir up a hornet's nest of problems.

34 An attempt to insist upon breaking up unions within a single enterprise, in my opinion, might increase rather than lessen industrial strife anyway. When the unions were weak they fought all the harder for survival with every means at their disposal. The objective, in the interest of the public, is to lessen rather than to increase industrial strife, and the fragmentizing of union power isn't going to do this.

35 Another alternative is some form of definitive binding arbitration. You notice I refrain from using the word compulsory. The word identification seems to arouse an emotional rejection. We, as free people, automatically resent the implication of compulsion. Yet, the enforcement of any law duly enacted by representatives of a free people has the element of compulsion. In fact, "compulsory" compliance affects us all. The immediate illustrations which occur to me are compulsory military service and compulsory education. In fact, the management side of transportation is already subject to compulsory stringent controls on the theory that the national and public interests demand it. To preserve public protection in this basic industry, it is becoming apparent that it is equally necessary to subject its employees to some limitations. The trend seems to be in this direction. It is becoming a practice to voluntarily agree on binding arbitration. The Pan American Airways and the Railway Clerks agreement signed last July 8th sets up a board with binding power to decide disputes when the processes of the Railway Labor Act fail. And, after a few days' strike, National Airlines and the employees recently agreed to binding arbitration if no agreement was reached in five days.

36 We in this country are the direct heirs of the long tradition of Anglo-American common law which encompasses the vital idea that all parties have rights which are subject to adjudication, binding adjudication, by an independent, impartial court in which the proceeding is processed according to established rules. This principle, in view of the fact that we are dealing with mature powers—labor and management, can be used to set up a permanent machinery which will effectively adjudicate labor disputes on their merits.

37 Some people feel that this is nothing but compulsory arbitration in another guise. I think that it has a serious and important difference. The reason why compulsory arbitration on a case-by-case basis is not always trusted by both management and labor is that the decision of the arbitrators may depend upon the current political considerations and other extraneous factors which will influence the arbitrators selected for a particular dispute at a particular time. They also feel that arbitrators selected might already be biased. Past experience has shown that it sometimes has the effect of bludgeoning parties into an otherwise unacceptable settlement.

38 I think that the only way to implement this ad hoc approach is by the establishment of an independent tribunal, whose sole function would be to adjudicate labor disputes after all efforts to negotiate and mediate have failed. The personnel of such tribunal, or court, would have to be carefully selected. Its beginnings would be highly important to its future success. Its members should be of the highest calibre and their tenure should be for long terms or for life. They should be above political influence or public pressures of any kind.

39 It has been said by both management and labor that binding arbitration is not compatible with free enterprise; that it is an invitation to Government dictatorship. If, for any reason, there is any feeling that a final decision of a court might still be unjust or unfair, there is a further protection for the rights of the parties which can be added. The law could provide that a decision be effective for a temporary period only, say of two years, using the same technique that was used in the Adamson Act. During this period both parties could live with the decision and, if during the actual experiment it appeared that certain issues were not actually resolved and the parties could not voluntarily reconcile them, then the whole matter could be again reviewed in the light of the experience gained. Thus, there would be no danger that the status quo would be frozen in spite of changed circumstances and experience.

40 The provision for a temporary mandatory order postponing the right to strike for a definite period of time has some precedent; for instance, the 80-day period of injunction specified in the Taft-Hartley Act. Furthermore, when the parties have lived with a situation for two years, such as happened in the case of the Adamson Law, the decision on the merits will either become acceptable or, at worst, will become narrowed. Perhaps matters which were previously considered important may not turn out to be so. The chances are good that any unresolved problems would be handled by the parties themselves during this period.

41 What type of disputes should be referred to such a tribunal? Congress, of course, could define an emergency dispute in the law. I think this would be difficult and controversial. Any dispute of sufficient emergency would become so defined by the circumstances and public pressure. The judgment in such matters might well be left to the discretion of the President. Our last several chief executives have had to take action whenever the public interest was seriously threatened and they have exercised admirable restraint in refusing to act except where truly essential industries were involved and the hurt to the non-participants and the nation outweighed the damage to the antagonists.

42 There is one class of disputes which should be referred to the court automatically. These are jurisdictional or inter-union disputes. In such instances the employer and the public are merely pawns in a power struggle between two unions or branches of a union in which management is, in effect, a nominal party. Such strikes are vicious in their effect on innocent parties and the public.

43 Does the machinery for binding adjudication of an emergency type labor dispute eliminate genuine collective bargaining? I don't see why it should. I see no reason why the knowledge that disturbing the entire national economy, health and welfare will land the parties in court should prevent voluntary agreement through the collective bargaining process.

44 Parties can and probably would exhaust every effort to negotiate in good faith in the great majority of cases. But, when they have reached a stalemate which threatens serious harm not only to them but to the general public and to the economy of the country, then some specific alternative should be provided by our society.

45 Labor unions and management have the maturity, the financial strength, the ability to hire competent counsel and economic advisers. With the high calibre of talent available to them, a detached, impassionate approach can effectually determine the merits of a dispute. It would be good for the parties and the public.

46 In my opinion, we have reached a plateau in labor-management relations from which we can now step up to an era of intelligent action as a substitute for brute force. We have reached the point where, in this competitive world, trial by combat has become a danger to the national interest and security. Where permanent damage is going to occur, we should get the third man in the labor-management ring when national health, safety and welfare are seriously threatened. We have banned atomic testing in the atmosphere. We certainly can protect ourselves from devastating national economic and personal damage to innocent bystanders by practices which are just as futile in permanently producing any real winners.

TRIAL OUTSIDE THE COURTROOM

Bert C. Goss

On November 21, 1962, Bert C. Goss, who is president of the public relations firm Hill and Knowlton, Inc., gave this speech concerning the effects of antitrust actions on public opinion toward business to the Antitrust Committee of the Chicago Bar Association.

Goss devotes most of his time to exploring and documenting his problem. The amount of time a speaker spends on this kind of analysis and documentation should correspond directly to his listeners' awareness of the facts surrounding an issue and whether or not they agree that the situation constitutes a problem. Do you think that Goss dwells too long on the effects antitrust actions have on public opinion?

In advocating a policy of closer cooperation between corporation lawyers and public relations men, Mr. Goss relies heavily on the use of testimony, which he employs both for proof and illustration. As part of your analysis of the speech, apply the appropriate textbook criteria for soundness to this testimony.

This speech is reprinted by permission from Vital Speeches of the Day *(December 15, 1962), pp. 137–141.*

1 An executive in our firm recently discussed press coverage of an antitrust action with the business editor of one of the largest newspapers in the East. He reminded the editor of the headlines which had proclaimed charges of monopoly when the government filed its suit some five years earlier—and of the spate of stories in subsequent years, alluding to the charges.

2 And he pointed out that the company's aquittal—the full clearance of the company by a federal court—received no attention in this paper whatsoever.

3 The editor, one of the most astute in the business, made this observation: "I know that sometimes a big story is carried when charges are made, and that when a company eventually is vindicated, it may be overlooked."

4 I mention this today because it lies at the root of a mutual problem which legal counselors and public relations practitioners face in the antitrust field.

5 The Justice Department's practice of encouraging public attention to its unadjudicated charges has confronted American business with public relations problems of serious proportions. You may win your case in a court of law but lose it before the bar of public opinion.

6 There is no question that the damages incurred go beyond those for which there may be legal redress. For this reason, the announcement of an indictment or antitrust investigation calls for the closest collaboration of legal counsel and public relations counsel to hold damage to a minimum.

7 Several years ago, the founder of my firm, John W. Hill, expressed this conviction in an article in "The Business Lawyer."[1] He said the time is past when corporate management can prudently act on a "strictly legal or strictly public relations point of view." Legal and public relations activities, he asserted, "are inextricably bound, so that in advising corporate management, informed public relations people must have a knowledge of the legal implications of their counsel, and the legal department must be able to take into account the public relations aspects of its advice."

8 This is particularly true in the antitrust field. The tangled webs and labyrinths of antitrust law are indistinct and ill-defined. Actions, charges and allegations, both inside and *outside* the courtroom, have profound implications on the ability of a corporation to continue operating successfully.

9 Publicity caused by antitrust moves and charges has—in specific instances—complicated the problem of corporate financing . . . furnished ammunition for union attacks against management . . . depressed the market price of corporate securities . . . impaired the morale of company employees . . . resulted in public antagonism, and raised the threat of consumer resistance to certain products.

10 The negative effect of such publicity thus extends into virtually every aspect of corporate activity.

11 In dealing with this question, lawyers and public relations men recognize that the antibusiness publicity of the Justice Department and Federal Trade Commission is no accident. It is not self-generating.

12 Both agencies have a vested, bureaucratic interest in publicizing themselves. They must woo the public and the Congress if they are to get the support and appropriations that enable them to stay in operation.

13 In their self-promotion, the antitrusters have a unique advantage over businessmen. The press regards the Department of Justice and FTC as primary news sources. Reporters call on these agencies regularly, eagerly seeking news and publishing it promptly. This is not the case with most business establishments.

14 Government officials are presumed by the press to be disinterested and thus worthy of more credence than businessmen who are, by contrast, interested parties and protective toward their companies.

[1] "Corporation Lawyers and Public Relations Counsel," by John W. Hill, in *The Business Lawyer,* April, 1959.

15 Almost every pronouncement coming from an official of Justice or FTC has the advantage of taking the offensive. Normally an accusation of guilt, even when unsupported, is more newsworthy than an expression of innocence, even when documented.

16 Moreover, the power of these government agencies to whip up hostility toward business has been tremendously increased by modern public relations techniques.

17 The Justice Department is well aware of the effect of this publicity on business.

18 Discussing consent decrees in 1957, then Antitrust Chief Victor Hansen commented: "Consent settlements may . . . avoid the possible adverse publicity of a protracted public trial. . . . In some instances, this publicity, largely avoidable in a consent settlement, may prove as damaging as the remedy decreed. . . ."[2]

19 On this point, Thurman Arnold recognized the publicity considerations which partially motivate the Department of Justice. He observed in 1961 that ". . . the government is ready to settle (for consent decrees) so that it can rush on to the next big case and the next headlines, and build up a big record of suits."[3]

20 The press conference, the television interview, the press release, the carefully calculated "leak," the speech before important audiences, the prime forum of a Congressional hearing—all provide channels for inciting the public with accusations and charges of illegality, monopoly, conspiracy and skulduggery of all kinds.

21 These agencies cleverly use dramatic data to buttress the charges and criticisms in their complaints, indictments, speeches and testimony. Both the Justice Department and FTC draw not only upon their own large staffs of lawyers, economists and research workers, but upon facilities of other government agencies. They receive a flow of complaints from disgruntled and embittered competitors—who in many cases are concerned less with the public interest and less with preserving competition than with hoped for protection against consequences of their own inefficient management.

22 Certainly, any observer must recognize the success of the public relations efforts of the antitrust division and the FTC. Surveys show that virtually all politicians and most thought leaders today

[2] Address by Victor R. Hansen before the American Management Association, New York City, 1957.

[3] Interview with Thurman W. Arnold, *Dun's Review and Modern Industry,* December, 1961.

support "more vigorous" enforcement of the antitrust laws. And the direct payoff, of course, has been in winning increased appropriations so frequently throughout recent years.

23 But let us look at some of the consequences to business.

24 This self-promotional activity has force-fed public suspicion of business, particularly big business. And it has encouraged the public to assume that damaging allegations are true, even though a trial date may not have been set.

25 The ultimate effect of this adverse opinion on problems of legal defense against antitrust suits is one which lawyers themselves are best equipped to appraise.

26 Unquestionably, however, headlined antitrust charges and supporting activities provide good fuel for Congressional debate, and for speeches by Congressmen, political leaders and other national figures. Thus the unproved accusations are doubly publicized. News and interpretive accounts of antitrust charges, not the cases alone, become part of the nation's permanent economic literature. This is true of inaccurate and biased accounts, as well as those of legal record and of scholarly and responsible origin.

27 Arguing that patents give drug manufacturers monopolistic control over prices, Senator Kefauver tried to prove that the patent amendments he proposed would encourage rather than discourage new drug discoveries. He offered highly publicized but wholly inaccurate figures to support the case. The industry devastated this argument by showing the figures to be so erroneous that they actually proved the opposite. Nevertheless, the discredited figures are repeated in speeches, and in newspaper and magazine articles. No doubt they will continue to turn up in economic studies and industry-baiting books.

28 Economists draw upon contemporary literature—including newspapers and magazines—when they prepare economics textbooks that influence college teaching for years to come. The authors of masters' and doctors' theses go to these same sources.

29 The chances are that if you'll thumb through your high school child's social studies textbook you'll find an account of the forcible dissolution of the old Standard Oil Company, but little other reference to antitrust history. Is it any wonder that young people so instructed tend to regard antitrust charges uncritically?

30 The reservoir of material hostile to business perceptibly rises higher and higher. It has spilled over from contemporary literature, and affects all those who write about economics and business, all those who study economics and business, all those who speak on business and economic subjects.

31 It is not surprising that these attacks have created a chronic mistrust of American business, and that for its own protection, business has had to learn how to tell its story. As a result, the public generally recognizes the essential role of the large corporation. A recent Opinion Research Corporation survey[4] shows that 83 percent of the public believes that large companies are essential for the nation's growth and expansion. But the poison has had its effect. The survey also shows that 61 percent of the public fears the power of big business—and believes this power is rising. And poll after poll of public opinion demonstrates that a large percentage of our citizens is convinced that businessmen regularly conspire to fix prices.

32 One cannot fail to see the parallel between the rising tide of antibusiness propaganda and the growing demand for restrictive anti-business legislation and regulation. Such proposals have ranged over a broad spectrum—from advocacy of public utility status for certain major industries, to control over industry's pricing practices.

33 Professor Corwin D. Edwards of the University of Chicago has pointed out that a major critical development could precipitate action on one or another of these extreme proposals. He has written:

34 "From time to time, a depression, an inflation, a business scandal, or some other dramatic influence in the political environment creates effective pressure for legislation. But when this happens the pressure is usually generated quickly, and the particular provisions of law in which it finds expression are seldom devised anew for the occasion.

35 "Typically, reformers find their programs in proposals that had been previously formulated and disregarded. Some of the impossibilities of one decade are likely to be the legislative enactments of the next. The thinking of people who believe that the curbs upon big business are not adequate suggests the directions which any future intensification of these curbs may take."[5]

36 Even if no legislative threats confronted us, the criticism and hostility fostered by the antitrust division and the FTC would still

[4] "The Antitrust Controversy," research report of *The Public Opinion Index for Industry*, February, 1962.

[5] "Large Enterprises and Antitrust Policy," by Corwin D. Edwards; presentation before 45th Annual Meeting of National Industrial Conference Board, May, 1961.

exact another serious consequence. This is the creation of an environment in which business is hampered in winning public support for legislation and regulations aimed at *stimulating*, rather than restricting, the growth of our economy.

37 It seems beyond argument that lawyers, public relations executives, and corporate officials have common cause in seeking to counter the flow of hostile comment. We must strive to conduct the antitrust defense of American business as capably *outside* the courtroom as inside the courtroom.

38 Business has a responsibility to tell the positive story of its adherence to sound policy, and its performance in the public interest. Business must build good will all the time so that it can effectively resist attacks when they occur.

39 A requisite is that business itself establish and adhere to sound policy, that it comply with the law.

40 The public, however, is not generally aware that compliance with the vague, conflicting and imprecise provisions of the antitrust statutes presents staggering difficulties. Nor does the public appreciate the difficulty of determining, before a court test, whether normal and traditional business practices may be construed as violations of the law.

41 The lead editorial in the current issue of *Fortune*[6] is titled: "Antitrust: The Sacred Cow Needs a Vet." This editorial comments on a thought-provoking article in the same issue by Professor Sylvester Petro of New York University School of Law. Professor Petro concludes with this observation:

42 "If our economy were to lose its drive, the record ought to show the real cause of the stagnation. Free enterprise and free competition have not failed. The failure would lie in the principle of government control and tutelage that the antitrust laws, properly understood, exemplify so clearly."

43 Both the *Fortune* editorial and Professor Petro's article sound the alarm over the rising scope of antitrust laws which has occurred in recent decades. It is not surprising that confusion has arisen, when as Professor Petro points out:

> Companies are sued because of actions that occurred a quarter of a century earlier (as in the case of the aquisition of Richfield Oil stock by Cities Service and Sinclair)—or 40 years earlier (as in the case of Du Pont and General Motors).

[6] *Fortune,* November, 1962.

> Business is told by the courts that it can achieve dominance in any field only if its leadership is "thrust upon it."
>
> Some businessmen are sued because they *cut prices;* other businessmen are sued because they *raise prices;* and still others are accused of violating the antitrust statutes because they have *similar prices.*

44 This confusion is exemplified by recent history of the oil industry. Three radically different situations have been cited to justify the same accusation: When competitive conditions are normal and prices uniform in a given area, "identical prices" are cited as evidence of monopoly. When price wars break out, critics say the "monopolists" are trying to "drive out" competitors. When the price wars peter out and prices are restored to normal levels, critics claim the companies have "gotten together" and "hiked prices."

45 Other developments in antitrust enforcement, if generally known by the public, would cause even greater consternation and confusion. The public is not aware that antitrust cases are often brought to protect inefficient and marginal businesses against more efficient competitors, to the detriment of the consumer. Clearly, certain antitrust actions have been pressed even though government lawyers themselves were aware that, if successful, their suits would result in higher prices to the public.

46 In this connection, Professor James A. Rahl of the Northwestern University School of Law has commented: "On a given product in a given market a seller's price could be so low over a period of time that competitors might be driven out of business. This could lead to a charge of monopolization under the Sherman Act, or of unfair method of competition under the FTC Act, or of selling at an 'unreasonably low price' under the criminal provisions of the Robinson-Patman Act."[7]

47 Then, too, the public has little awareness of the role which politics plays in the filing of antitrust charges. As long ago as 1951, Supreme Court Justice Jackson was quoted as saying that cases often were picked for prosecution on a political basis. "After all," he said, "they had to be picked on some basis. We might as well be candid about it."[8]

[7] "New Directions in Pricing Policy," by James A. Rahl; presentation before 45th Annual Meeting of National Industrial Conference Board, May, 1961.

[8] *The New York Times,* January 24, 1951; *The Wall Street Journal,* January 26, 1951; reporting on January 23, 1951 address by Justice Robert H. Jackson before antitrust section of New York State Bar Association.

48 Since then more than a few of those suffering antitrust accusations have had reason to agree with Justice Jackson. Of course, the actions last April when the FTC, the Department of Justice and Senator Kefauver all were called into the steel price controversy on a moment's notice, provide graphic illustration of the use of antitrust to support a political objective.

49 In view of the complexities of the laws, it is difficult to insist that businessmen must assert an absolute compliance with the law as a condition of entering a defense in the public arena. No one condones the exceptional flagrant conspiracy or price fixing agreement. The flagrant violation of the law by any business or individual serves only to damage business itself—and to do great long-term harm to the public relations of all industry.

50 But businessmen have an obligation to the public, to our economic system, and to their stockholders to defend themselves publicly when the Justice Department or the FTC sallies into totally new and hitherto untested areas.

51 In this connection, Antitrust Chief Lee Loevinger was candid in an interview last year.[9]

52 He was asked: "Do you get many complaints from businessmen to this effect: 'We just don't know whether a thing is going to be legal or not; we can't find out'?"

53 And his answer was that there are many uncertainties in a responsible executive's life—that the businessman isn't pleased with them, but he must deal with them.

54 Then Loevinger was asked whether the law shouldn't be clear, so that a man would know just what it means.

55 His answer: "The law is clear, and people do know what it means, in general terms. It is not always clear, and it is not always certain with respect to borderline cases in application to specific circumstances. . . ."

56 A following question was: "Is there anything you can do to clarify the meaning of the law?"

57 His answer was: "We can bring more cases, and get more court decisions."

58 The need for court tests is apparent to lawyers. But to the layman, the implications of Loevinger's statement are surprising. He

[9] Interview with Lee Loevinger, Assistant Attorney General in Charge of the Antitrust Division, Department of Justice, *U. S. News & World Report*, June 26, 1961.

appears to say: If we're not sure whether an action is against the law, we charge a corporation with a violation, we attack it in the press, we haul it into court, we saddle it with burdensome legal costs, we tie up the time of its executives, we spend untold amounts of the taxpayers' money. And even *we* don't feel certain that it has broken the law.

59 Few would disagree that businessmen have a right—indeed, an obligation—to defend themselves publicly against these extensions of the antitrust laws, and to seek administrative or legislative redress when such extensions are harmful.

60 In any such public defense, let me make it clear, the public relations executive recognizes that legal considerations must be paramount. Nothing should be done or said which might compromise a successful legal defense. The ultimate decisions must be made by legal counsel, on the basis of the legal requirements of the situation.

61 We do say this: Within such limitations, both legal counsel and public relations counsel have a mutual obligation to protect their client's reputation, on which he depends for profitable operation, with the same zeal and care that his case is defended before the bar.

62 All of us recognize that there have been obstacles which, in the past, have tended to limit such cooperation between lawyers and public relations people.

63 Perhaps the most common roadblock can be summarized with a statement we have all heard many times: "We must not try the case in the newspapers."

64 Let me make clear the attitude of public relations people. We would modify this statement slightly, like this: "We must not try the case in the newspapers—if it can be avoided."

65 Conscious as we are of the need for preserving a company's good name, we prefer never to see any mention of antitrust activities, complaints, indictments or charges in the press.

66 But we don't have the option.

67 The prosecutors, the enforcers, *do* try their cases in the newspapers. They announce an intent to make a complaint—with headlines. They publicize the filing of a complaint—with press releases. They make speeches about their cases—with headlines. "Plants" and "leaks" stream out to reporters while cases are pending. And during the course of the trial, the tendency of the press is to give strongest weight to the government's charges rather than the company's defenses.

68 We all know of cases in which accused corporations have gained their first hint of an antitrust charge from a story in the newspapers. Indeed, I recall one case in which the companies involved were not even served with a complaint until some two weeks after news stories announced the government action.

69 That, I submit, is trying a case in the newspapers.

70 We in public relations feel that a company's policy should be to respond to, and to rebut, all hurtful charges when the response in legal counsel's judgment may be made without compromising the effectiveness of the legal defense.

71 Another concern which has been expressed by some lawyers and corporate officials is this: "We mustn't publicize the charges."

72 Public relations people agree. Nothing should be done to stir up interest in an accusation, if the accusation is receiving no attention. But we would add one word again. If the charge is being publicized, don't allow only one side of the story—the *other* side—to be told.

73 There is another admonition that often affects public relations action with respect to antitrust cases: "Don't make the Justice Department mad."

74 Fear occasionally is expressed that a strong, forceful, accurate answer to a Justice Department or FTC charge might antagonize the government's lawyers. The idea is that such aggravation might incite more vigorous enforcement or other undefined liability. The record, however, indicates that the antitrust division and FTC have been singularly consistent. The evidence seems clear that their hundreds of lawyers and economists pursue every complaint possible in order to earn their salaries and to protect their position in the bureaucracy.

75 If anything would deter action by an agency responsible to the Congress and the public, it would be the fear that the charges could be publicly exposed as groundless.

76 When antitrust actions are expected or pending, legal considerations are paramount. But there are steps which both legal and public relations counsel should take to protect the public reputation of their clients.

77 These steps can work to the direct benefit of legal counsel, as well as the client's reputation. No lawyer would choose to try a case in an area where hostile or critical public and editorial comment predominates. In fact, unfavorable public attitudes and editorial criticisms have been cited on occasion as a reason for a change of venue.

78 A company must plan carefully to protect its public position to the maximum extent possible. The filing of charges and the conduct of a trial against a major corporation or industry unavoidably causes editorial comment, feature and interpretive articles, and other news coverage. If the accused corporation or industry foregoes public relations activities, all such comment usually reflects only the government's complaints and briefs.

79 As far in advance as possible, the company should develop plans for handling public relations as well as legal aspects of the pending litigation. This should involve initially a conference of company officials, legal counsel, public relations staff, and public relations counsel, if any.

80 This conference should consider:

81 First, the government's probable publicity policy—including charges likely to be made in public statements, the kinds of publicity which might be expected to develop both before and during the proceedings, and the public attention these charges would receive.

82 Second, company policy or strategy with respect to the proceedings, including consideration of the need for a company reply to the government's charges, or to expected testimony of principal government witnesses.

83 Third, public relations values to be included in company testimony and trial strategy.

84 Fourth, coordination of public relations and legal activities during the trial—with particular attention to providing appropriate assistance to the press and helping to assure accurate, balanced coverage of the proceedings.

85 Whenever legal strategy allows, a company facing antitrust attack should be prepared to make rebuttal to public accusations, when and if they are made. To do this effectively, corporate officials, lawyers, and public relations people must prepare procedures for the rapid development and quick clearance of company statements. A leading antitrust lawyer for one of the country's largest corporations told me several days ago that he was convinced that most companies can—if they work in advance on the basis of information available to them—prepare rebuttals that are forceful and with enough news material to make the refutation attention-getting. He added that in actual practice his own company had done this and had captured its share of the news coverage and headlines. The benefits, in keeping the record straight, were substantial.

86 Rapid development of such statements is important. News is perishable. In most cases, the news media will publish a rebuttal along with an attack—but they are much less likely to do so in a separate story which limps along 24 hours or so after the charge is made.

87 Sometimes even the best planned handling of the news may be ignored or unduly subordinated in the press. Thus it is also advisable to have an alternative plan for getting the facts directly to such thoughtful and interested individuals as stockholders, suppliers, customers, other businessmen, city officials, and others important to the particular company involved. This may be done quickly by letters designed for each audience. Or by adding such groups to the release distribution list. Or by other means. The company's own employees are a particularly important and effective group. They should be kept informed about the charges and the company position so they can reflect the company's story in their own communities.

88 And in those cases where the defendant is ultimately exonerated, a company should undertake strong efforts to gain public awareness of the outcome of the trial. This should, whenever possible, include a concise summary of the company's positive position—a "white paper" which can help to preserve perspective and tell the facts of the acquittal. As I mentioned earlier, charges and accusations are news. When the antitrust division files suit, it issues a press release and the charges frequently are emblazoned in headlines stretching across the continent.

89 But when a company wins, the Justice Department demonstrates no similar devotion to the public's need for "government information services."

90 In a case involving Du Pont, charges were filed in a blaze of publicity. Four years later, the entire matter was quietly quashed by the government's lawyers. Not surprisingly, this development received no publicity whatever from the excellent information facilities of the Justice Department.

91 Du Pont moved immediately to rectify this omission by the government's information service, and through a formal statement and wide press contacts was able to gain public recognition of the Justice Department's action.

92 At that time, Crawford H. Greenewalt, Du Pont president, said: "Although the antitrust division showed no distaste for publicity at the time the indictment was obtained, it seems now as though its attitude has changed. It is now apparent that if anybody is going to tell the public that this case against Du Pont was dropped, it will have to be the defendant.

93 "This seems a trifle inconsiderate," Mr. Greenewalt continued, "to those of us who squirmed under the initial publicity, but I suppose we should be sympathetic with a human reluctance to admit error . . . In any event it is my privilege to announce to the public generally that the Department of Justice, on December 2, 1952, dropped this case against us."[10]

94 The problem we have been talking about today is one that appears certain to get worse before it gets better. The number of antitrust cases filed by the Justice Department in the first two years of the Kennedy Administration (132), was double that of the first two years of the Eisenhower Administration (65).

95 A distinguished antitrust lawyer for an oil company told one of our executives not long ago that he feared a new juridical theory is evolving from the pattern of antitrust prosecutions of recent years. "Throughout our history," he said, "the accused has been considered innocent until proved guilty. But now in antitrust cases the reverse appears to be true. The accused often seems to be considered guilty until he proves his innocence."

96 I'm not qualified to judge the legal validity of his theory. But it struck a spark in me, because what he said applies fully to the court of public opinion. I'm afraid that your clients and mine are automatically considered guilty by the public when the charges are made. There is virtually no understanding of the strenuous attempts made by businessmen to adhere to antitrust requirements in the face of statutes which are so written that they cannot be interpreted precisely. All too often, the public—lacking knowledge of complexities in the law and of the many court vindications—continues to think industry is guilty. This has been going on so long that opinion polls clearly show people to be misinformed and hostile about price-fixing charges. A hostile public is one step removed from hostile legislation.

97 Nobody argues that there is any public defense for price-fixers. The best public relations is compliance with the law. But lawyers and public relations men alike recognize that there is often a delicate problem, in the evolving body of antitrust law, in determining what is, and what is not, compliance. We believe this: if a company tries to comply with the antitrust statutes—and thinks it has complied—then it should defend itself vigorously against all public charges, indictments, investigations, leaks and slurs to the contrary.

98 We believe the legal profession is coming to recognize that many antitrust cases, won by industry in the courts, are lost in the newspapers. The problem, gentlemen, is to win outside the courtroom,

[10] Statement to Press, E. I. du Pont de Nemours & Company, Inc., December 21, 1952.

as well as inside; and, in any case, to make clear the company's efforts to comply with the law. For the continued erosion of the public's good will toward industry contains the germ of destruction for free enterprise.

99 The fanfare with which antitrust actions are greeted is no accident. It is planned that way. The company which fails to respond to the highly adverse publicity is like a citizen taking the Fifth Amendment. This is perfectly proper and in law it implies no guilt. But the public cannot be blamed if it suspects complicity.

100 Yet, once an antitrust case has been set in motion, a company must consider carefully what it says and how it says it, lest it create vexing and unnecessary problems for itself. This makes it essential that legal counsel and public relations counsel collaborate closely. They must exercise a nice balance of judgment to do what is best, overall, for the company.

101 We have found that this balance of judgment can best be arrived at when the lawyers and public relations men plan jointly how they will handle situations that can be foreseen. Good planning, in our experience, eliminates 90 percent of the problems that may otherwise arise, and sharply cuts back the hazards of saying the wrong thing at the right time, or of being caught without a statement when one is sorely needed.

102 To me, one of the encouraging developments of recent years is this growing collaboration between legal counsel and public relations counsel on antitrust and other problems. We are all caught up in the same worthwhile cause—the maintenance of a free and competitive business economy. You, as advocates at law, and we, as advocates in public opinion, have similar and overlapping aims. The more we can coordinate our efforts, the more certain we can be of the successful and lasting defense of our clients and of the competitive enterprise system.

MAN'S OTHER SOCIETY

Richard M. Duesterbeck

This speech was delivered by Richard M. Duesterbeck in the Interstate Oratorical Contest of 1961. Duesterbeck, who earlier in life had been imprisoned for misapplication of federal funds, was a senior student at Wisconsin State College in Eau Claire at the time of the contest.

Duesterbeck bases his plea for prison reform largely upon his personal experience. Although personal experience usually has a strong persuasive appeal, in this instance it creates a special problem of source credibility. What possible effects does his prison record have upon the persuasiveness of his message? How is his credibility as a source similar or dissimilar to that of Ralph Zimmermann in "Mingled Blood"? Are there any factors in Duesterbeck's personal narrative that make the problem especially compelling?

Duesterbeck clearly enumerates the parts of his solution, but he does not develop any of them extensively. However, do you think that he sufficiently develops each aspect of his plan for prison reform to make it seem plausible and workable?

This speech is reprinted by permission from Winning Orations, 1961 (*Evanston, Ill.: The Interstate Oratorical Association, 1961*), *pp. 100–102.*

1 When you look at me, it is easy to see several similarities between us. I have two arms, two legs, a brain, and a heart just like you. These are my hands, and they are just like yours. Like you I also have wants and desires; I am capable of love and hate. I can laugh and I can cry. Yes I'm just like you, except for one very important fact—I am an EX-CON.

2 The word EX-CON is a rough word. It means that I committed a crime, was arrested, convicted of Misapplication of Federal Funds, sentenced, and served time. For eleven months and eleven days I was part of Man's Other Society.

3 On June 16, 1959, I was sentenced to a term not to exceed two years in a federal institution. I was taken to the United States Federal Penitentiary, Terre Haute, Indiana, where I stayed for two months. I was then transferred to the Federal Correctional Institution at Sandstone, Minnesota, where I served until my parole was granted.

4 You have read about prison life in books and periodicals. You have seen in the movies and on television, dramatization concerning prison activity. Maybe you have wondered—What is it really like? I no longer wonder. I have served time. I know what it is like to live behind prison bars.

5 Until a person has his freedom taken from him, he can never fully appreciate how precious it really is. Think what it means to go for a walk, a long walk in one direction—to be able to take your car and drive through the countryside—to pick up a child, hold him in your arms, and listen to his childish chatter—to reach into your pocket and take a nickel—to gaze upon the third finger of your left hand and to see your wedding ring. These are some of the things which you cannot have in the prison community.

6 How many of you know that as an inmate in a federal institution I was allowed to write three letters a week, to an approved correspondent? Did you know that I could spend five hours per month visiting with my family, or that I was allowed to receive one package a year, at Christmas time, and it had to be of a certain size, weight, and could contain only specific items?

7 During my three-hundred-and-forty-six days as an inmate I saw many things. I met men I never knew existed before. My dorm mates were murderers, rapists, and dope addicts. You name them and I dormed with them. I had the opportunity to talk with them and to hear the very twisted thoughts which they had.

8 During this period of time I also learned many things. I can go out on the parking lot, take your car, start it, and I don't need your keys. I have acquired the ability whereby I can take my bare hands and kill you, just like this. I know more ways of taking your money from you than I can possibly remember. I have become an accomplished poker player, and believe me when I say that I can deal from the bottom of the deck with the best of them.

9 Oscar Wilde put it this way in his poem entitled "Ballad of Reading Gaol":

> The Vilest deeds like poison weeds,
> Bloom well in prison air,
> It is only what is good in Man,
> That wastes and withers there.

10 Now you may be thinking: Well what did he expect; he asked for it, didn't he? And you are right, I got exactly what I deserved. I am ashamed of having done time, but I did; and although I would give my right arm to be able to turn back the pages of time, it cannot be done. The purpose of the prison, however, is not only to confine a man, it also has the obligation to take that individual and return him to society as a rehabilitated human being. Does the taking of a man's wedding ring from him, allowing him to write three letters a week, or allowing him to visit with his family but five hours a month—do these things aid in rehabilitation of an inmate? The answer is NO. They do not.

11 It is easy to stand here and criticize the prison community, especially after one has done time in it. Criticism of this nature, however, bears with it very little validity, unless the person making the accusations stands ready to propose a program that will eliminate the evils to which he objects.

12 The problems of the prison are many and they are varied. In my estimation, however, there is one that stands out above all others. It concerns itself with the mistaken idea, which still persists, that there is a direct relationship between the seriousness of a man's crime and his potential for rehabilitation. William Krasner, a noted writer in the field of criminology, states that the dominant correctional philosophy is that the penitentiary is a kind of purifying flame into which the sinner must be thrust and held until he is punished, purged, or consumed. Mr. Krasner then goes on to say that society fails to realize that the prison door swings both ways, and unless a man dies in the institution he will some day return to society.

13 The program which I propose consists of three steps and if they are followed, they will go a long way towards elevating rehabilitation to its proper position in the field of prison operation.

14 Step number one—segregation. The first time offenders will have to be segregated from the general prison population. Once a man has become institutionalized, it is almost impossible to change him. I recall a young man I met in Sandstone who was 27-years old. His life of crime began when he was sixteen and in the eleven years that followed he spent a total of less than six months in free society. He did time in five different state and federal prisons. Then there was the man who was sentenced the same day I was. He was fifty-one years of age and in the past twenty-seven years had spent less than two years as a free man. I could give you many other examples that would illustrate the fact that the prison is not returning men to society in a reformed condition. I am not trying to get you to believe that all of us criminals are reformable. You know and I know that is not so. What I am saying is that the best chance for rehabilitation lies with that first time offender provided he can be kept from association with the time hardened inmate.

15 Step number two—social education. You would be surprised at the number of men who enter the institution with the idea that society owes them a living. Unless this attitude is changed in the institution he will return to society in the same frame of mind. This part of my program demands very careful planning so that the desired results can be achieved.

16 Step number three—educate society. In order for this program to be accomplished society will have to be made to realize that an inmate is a human being. Father Clark of St. Louis, Missouri, who has been called the "Hoodlum Priest" because of his work with released prisoners, gives the following point of view on how society treats the released inmate. He says: "We boycott him all the way down the line—economically, socially, morally. It's very tough to get a job, own a home, lead any kind of normal life. The unions don't want him; the bonding companies and Armed Forces won't have him." Society will have to be willing to accept him upon his release and even more important, they will have to be willing to provide him with gainful employment.

17 To succeed this program needs the interest of the general public. How many of you know what goes on behind the walls of your state institutions? How is the inmate treated? Is the correctional program of a progressive nature? Do the prison and the personnel therein provide an atmosphere that is conducive to rehabilitation? These are questions that need answers. Unless we are willing to take an active interest in this problem, rehabilitation will always occupy a position of secondary importance rather than being the number one goal of prison operation.

18 In June of this year I will receive my Baccalaureate Degree with a Bachelor of Science in Education. I hope to join the Federal Prison System as an Assistant Director of Education in one of its thirty-two federal institutions. There I will be given an opportunity to set up and conduct a program of social education. I am one of the lucky ones. For everyone like me there are hundreds who are allowed to fall by the wayside because of the indifference of society. I ask of you to keep in mind that the prisoner doesn't need your sympathy and he doesn't need your charity, but he does need your help and this he needs most desperately. The Bible puts it in no uncertain terms when it tells us that you should do unto others as you would have them do unto you, for you are your brother's keeper.

WHY NOT LET COMPETITION GO TO WORK IN TRANSPORTATION?

Daniel P. Loomis

Daniel P. Loomis has been connected with the railroad industry most of his life: first as general counsel for the Delaware and Hudson Railroad; then as chairman of the Association of Western Railways; and, since 1957, as president of the Association of American Railways. He has also served as a lecturer on railroad labor relations at various universities, including the University of Chicago, Northwestern University, and the University of Minnesota. Loomis delivered this speech on transportation before the Economic Club of Detroit, Michigan on January 14, 1963.

Loomis's railroad background and the fact that he is addressing the Economic Club of the "Automobile City" make the introduction to his speech crucial. He must immediately win enough sympathy for himself and his subject to assure a sympathetic hearing. Analyze how he tries to cope with the situation in his initial remarks.

Different from the other speeches in this chapter, which advocate new plans, this policymaking address advocates the removal *of government obstacles to competition. Loomis proceeds by citing which restrictions could profitably be removed and why this action would be desirable. Do you think that he argues for the removal of these restrictions because of necessity or because of advantage to the railroad industry? To what great American value does his argument appeal? How is this speech an appeal for the restoration of a value?*

Loomis frequently asks rhetorical questions in his argument; in fact, he devotes paragraph 28 entirely to a series of questions. Skillfully worded rhetorical questions embody arguments and have the advantage of forcing the listener to answer in his mind. Why do you think Loomis placed these questions in one paragraph? Does this technique have any special persuasive impact?

As you read this speech, observe the visualization technique Loomis uses in paragraphs 34–38. Through this means he expects his audience to visualize the desirable consequences likely to occur from the removal of government regulations. What special persuasive effect does such a visualization achieve?

This speech is reprinted by permission from Vital Speeches of the Day (*March 15, 1963*), *pp. 322–325.*

1 May I express my great pleasure at having the privilege of addressing this outstanding body. When a fellow railroader heard I was coming to Detroit to talk before this great forum of leaders of the auto industry, he remarked that this must surely be a case of "Daniel walking into the lion's den."

2 Now, in a narrow sense, he was right. For if there is anything certain in transportation history, it is that the near-monopoly on inland transport which railroads held in the last century was doomed once and for all time when your managerial ancestors developed the motor vehicle—and when you yourself, in turn, produced these in such fabulous quantities as to park one alongside practically every home in every village and town in the land. Your wondrous assortment of automobiles dealt a body blow to that one-time transport monopoly. So did your trucks and buses. Other blows have rained down from airplanes, pipelines, towboats and the long lakers that sail by on your Detroit River. Today's picture of transportation is thus one of all-pervading competition—a rough-and-tumble struggle of many, many contenders. Small wonder the railroads occasionally emerge in groggy condition!

3 Yet I did not come here today to recall with nostalgia the "good old days" or seek your sympathies. Nor did I come to record any railroad resentment for the whirlwinds of competition you unleashed in the transportation industry. I came not to oppose progress in automaking but to serve it.

4 If you can now build cars economically (and who would contend you cannot!), we railroadmen will show you how to build them even more economically.

5 If your state's road officials can build highways economically, we will show you how to build them with even greater economy.

6 If you factory managers and investors are worried about coping with the profit squeeze exerted by rising internal costs, we will show you how to cut those costs.

7 If all of you who buy cars and automotive products are worried about the prices you pay, we will show you how to get even lower prices.

8 And I might add, gentlemen, that you don't need an Aladdin's Lamp to perform such magic. In fact, there's no magic to it at all. We need only use plain old common sense based on giving the competi-

tion that now pervades our transport system an open, honest chance to go to work for your interest and for the public's interest.

9 I remarked earlier that any interpretation of conflict between rail and auto interests could be based only on the most narrow look. Mass production and nationwide marketing of autos or any other product would be impossible without the railroads' mass transportation services. Yet I submit, gentlemen, that we have a mutuality of interest that far transcends the classic relationship between industry and carrier, supplier and customer. We are partners in preserving and strengthening the competitive enterprise system that underlies America's productive might. Like you, we railroaders believe that the man who makes the best product at the best price and offers the best service, should get the public's business. This is the very soul of the competitive enterprise system. It is what has made Detroit, and what has made America.

10 I come with a message of grave danger to that system in a most vital segment of our economic and national life, however. And I come to appeal for your help in putting transportation on the competitive track that leads to a strengthened industry, better services and lower prices for everyone.

11 You will have noticed that I titled my talk "Why Not Let Competition Go to Work in Transportation?" I chose that to point up the strange government regulatory roadblocks that hang over from the 19th Century thinking and which prevent railroads and other carriers from passing on to you the public the full benefits of technological progress in hauling people and goods. I will deal mainly with this subject for I consider it an area where you and all America have the clearest stake and where remedial action can result in the most immediate benefits to everyone. Even so, I am tempted to take up the almost equally meaningful effort of rail management to update outworn work rules in the industry and to clear away featherbedding. The railroad merger movement and the plant modernization programs aimed at changing the face and structure of the rail industry offer further temptations. I will touch on these developments briefly—for they are all parts of the great story of an industry which is changing dramatically and is crossing the threshold to a new era of service to the nation.

12 This new year opens to the echoes of significant 1962 events signaling these changes. Last year witnessed a modest traffic comeback for railroading from the rock-bottom years that have haunted us, as well as much of the nation, since the recession of 1958. It witnessed the end of the onerous 10 per cent federal excise tax on travel tickets and some long-overdue changes in policies to spur investment. It witnessed a ringing indictment by President Kennedy of the punishing inequities in the nation's transportation laws and an urgent call for correction by Congress. And it witnessed further steps along the rough road which we set out on years ago to end those featherbedding work practices which bleed railroads of nearly $600 million a year in pay for work not performed or not needed.

13 All in all, these developments of 1962 add up to the brightest outlook for railroads in recent years. Yet, at the present time, a brighter outlook is all it is. Fulfillment of the railroads' truly great potential for service to the American people will result not so much from the actions taken in 1962 as from what remains to be done in the year ahead. Specifically, it will depend largely upon the progress that is made along the three vital fronts I mentioned.

14 Let no one deceive you as to railroad intentions on featherbedding. Despite union refusal to bargain on this issue, despite court delays and other forms of filibuster, we will not stop until we have rid ourselves—and you, our customers—of the expense of outmoded work rules and unneeded positions, including those of firemen with no fires to tend on diesel freight and yard locomotives. Imagine auto unions telling auto-makers they could not put in more efficient machinery on an engineblock line—or if they did, they would have to keep all present employees on the payroll permanently. Or imagine installing push-button elevators in an office building, then being required to keep idle operators on board, and on full pay. Ludicrous as such things sound, these are the kind of paralyzing situations we are up against today in railroading. We not only cannot stand it any longer; we *will* not stand for it.

15 It is tragic that the unions representing train operating employees have refused to cooperate with railroads in this obviously essential streamlining program. They have chosen instead to follow the dead-end road of insistence upon retaining every possible job regardless of need or justification for it. One is forced to wonder if union officials are not more interested in maintaining dues-paying membership rolls than in helping workers adjust to change and getting better pay and building genuine security into really necessary jobs.

16 The second vital front on which a breakthrough could be attained in 1963 is one on which the principal opposition again has come from unions of railroad employees. This involves the numerous applications for railroad mergers and consolidations now on file with the Interstate Commerce Commission. The unions profess to see dire

consequences in these proposed railroad mergers, regardless of their economic need or justification. However, it appears to virtually all informed people that they really oppose mergers for the same short-sighted reason that they oppose changes in work rules, and that is the fear of losing jobs . . . or dues-paying union members.

17 As no one knows better than you in the auto industry, soundly conceived mergers that increase efficiency and contribute to more economical operation are in the long-range best interest of employees, exactly as they are in the best interest of the public as a whole. No one, least of all a company's employees, benefits from an inefficient operation, for the company or industry that does not keep pace in today's highly competitive, fast-moving world cannot hope for long even to stay alive and maintain jobs that are needed, much less to provide jobs that are not needed.

18 The railroad industry today is the product of literally hundreds of mergers, and the nation can only be thankful that it did not follow in the past the unsound philosophy now being advocated by unions for the future. There remain over 100 major railroads in this nation, and the process of consolidating facilities and streamlining services must be continued if rail survival is to be assured in the face of red-hot competition from other forms of transportation. The Interstate Commerce Commission just two weeks ago approved the stock-purchase control plan of the Baltimore and Ohio by the Chesapeake and Ohio, and we trust this action signals early decisions on other long-pending merger proposals.

19 The third critical front on which significant progress must be made in 1963 is the one I came here mainly to tell you about today—the one that has as its objective the removal of excessive, capricious and unnecessary regulations that handicap railroads in meeting the competition of other forms of transportation and in better serving all of you. These regulations, for the most part, were adopted when railroads were the only form of transportation worthy of the name and when business standards and laws were a far cry from what they are today. They were needed then because competition, which has no peer as a protector of the public interest, simply did not exist in the field of transportation.

20 Obviously, this is not the situation today, where shippers and travelers have not only an abundance of for-hire carriers from which to choose, but also a great and growing capability to provide private transportation service for themselves in their own vehicles, both for travel and freight. Already the private automobile accounts for more than 90 per cent of all intercity travel in the United States, leaving only 10 per cent to be divided up among airlines, railroads, buses. And in the transportation of goods on the highways, traffic handled by industry-owned and unregulated carriers outnumbers that handled by general for-hire carriers in the ratio of about two to one.

21 In fact, the common carriers of today are fighting among themselves for a steadily diminishing share of the total transportation pie when the real threat to common carriers of all modes is private transportation, which is growing by leaps and bounds. If common carriers are to reverse this trend, as they must, then it is obvious that common carriers must be able to provide the service shippers want at a price no higher, and preferably lower, than shippers can provide it for themselves. To do this, common carriers must be given the freedom to meet competition in whatever form it exists, private carriage or otherwise. No scheme for extending or tightening up regulations will solve this problem: Less regulation over common carriers is the only answer.

22 I say common carriers, but what I really mean is railroads. For it is only railroads that are fully regulated with respect to all their traffic. Motor common carriers have what is known as the agricultural commodities exemption of the Interstate Commerce Act which enables them to escape regulation in the movement of vast tonnages of agricultural commodities. This is one of the reasons why up to 98 per cent of the tonnages of certain agricultural commodities have shifted to truck. Operating outside regulation, truckers, including common carriers, are able to charge any rate they choose on the movement of any exempt agricultural commodity.

23 Yet, when the same commodities move by railroad, they are subject to full regulation by the ICC, including the requirement that rates must be published for all competitors to see, and cannot be changed except upon 30 days' published notice or by special permission of the ICC. With this enormous advantage, trucks are able to undercut railroad rates at will, which is exactly what they do.

24 A similar advantage is enjoyed by barge lines operating free of charge on inland waterways improved and maintained at public expense. Largely as a result of the bulk commodities exemption, which enables even the common carrier barge lines to escape regulation merely by limiting the number of bulk commodities they carry on a single barge or tow, an estimated 90 per cent of all waterway traffic goes unregulated. This especially hurts, for the handling of bulk commodities is the railroads' bread-and-butter business—a job they do best. Yet in competing for this type of traffic with barge lines, the railroads suffer an almost fatal disadvantage in having to publish and abide by strict rates while their barge line competitors are free to charge whatever they choose.

25 I mentioned earlier the transportation message which President Kennedy sent to Congress last year. In that message the President referred specifically to the two inequities I have just described and gave his suggestions for affording the railroads some relief. His recommendations were incorporated in bills, but committee action was not completed before Congress adjourned. Administration sources have announced that the proposals will be renewed early in this Congress.

26 Essentially what the President proposes is to achieve greater equality of treatment and opportunity by relaxing the regulatory restraints imposed on railroads and allowing the forces of competition to assume something of their proper role in protecting the public interest. Specifically, as to those commodities now entirely exempt when moving by motor carrier or barge, the President would relieve the ICC of its power to stop railroad rate reductions—a power which the ICC too frequently exercises to protect competing forms of transportation. Any rate *increases* by railroads, on the other hand, would continue to be subject to ICC control. Moreover, the ICC still would retain full power to prohibit rates that are unduly discriminatory, exactly as it does today. The only change is that railroads, instead of having to hold up a protective price umbrella over competitors, would also be free to make competitive rate reductions.

27 What present regulatory exemptions have done, in effect, has been to make competition in transportation a one-way street. Exempt road and water carriers can set rates at any level they wish and cart off the railroads' traffic with impunity: When the railroads try to hold onto their traffic or get it back by reducing their rates, the public regulator blows the whistle and swings the night-stick.

28 Isn't it about time the railroads were allowed to do the same as their competitors? Isn't it about time government started treating all carriers alike? Isn't it about time to do away with a Big Brother type of regulation which protects and coddles road and water carriers while hamstringing our indispensable rail carriers? What's wrong with giving competition a chance to help transportation blossom out into full flower, just as it has spurred progress in the great auto industry?

29 I might point out that the President also considered the alternative step of achieving greater regulatory equality by extending government price controls to carriers now free of these. To his credit, he expressed clear preference for placing greater reliance on the forces of competition and less on the restraints of regulation. My own conviction is that in a fast-moving, complex economy like America's, the only practical and workable approach is to return to less regulation and freer competition.

30 Detroit can provide abundant examples to point up the damage done by cobweb-covered controls in transport. Imagine, for instance, that General Motors' pricing was completely regulated by government (God forbid!) but that other auto companies could wheel and deal and price their products in freedom as they do today. How long do you suppose GM would survive such an inequity?

31 Or suppose an auto-maker announced that as a result of operating efficiency or market pressures, his auto prices were to be cut by $100. Imagine the cheers from the public . . . the laudatory editorials over this statesmanlike action . . . the speeches at Lansing . . . the statements from Washington!

32 But if the same regulatory fabric surrounded the auto industry as now enmeshes railroads, the price-cutting auto-maker would immediately be hailed before a governmental tribunal by his competitors and forced to defend and justify his action. They would make it out to be practically a crime to cut prices. And even if the regulator finally approved the reductions, so many months or years of arguing and litigation may have elapsed that markets might have disappeared, along with all those savings for the public . . . and perhaps the auto-company, too.

33 Well, gentlemen, that's railroading for you! Anyone here want to change places?

34 What would railroads do with greater pricing freedom? One example came out just a few days ago when Commonwealth Edison of Chicago proposed to begin next year to receive coal at its Hammond, Indiana, generating plant by a special new integrated train. This would run non-stop as a unit of 100 or more cars from coal mines 250 miles away, carrying a whopping 10,000 tons per trip, cutting days off normal delivery schedules and resulting in fuel savings of more than $1 million a year.

35 Another example lies in the extended effort by one of our southern railroads to obtain ICC approval for deep rate reductions on movements of grain in specially built, lightweight covered-hopper cars. Again, the principle was the same: Railroaders developed a better way to haul products more cheaply, then tried to pass on the economies to the public in lower prices. And up went the regulatory bars!

36 We would also like to give you shippers the privilege of contracting for rail transportation over a long period, getting lower rates in exchange for guaranteed volume or shares of your shipments. Detroit factory managers do this sort of thing every day in signing up suppliers of materials and sub-assemblies. But when the railroads tried to develop such a contract system in one recent case, the ICC found this unlawful.

37 Other developments that point up the need for greater flexibility in transport pricing include the spectacular growth of piggy-backing of truck trailers on flatcars, the expanding use of universal containers that can be transferred from train to truck to ship to airplane without reloading contents, and the return of much new automobile traffic to railroads. Underlying the latter development was a combination of lower rates and better service made possible by important breakthroughs in the development of new bi-level and tri-level "rack" cars for transporting 12 to 15 automobiles on one freight car and as many as a thousand in one freight train. This, gentlemen, is what we mean when we talk about the super-railroads to come.

38 Latest statistics covering the movement of new automobiles by railroad in the first quarter of 1962 show that volume was more than double that of the first quarter of 1960 and 1961 and nearly four times that of the 1959 quarter. The railroads' gross freight revenue from automobile traffic more than doubled, from $16¼ million in the 1959 quarter to more than $35½ million in the first quarter of 1962. And wherever railroads received more money for these expanded services to auto-makers, the latter reaped huge savings in costs compared with older shipping methods. On a standard size automobile of 4,000 pounds, the transportation savings to auto companies have averaged nearly $50 as compared with the rates in effect during 1959. Thus railroads have attained a significant increase in their productive capability at a very substantial decrease in unit cost. The result is a combination of lower rates to customers and higher volume for railroads that has tended to maximize rail earnings while helping manufacturers in their constant battle to hold the cost and price line on new automobiles. This is truly an example at its best of mutual interest working toward mutual benefit.

39 What could be fairer or more desirable than this? Nothing, you would say. Yet President Kennedy's modest proposal to give greater leeway to competitive forces brought forth from the top spokesman for the American Trucking Associations this amazing statement: "Our industry," he said, "has no confidence in the ability of free competition in the market place to produce orderly transportation."

40 Coming from a Marx or Lenin, such a vote of "no confidence" in what is the keystone of the American system would surprise no one. Coming from the top spokesman for a major American industry, it is something else again.

41 You might well ask, just what is there that is so peculiar, so unique, about transportation that warrants retaining the singular, severe restrictions on the pricing freedom of railroads, while allowing railroad competitors free rein in the broad areas covered by the exemptions?

42 Certainly, it is not a well-grounded fear of monopoly, for the existence today of extensive networks of highways, airways, waterways and pipelines, in addition to railroads, makes the attainment of monopoly by any one transportation mode a practical impossibility.

43 Certainly it is not for lack of adequate safeguards to protect the public interest against discriminatory pricing, for the President, in making his proposal said: "To prevent the absence of minimum rate regulation . . . from resulting in predatory, discriminatory trade practices or rate wars . . . the Congress should make certain that such practices by carriers freed from minimum rate regulations would be covered by existing laws against monopoly and predatory trade practices." Railroads are in full accord with this objective.

44 Could it possibly be that barge lines and trucks are fearful of their ability to compete with railroads on fair and equal terms? Not if you can believe what you hear. Spokesmen of both forms can be heard almost daily proclaiming their alleged superiority over railroads in either pricing or service or both. In fact, it was only a few weeks ago in New York that the top trucking spokesman in the United States virtually wrote off the railroads as being over the hill, while the trucking industry, he candidly acknowledged, was "mature."

45 Frankly, we get awful tired of hearing highway haulers talk about the need to shield "small" operators against the "big, powerful" railroads. Gentlemen, don't be misled! What the trucking industry isn't telling is that truckers are now grown big and powerful themselves and as able as anyone to stand on their own feet in competition. The Transportation Association of America estimates that the freight bill for intercity highway carriage—including both private and for-hire trucks—totaled approximately $19 billion in the year 1961, or *more than twice* the freight revenues of all the nation's railroads. This, I repeat, is traffic *between* cities and does not include local truckers' revenues.

46 Individual companies are also giants in their own right. In 1960, nearly a thousand intercity motor carriers had operating revenues of over $1 million. Over 100 truck companies had revenues of more than $10 million, and one giant trucking corporation took in a total of $99 million.

47 What is it then that denies to transportation and the public the benefits to be had from competition? It is simply that to barge and truck interests, the protection they enjoy against fair railroad competition has become a way of life. The prospect of their having to venture forth and face the rigors of fair competition must be distinctly unappealing. Yet, in the nation's interest, I would suggest to our truck and barge friends that instead of striving to retain the artificial and unfair government protections they now enjoy, why not strive to establish a system in which every form of transportation will be allowed to give the public its best possible service at the lowest possible cost. When this is done, traffic will flow naturally to all carriers according to the true economic capabilities of each. Then, we'll finally begin to see some rational division of transport functions and a strengthened industry operating at lower costs and far more capable of meeting peacetime needs and wartime emergencies.

48 Continued government protection of big truck and barging businesses against fair railroad competition is not only a monstrous injustice against one of America's most essential businesses. It picks the public's pocket by denying you the benefits of vigorous price competition in transportation. And equally alarming, it promotes the tightening grip and inexorable expansion of a Big Brother philosophy that will ultimately sound the death-knell for competitive enterprise *unless checked here and now*. Gentlemen, we ask your help in doing just that.

THE INTELLECTUAL AND THE POLITICIAN

John F. Kennedy

As Senator from Massachusetts, John F. Kennedy delivered this speech on June 14, 1956, at a Harvard University commencement, during which his alma mater awarded him an honorary LL.D. degree.

He took this opportunity to plead for a closer link between American intellectuals and American politicians.

Kennedy's speech offers no detailed plan or machinery for action; it simply calls for a policy of cooperation and understanding between the two groups. In his first point he tries to show the common ancestry of the two groups; in the second, he reminds them that both operate within a common framework—liberty. In the third point he stresses "the great potential gain for both groups resulting from increased political cooperation." What is the persuasive function of the first two points? How does Kennedy support his third point? Does he adequately develop the advantages of a policy of increased cooperation to make the ideas convincing?

As you read this speech, compare Kennedy's style with that of his Presidential "Inaugural Address." Which speech has the more natural approach as revealed by the sentences? Which approach is more effective? How does the nature of the subject, audience, and occasion bear upon the previous question? "The Intellectual and the Politician" paraphrases and briefly quotes statements of others. Do you find that this technique achieves any special effect?

This speech is reprinted by permission from Representative American Speeches: 1956–1957, *ed. A. Craig Baird (New York: H. W. Wilson Co., 1957), pp. 165–172; and by permission of Mrs. John F. Kennedy.*

1 It is a pleasure to join with my fellow alumni in this pilgrimage to the second home of our youth.

2 Prince Bismarck once remarked that one third of the students of German universities broke down from overwork; another third broke down from dissipation; and the other third ruled Germany. As I look about this campus today, I would hesitate to predict which third attends reunions (although I have some suspicion), but I am confident I am looking at "rulers" of America in the sense that all active informed citizens rule.

3 I can think of nothing more reassuring for all of us than to come again to this institution whose whole purpose is dedicated to the advancement of knowledge and the dissemination of truth.

4 I belong to a profession where the emphasis is somewhat different. Our political parties, our politicians are interested, of necessity, in winning popular support—a majority, and only indirectly truth is the object of our controversy. From this polemic of contending

factions, the general public is expected to make a discriminating judgment. As the problems have become more complex, as our role as a chief defender of Western civilization has become enlarged, the responsibility of the electorate as a court of last resort has become almost too great. The people desperately seek objectivity and a university such as this fulfills that function.

5 And the political profession needs to have its temperature lowered in the cooling waters of the scholastic pool. We need both the technical judgment and the disinterested viewpoint of the scholar, to prevent us from becoming imprisoned by our own slogans.

6 Therefore, it is regrettable that the gap between the intellectual and politician seems to be growing. Instead of synthesis, clash and discord now characterize the relations between the two groups much of the time. Authors, scholars and intellectuals can praise every aspect of American society but the political. My desk is flooded with books, articles and pamphlets criticizing Congress. But, rarely if ever, have I seen any intellectual bestow praise on either the political profession or any political body for its accomplishments, its ability or its integrity—much less for its intelligence. To many universities and scholars we rear nothing but censors, investigators and perpetrators of what has been called "the swinish cult of anti-intellectualism."

7 James Russell Lowell's satiric attack more than a hundred years ago on Caleb Cushing, a celebrated attorney general and member of Congress, sets the tone:

> Gineral C is a dreffle smart man,
> He's ben on all sides that give places or pelf,
> But consistency still wuz a part of his plan—
> He's been true to *one* party, that is himself.

8 But in fairness, the way of the intellectual is not altogether serene; in fact so great has become popular suspicion that a recent survey of American intellectuals by a national magazine elicited from one of our foremost literary figures the guarded response, "I ain't no intellectual."

9 Both sides in this battle, it seems to me, are motivated by largely unfounded feelings of distrust. The politician, whose authority rests upon the mandate of the popular will, is resentful of the scholar who can, with dexterity, slip from position to position without dragging the anchor of public opinion. It was this skill that caused Lord Melbourne to say of the youthful historian Macaulay that he wished he was as sure of anything as Macaulay was of everything. The intellectual, on the other hand, finds it difficult to accept the difference between the laboratory and the legislature. In the former, the goal is truth, pure and simple, without regard to changing currents of public opinion; in the latter, compromises and majorities and procedural customs and rights affect the ultimate decision as to what is right or just or good. And even when they realize this difference, most intellectuals consider their chief function that of the critic—and politicians are sensitive to critics (possibly because we have so many of them). "Many intellectuals," Sidney Hook has said, "would rather 'die' than agree with the majority, even on the rare occasions when the majority is right."

10 It seems to me that the time has come for intellectuals and politicians alike to put aside those horrible weapons of modern internecine warfare, the barbed thrust, the acid pen, and—most sinister of all—the rhetorical blast. Let us not emphasize all on which we differ but all we have in common. Let us consider not what we fear separately but what we share together.

11 First, I would ask both groups to recall that the American politician of today and the American intellectual of today are descended from a common ancestry. Our nation's first great politicians were also among the nation's first great writers and scholars. The founders of the American Constitution were also the founders of American scholarship. The works of Jefferson, Madison, Hamilton, Franklin, Paine and John Adams—to name but a few—influenced the literature of the world as well as its geography. Books were their tools, not their enemies. Locke, Milton, Sydney, Montesquieu, Coke and Bolingbroke were among those widely read in political circles and frequently quoted in political pamphlets. Our political leaders traded in the free commerce of ideas with lasting results both here and abroad.

12 In these golden years, our political leaders moved from one field to another with amazing versatility and vitality. Jefferson and Franklin still throw long shadows over many fields of learning. A contemporary described Jefferson, "A gentleman of thirty-two, who could calculate an eclipse, survey an estate, tie an artery, plan an edifice, try a cause, break a horse, dance a minuet, and play the violin."

13 Daniel Webster could throw thunderbolts at Hayne on the Senate floor and then stroll a few steps down the corridor and dominate the Supreme Court as the foremost lawyer of his time. John Quincy Adams, after being summarily dismissed from the Senate for a notable display of independence, could become Boylston Professor of Rhetoric and Oratory at Harvard and then become a great Secretary of State.

(Those were the happy days when Harvard professors had no difficulty getting Senate confirmation.)

14 The versatility also existed on the frontier. An obituary of Missouri's first senator, Thomas Hart Benton, the man whose tavern brawl with Jackson in Tennessee caused him to flee the state, said:

> With a readiness that was often surprising, he could quote from a Roman law or a Greek philosopher, from Virgil's *Georgics*, the *Arabian Nights*, Herodotus or Sancho Panza, from the Sacred Carpets, the German reformers or Adam Smith; from *Fénelon* or *Hudibras*, from the financial reports of Necca or the doings of the Council of Trent, from the debates on the adoption of the Constitution or intrigues of the Kitchen Cabinet or from some forgotten speech of a deceased member of Congress.

15 This link between the American scholarship and the American politician remained for more than a century. Just one hundred years ago today in the presidential campaign of 1856, the Republicans sent three brilliant orators around the campaign circuit: William Cullen Bryant, Henry Wadsworth Longfellow and Ralph Waldo Emerson. Those were the carefree days when the "egg-heads" were all Republicans.

16 I would hope that both groups, recalling their common heritage, might once again forge a link between the intellectual and political professions. I know that scholars may prefer the mysteries of pure scholarship or the delights of abstract discourse. But, "Would you have counted him a friend of ancient Greece," as George William Curtis asked a century ago during the Kansas-Nebraska controversy, "who quietly discussed of patriotism on that Greek summer day through whose hopeless and immortal hours Leonidas and his three hundred stood at Thermopylae for liberty? Was John Milton to conjugate Greek verbs in his library or talk of the liberty of the ancient Shunammites when the liberty of Englishmen was imperiled?" No, the duty of the scholar—particularly in a republic such as ours—is to contribute his objective views and his sense of liberty to the affairs of his state and nation.

17 Secondly, I would remind both groups that the American politician and the American intellectual operate within a common framework—a framework we call liberty. Freedom of expression is not divisible into political expression and intellectual expression. The lock on the door of the Legislature, the Parliament or the Assembly Hall—by order of the King, the Commissar or the Fuehrer—has historically been followed or preceded by a lock on the door of the university, the library or the printer's. And if the first blow for freedom in any subjugated land is struck by a political leader, the second is struck by a book, a newspaper or a pamphlet.

18 Unfortunately, in more recent times, politicians and intellectuals have quarreled bitterly—too bitterly in some cases—over how each group has met the modern challenge to freedom both at home and abroad. Politicians have questioned the discernment with which intellectuals have reacted to the siren call of the extreme left; and intellectuals have tended to accuse politicians of not always being aware, especially here at home, of the toxic effects of freedom restrained.

19 While differences in judgment where freedom is endangered are perhaps inevitable, there should nevertheless be more basic agreement on fundamentals. In this field we should be natural allies, working more closely together for the common cause, against the common enemy.

20 Third and finally, I would stress the great potential gain for both groups resulting from increased political cooperation.

21 The American intellectual and scholar today must decide, as Goethe put it, whether he is to be an anvil—or a hammer. Today, for many, the stage of the anvil, at least in its formal phases, is complete. The question he faces is whether he is to be a hammer—whether he is to give to the world in which he was reared and educated the broadest possible benefits of his learning. As one who is familiar with the political world, I can testify that we need it.

22 For example: The password for all legislation, promoted by either party, is progress. But how do we tell what is progress and what is retreat? Those of us who may be too close to the issue, or too politically or emotionally involved in it, look for the objective world of the scholar. Indeed, the operation of our political life is such that we may not even be debating the real issues.

23 In foreign affairs, for example, the parties dispute over which is best fitted to implement the long-accepted policies of collective security and Soviet containment. But perhaps these policies are no longer adequate, perhaps these goals are no longer meaningful—the debate goes on nevertheless, for neither party is in a position to undertake the reappraisal necessary, particularly if the solutions presented are more complex to, and less popular with, the electorate.

24 Or take our agricultural program, for another example. Republicans and Democrats debate long over whether flexible or rigid price supports should be in effect. But this may not be the real issue at all—and in fact I am convinced that it is not, that neither program offers any long-range solution to our many real farm problems. The scholars and the universities might reexamine this whole area and come up with some real answers—the political parties and their conventions rarely will.

25 Other examples could be given indefinitely—where do we draw the line between free trade and protection, when does taxation become prohibitive, what is the most effective use we can make of our present nuclear potential? The intellectuals who can draw upon their rational disinterested approach and their fund of learning to help reshape our political life can make a tremendous contribution to their society while gaining new respect for their own group.

26 I do not say that our political and public life should be turned over to experts who ignore public opinion. Nor would I adopt from the Belgian Constitution of 1893 the provision giving three votes instead of one to college graduates; or give Harvard a seat in the Congress as William and Mary was once represented in the Virginia House of Burgesses.

27 But, I would urge that our political parties and our universities recognize the need for greater cooperation and understanding between politicians and intellectuals. We do not need scholars or politicians like Lord John Russell, of whom Queen Victoria remarked, he would be a better man if he knew a third subject—but he was interested in nothing but the Constitution of 1688 and himself. What we need are men who can ride easily over broad fields of knowledge and recognize the mutual dependence of our two worlds.

28 "Don't teach my boy poetry," an English mother recently wrote the Provost of Harrow. "Don't teach my boy poetry; he is going to stand for Parliament." Well, perhaps she was right—but if more politicians knew poetry, and more poets knew politics, I am convinced the world would be a little better place to live on this Commencement Day of 1956.

"LET US WORK WHILE IT IS YET DAY"

Adlai E. Stevenson

The University of California at Berkeley honored U Thant, Secretary General of the United Nations, at a Charter Day convocation, on April 2, 1964. The American Ambassador to the United Nations, Adlai E. Stevenson, delivered the major address. In his speech, Ambassador Stevenson argued against reversion to a policy of isolationism and "passionate nationalism" and in favor of a policy of greater internationalism and universalism.

Stevenson used an inductive approach to meet the constraints of the occasion. Before divulging any general policy position, he developed a rationale for it. This technique is most often used when a speaker anticipates initial resistence to his course of action, since it has the advantage of getting the audience to view the evidence before prejudices become operative. Do you see any special reason why Stevenson, who very likely had high source credibility with his audience, used the inductive approach? Do you think that the persuasive strategy of the speech effectively leads one to the policy he is supporting? Does the way he develops the problem direct the listener to one, and only one, course of action—namely, the one he is advocating? Is his policy a new course of action or is he essentially defending the policy of the American government in 1964?

Rhetorical critics have often praised Stevenson's speech style. Some critics say that his style is unusually fresh and invariably stimulating. A truly excellent rhetorical style, one which makes ideas convincing and compelling without apparent artifice, is the supreme objective of an orator. As you read this speech, carefully note the source of Stevenson's stylistic effectiveness. Does it stem from word choice? Sentence construction? Allusions and pithy quotations? Imaginative ideas? Do you think his style as exemplified in this speech deserves the critics' praise? As a matter of interest, compare the style of this speech and that of Kennedy's "The Intellectual and the Politician." What do they have in common? Are there any essential differences?

This speech is reprinted by permission of Adlai E. Stevenson from a pamphlet by the World Law Fund, 11 West 42nd Street, New York, N.Y.

1 For me it is a two-fold honor to participate in these ceremonies marking the University of California's 96th Charter Day.

2 First, in honoring U Thant, Secretary General of the United Nations, you honor a man dedicated to the proposition that peace is nothing less than a human right. His dedication, I would add, is exceeded only by his labors to make that right universal. He is the symbol today of Lincoln's hope for a world in which right makes might. One cannot ask more of any man, and I am privileged to be here today in the company of a dear friend, a colleague and a great citizen of Burma and the world.

3 Second, coming as it does from a university that not only stands for, but has created some of the finest traditions of higher education, the degree you confer on me has meaning far beyond its flattering citation. I accept it with pride and gratitude.

4 This is by no means the first time I have spoken on the campus of the great university of my native state of California. And I well remember the last time. It was here in the Greek Theatre before a huge international conference of astronomers. Today, decorated with a Doctor's hood of the University of California, I feel even more—astronomical. I shall try to reciprocate by not abusing your kindness.

5 It was King Solomon who said, "Knowledge is a wonderful thing; therefore get knowledge; but with all thy getting, get understanding."

6 I could suggest no harder task, no greater challenge to a university in our complex world. And that is why we must see to it that no one, for whatever reason or in the service of whatever interest, diverts a university from its basic objective. For the university is the archive of the western mind, it is the keeper of the western culture; the fountain of western culture is freedom—freedom to inquire, to speak, to write, to worship in security. Men may be born free, but they cannot be born wise. It is the aspiration of the university to make free men wise.

7 Thomas Jefferson proclaimed that the United States was the strongest nation on earth not because of its military might or its productive capacity, but because of its revolutionary ideas. The American Revolution, he said, is intended for all mankind. And I would remind you that there would have been no American Revolution had we not had men who were free and wise and, therefore, not afraid to stand up and rock the boat.

8 Such an audacious and revolutionary heritage poses certain dangers nowadays, especially in education. But education itself can be dangerous. My friend, Robert Hutchins, has pointed out that the only way to avoid this danger is an educational system in which the student is exposed to no ideas whatever. But that, I think, would be a greater danger by far.

9 So I am happy, Dr. Kerr, that in this great university on the rim of the Pacific, which is not pacific, faculty and students alike search for the truth and tackle the great ideas and tough problems of our time.

10 It is about some of these problems and ideas that I want to speak.

11 Chesterton once said that the trouble about truisms is that they are still true. No truisms have been more pitilessly overworked than those affecting our new post-scientific, post-technological world environment. How often are we told that space has been conquered, that communication from one end of the world to the other is instant! How often we hear about the interdependence of the world economy! Our ears have been all but stunned by reminders that a few nuclear bombs could finish off the human experiment. In fact, we are so stunned that, like Dr. Strangelove, we can learn to live with the bomb and stop worrying.

12 Repetition, reiteration, rhetoric have all rubbed off the cutting edge. What can one say to restore it, to discover once again the truth under the truism? Does it just add to the cozy fog to remind ourselves that year by year the proximity, the instant contact, the fateful interdependence actually grow by a sort of geometrical progression—each invention speeding the next, each advance mobilizing the means for more?

13 Ten years have passed, I recall, since I gave the Godkin Lectures at Harvard and tried to explore some of the implications of our narrowing world. Only ten years—and in that time we have halved our flight time within space and propose, within another decade, to halve it again. We have sent Telstar in the heavens. We have catapulted men into outer space. One man in 24 hours has lived through a dozen dusks and dawns and swung above our planet, seeing it for the first time for what it is—a little ball in infinite space—and seeing it perhaps with a new eye of understanding.

14 "Our Earth, how beautiful it is!" cried one of the Soviet Cosmonauts. Notice our Earth, mankind's Earth, the only little space in all infinity where man can breathe and live and sleep, the little space which now, with a casual flip of a switch, he can annihilate so that the breathing and the sleeping and the living come finally to their end.

15 If this interdependence—this interdependence of mutual destruction—does not move us, what can, what will? We have to accept it as the new irrevocable environment of our age. And if there is one lesson above all that history should impress on us, it is that we ignore our environment at our peril.

16 From the origins of man, the collective group—call it tribe, call it state, call it nation—has battled with its neighbors, disputed the earth's surface, and in bloody engagement after bloody engagement marked the rise and fall of empires, confederacies, alliances and all kinds of dominations. It had one rationale. In the pre-scientific world, there were not enough resources to go round, and often the survival of one tribe meant the conquest of another's hunting grounds and the elimination of the other hunters. But however often and at whatever level this biting struggle for survival was renewed—in little wars or big wars—there was no extermination. Other groups took up the burdens. The human experiment went on.

17 Today the supreme expression of historical irony is that the real war of extermination is possible, the final destruction of the human species, and just as the pressure of competitive need is withdrawn. We no longer need our neighbors' hunting grounds. The rationale of separate, desperate sovereignty has all but vanished in the last two or three decades. But just as the reason vanishes, the means take over. We can wipe out the children of God just at the moment when, at last, the possibility of nourishing all of them begins to dawn. Irony of ironies!—The scientific means to end the need for war are twisted to ensure that the war of final extermination at last becomes a possibility.

18 In theory, of course, we know how to break away from these old fatalities. Within wider and wider areas of the earth's surface, men have contrived to rise above the rule of force and grab. Our large, peaceful, domestic societies prove to us that man is not condemned forever to clan and vendetta. An impartial government which provides police protection and the means, by law courts, to settle disputes is not a pipe dream. We live with it every day, and here in America we do so within a continental federation. Within these wide frontiers of law and order, the economic life of the land may be competitive, but it is not lethal. There is no compulsion either to rob or kill or to starve.

19 In short, the ground rules of our domestic society are not bad guidelines for international order. And in a world where wars can exterminate and at the same time economic life can begin to feed everyone, the guidelines that have worked to give peace and some sufficiency over a whole continent are sign posts to an inter-continental world society.

20 Nor do they represent a shift of scope of anything like the proportions which, in physical terms, we begin to accept every day. For a world of instant communication and increasingly instant travel, a few enlargements in the concepts of government, law, police and the general welfare are still—or should still be—much less startling than jumping into outer space. Can we, then, seriously expect to modify everything except our institutions, and turn every physical habit upside down while preserving every political tradition unchanged?

21 Yet we must admit it. We are blinded to the over-arching facts of our new environment, because they still seem unfamiliar and we feel more at home, more cozy with the old lethal habits of the past. We love the poison that slays us. Twice in my lifetime our vaunted western world has plunged the globe into near total war. And in nazism it reached a pitch of hysteria which betrayed the fact that uncontrolled nationalism is now in many ways an incurably pathological condition.

22 Yet we still live with our passionate nationalisms. In fact, the last decade has seen such a flowering of new sovereignties that 113 states now make up the roster of the United Nations. Since we met here in San Francisco just 19 years ago it has more than doubled. Nor is this revival of nationalism simply a reflection of the ending of old imperialisms. The monolithic communist world has broken up into separate nationalisms. Our defensive alliance has been invaded by nationalism and is in disorder. The march toward European unity has been halted. And where do we, the United States, stand? What about us—the inescapable leader of the coalition of free men, the keystone of NATO's arch, the United Nations' chief backer, the largest contributor to the world's assistance programs, the nation whose retreat to isolationism—if it ever occurred—would destroy every one of the frail, halting experiments to build up some kind of post-national order to counter the blinding risks of our day?

23 We must face the fact. We live with divided minds on this great issue. With a prescience unmatched at the time, the founding fathers spoke not for Americans, but for mankind. They sought to set up a government based not on the affinities of blood and culture, but on the universal rights of man—the rights of all men—and believed indeed that they were setting new standards of rationality and legality for the whole human race. But in a world still so totally unready for their ideals, they believed that their best chance of preserving them was to avoid contamination. The spokesmen for humanity avoided "entangling alliances" and kept their new hemisphere out of the clutches of the old. The feeling of America as at once universal and also apart is as rooted in us as our constitution.

24 In our own day, the conflict between our traditions has come fully into the open, as it had to do once physical aloofness ceased to be a possible option. "Two souls—alas!—dwell in my breast" said Goethe, and of America it may be said that the soul of universalism and the soul of particularism, or isolation if you prefer, struggle for mastery in all our debates.

25 We are no longer alone in this dilemma and we see today the leaders of Russia and China struggling to reconcile their own national interests with their claim to speak for a communist future for mankind—with the added difficulty that the two variants of communism, the true and the false (we will leave them to decide which is which), are now in open conflict from one end of the world to the other. But we need not be concerned here with their dilemmas. What are we to do with our own?

26 Let me quickly remind you once more of the background to our conflict. It is the environment of the post-scientific era—of instant communication, near-instant travel, and of outer space. And every hour, the world draws in, draws closer still.

27 In this shrinking universe, we have considered and partly pursued three lines of policy since the war.

28 The first, now only the belief of an irrational but noisy minority, is based on pure American self-sufficiency and isolation. Intellectually, the majority no longer accept this, and the government does not nakedly proclaim it. But national interest is nonetheless invoked from time to time as though it were a factor unconnected with the dense web of others' national interests and with the high interdependence of the world's economic structure.

29 In a second strand—which has made up the bulk of our policy—we have abandoned aloofness and self-sufficiency to seek with friendly nations a common safeguard against communist pretensions. An alliance, largely conceived and generously executed, has entered into our policy making for the first time, and within it we have achieved many things which carry us beyond the day of national separatism. This alliance was not just a block against communism. It was a building block for future world order. It was a recognition of more than national interests. It was a method of organizing the underpinning of a world society in which even continental limits are beginning to look parochial.

30 Today, as I say, this alliance is in grave disorder. It is not simply a question of the reversion of a narrower nationalism on the part of a decisive partner. It is not simply the risk that the contagion of separatism may spread. It is that we can no longer rely on fear of the outward thrust of Stalinism to hold us together. Indeed, we may well confront one day a Mr. Khrushchev who has more in common with a contented, prosperous bourgeois west than with a racialist, radical, aggressive and impoverished far eastern rival.

31 What then should be our attitude now that the political landscape of the post-war world—the landscape of alliances and blocs—is changing before our eyes? I suggest to you that this spectacle only adds to the significance of the third strand in our post-war policy—the strand which both goes back to the earliest universal vision of the founding fathers and also accepts the newest, latest evidence of the world's inescapable interdependence, the strand with which we seek, patiently, soberly, one step at a time, to build up our international policy in tune with man's new technological and scientific environment.

32 There are traces and hints of this policy at every turn. Little by little, for instance, many international agencies are bringing wider vision into focus on economic development, aid, trade and the financing of all of them. All these activities have behind them the realization that no nation can subtract itself from the close mesh of economic interdependence, that in a world in which a small minority are growing steadily richer, while everywhere else the gap increases between rich and poor, elementary considerations of justice, even peace itself, demand a better sharing of the world's resources and solidarity on the part of those whom destiny has placed on the better side of the world's tracks.

33 But these first tentative steps towards the concept of the "general welfare" on a worldwide scale are concerned with the lesser part of the problems which confront us when we seek to live in a community. The most vital, the most dangerous, the most fateful issues concern our security, the settling of our disputes, the ability to give ourselves the pre-condition of civilized living—life without violence, life lived under agreed procedures of arbitration, conciliation, of law itself. Can we see much progress here? Are we not as immersed as ever in the age of arbitrary violence?

34 Here, too, I believe there is evidence of new beginnings, of a recoil from the nihilistic terror of war and of the escalation that leads to it. The Cuban Crisis has been followed, after all, by the partial test-ban treaty and a pause in the arms race. More than this, I see growing up in the interstices of the old power systems a new readiness to replace national violence with international peacekeeping. The Near East, Korea, Kashmir, Congo, now Cyprus, the various frontier forces and observer groups, none of them in themselves completely satisfactory or efficient, and yet adding up to peaceful means of policing, controlling and resolving disputes—to cease firing and start talking.

35 There is, I believe a rapidly increasing realization that nations, like individuals, are "part of the main," part of that wider family living so precariously on this planet, part of a human species whose sheer survival is now at stake.

36 So we have reached a sort of turning point. Many of the old pressures which kept our western alliance in being are losing strength. We are beginning to be confronted with a choice. Shall we go back to a senseless separatism and isolationism—made no less senseless by the high style and rhetoric of some of its contemporary practitioners. Or shall we reach out to the fuller vision of our greatest traditions—to the rights of all men, to a society based upon human brotherhood, to a worldwide peace secure in justice and ruled by law?

37 As I have said before, I believe that now as in the days of the founding fathers, even the faintest possibility of achieving such an order depends upon the steadfast faith of this country. In their day, too, democracy in an age of monarchs and freedom in an age of empire seemed the most remote of pipe dreams. Today, too, the dream of a world which repeats at the international level the solid achievements —of law and welfare—of our domestic society must also seem audacious to the point of insanity, save for the grim fact that survival itself is inconceivable on any other terms.

38 And once again we in America are challenged to hold fast to the audacious dream. If we revert to crude nationalism and separatism, every present organ of international collaboration will collapse. If we withdraw our support from the embryonic organs of world policing and world law, there will be no other sources of support. If we turn in upon ourselves, allow our self-styled patriots to entice us into the supposed security of an impossible isolation, we shall be back in the jungle of rampant nationalisms, baleful ambitions and irreconcilable conflicts which—one cannot repeat it too often—have already twice in this century sent millions to their deaths, and next time would—literally—send everybody to final destruction.

39 Thus the only sane policy for America—in its own interests and in the wider interests of humanity—lies in patient search for the interests which unite the nations, for the international instruments of law and security, for the institutions of a stable, working world society, for the strengthening of what we have already built inside and outside the United Nations.

40 If the United States does not press on, no one else will. If we falter, if we lay down this burden, the world, I believe without rhetoric or exaggeration, is lost.

41 So, in the words of the Scriptures, "Let us work while it is yet day." Honoring U Thant, Secretary General of the United Nations, today, you pay a fitting tribute to the leader of us all in this mighty work.

INDEX OF RHETORICAL PRINCIPLES

INDEX OF RHETORICAL PRINCIPLES

The first numbers after a term indicate page numbers; the numbers in parentheses specify paragraphs within the speeches.